# The Educator's Guide to ADHD Interventions

T0383538

Designed specifically for middle and high school educators, this guidebook clearly and thoroughly breaks down effective classroom-based interventions for students with ADHD. Chapters walk readers through each intervention, providing step-by-step implementation guides, describing potential pitfalls, and offering critical tips and advice to help you ensure that your interventions are both culturally responsive and sustainable. Filled with helpful templates and tools, this book is essential reading for anyone who needs help creating effective, sustainable interventions for students with ADHD.

**Judith R. Harrison, PhD**, is Associate Professor in the Department of Educational Psychology, Co-Coordinator of Special Education Programs at Rutgers University, USA.

**Denise A. Soares, PhD**, is Assistant Dean, Director of Graduate Studies for the School of Education and Associate Professor of Special Education at the University of Mississippi, USA.

**Steven W. Evans, PhD**, is Distinguished Professor of Psychology Co-Director of the Center for Intervention Research in Schools, at Ohio University, USA.

# The Educator's Guide to ADHD Interventions

## Strategies for Grades 5–12

Judith R. Harrison, Denise A. Soares
and Steven W. Evans

Routledge
Taylor & Francis Group

NEW YORK AND LONDON

Designed cover image: Getty Images

First published 2023
by Routledge
605 Third Avenue, New York, NY 10158

and by Routledge
4 Park Square, Milton Park, Abingdon, Oxon, OX14 4RN

*Routledge is an imprint of the Taylor & Francis Group, an informa business*

© 2023 Judith R. Harrison, Denise A. Soares, and Steven W. Evans

ISBN: 978-0-367-62620-4 (hbk)
ISBN: 978-0-367-62240-4 (pbk)
ISBN: 978-1-003-10998-3 (ebk)

DOI: 10.4324/9781003109983

Typeset in Optima
by Apex CoVantage, LLC

*Judith*

*To my husband Randy, for all his editorial assistance, patience, and encouragement, as he has lived his neurotypical life surrounded by neurodiversity with a smile on his face (most of the time)!*

*Denise*

*To Barry, my husband; he makes me laugh, wipes away the tears, and keeps me strong! He is my love, my rock, and my greatest supporter.*

*Steve*

*To my grandparents Bert and Margaret Leversee, who have always been and still are the people whose lives and values I aspire to emulate.*

# Contents

Contents

# Meet the Authors

**Judith R. Harrison, PhD**, is Associate Professor in the Department of Educational Psychology, Special Education at Rutgers University.

Dr. Harrison was a special education teacher and counselor for over 20 years. Her research interests are classroom-based strategies for students with emotional and behavioral disorders and attention-deficit/hyperactivity disorder.

**Denise A. Soares, PhD**, is Assistant Dean, Director of Graduate Studies, and Associate Professor of Special Education at the University of Mississippi.

Dr. Soares served as a special education teacher, behavior specialist, and administrator for 18 years. Her research focuses on applied and practical experiences in academic and behavior interventions for at-risk students, as well as examining the efficacy of those interventions in classroom settings where teachers have competing time demands. Dr. Soares is dedicated to special education and bridging the gap between research and practice.

**Steven W. Evans, PhD**, is Distinguished Professor of Psychology at Ohio University.

Dr. Evans is also Co-Director of the Center for Intervention Research in Schools at Ohio University. He began his career as a special education teacher and has consistently focused his work on finding ways to help students with emotional and behavioral problems achieve success socially and academically at school.

# Acknowledgements

Like most endeavors, it took a village to write this book, and we are thankful for everyone that participated knowingly and unknowingly. Specifically, we are thankful for the artistic support from Alyssa Baran, Amy and Riley Williams, Alana Harrison, and Austin Newcomb. To our families who patiently awaited the final version as we continually said, "just one more chapter" and "I can't do that because I have to finish this book," we say "thank you" to each and every one of you. We could not have completed this text without your understanding! To Mary Bramlett, and our many students, children, and grandchildren who contributed to the making of the fictional characters in the scenarios at the beginning of the intervention chapters, thank you for letting us be part of your journeys. To Randy Harrison, your contributions are innumerable. In addition, we would like to thank our editors at Routledge (Taylor & Francis) Publishing for their patience, kindness, and support throughout the process. Finally, we must acknowledge George DuPaul for taking time out of his busy schedule to write the foreword to this book.

# Foreword

Middle and high school students with attention-deficit/hyperactivity disorder (ADHD) frequently engage in behaviors that not only disrupt their own learning but also interfere with their classmates' educational activities and progress. Regularly throughout the school day and across subject matter periods, students with ADHD are inattentive, distracted, and restless; interrupt teachers and students by calling out, talking to peers, or making noises; and, as a result, are not listening to instruction or completing assigned tasks. Over the long term, these deficits negatively impact educational progress such that students with ADHD are among those at greatest risk for underachievement and school dropout. Thus, secondary school teachers are faced with the ongoing and frustrating challenge of helping these students manage their behaviors and buckle down to pay attention and do their work. Given the relatively high prevalence rate of ADHD (i.e., about 5% of the child and adolescent population), teachers can expect to work with at least one student with ADHD in every class period they teach.

In many ways, the combination of adolescence and ADHD represents a "perfect storm" that compounds the challenges faced by students working with these students. At its core, ADHD is a disorder of self-regulation; individuals experience significant difficulties managing their behaviors and emotions, particularly in high-demand situations (e.g., when expected to follow rules, sustain attention to effortful assignments, and remain seated for extended periods of time). Meanwhile, adolescence is a period of hormonal, biological, and psychological turmoil that can disrupt the learning progress of all students, not just those with disabilities. In addition, as students progress through middle and high school, they are expected to take on a greater and more advanced workload while completing assignments with increasing independence from teacher and parent support. Thus, the very self-regulation deficits that comprise ADHD are diametrically in opposition to expectations we have for adolescents in secondary schools. As a result, teachers need feasible and practical strategies that can effectively support students with ADHD.

Fortunately, Drs. Judith R. Harrison, Denise A. Soares, and Steven W. Evans provide a comprehensive guide for middle and high school teachers that describes evidence-based intervention and support strategies to help adolescents with ADHD successfully navigate the "perfect storm." *The Educator's Guide to ADHD Interventions: Strategies for Grades 5–12* is one of a kind (i.e., most teacher guides for ADHD are focused on elementary school-aged children) and includes techniques and hands-on tools that teachers can use at the point of performance (i.e., the time and location when students are experiencing difficulties). This guide incorporates many of the principles and concepts that underlie effective school intervention for ADHD with a specific focus on target behaviors and skills that are typically lacking among students with this disorder. Specifically, strategies emphasize direct instruction in organization, study, and note-taking skills that are key for educational success, along with ongoing monitoring and frequent feedback regarding performance of these skills over time. Given that no single individual, including the teacher, can comprehensively address all of the challenges faced by adolescents with ADHD, readers are directed to adopt a team approach that involves clear, consistent, and supportive communication between school and home. Because adolescence is a time when peer relationships are increasingly salient, the guide describes methods (e.g., peer tutoring) that harness the power of the peer group to help students focus on academic concepts and assignments. Finally, we know that a "one size fits all" cookbook approach is ineffective in the long run, so Dr. Harrison and colleagues provide helpful guidance on how to use assessment data to design an intervention plan that addresses the unique needs of individual students with ADHD.

Teachers reading this guide should feel confident that they are getting the most current research-based information on how to help middle and high school students with ADHD. In following the strategies and adopting the techniques described by Drs. Harrison, Soares, and Evans, teachers will be able to promote better behavioral and emotional self-regulation in their students, and ultimately lead students to gain skills that directly counteract the challenging deficits faced by secondary school students with ADHD.

George J. DuPaul, PhD
College of Education
Lehigh University
Bethlehem PA

# An Introduction to ADHD

# Introduction to
# the Reader

If you are reading this book, you are probably one of millions of middle and/or high school teachers around the world who look out across their classrooms daily and see "that" student. The one that seems to defy all that you learned from your costly education and training and the skills that you have worked hard to develop. He is probably staring out the window at the snow or rain or bird in the tree, or at his peer sharpening his pencil, or simply off into space and thinking about what? You often wonder! He may be tapping his pencil, kicking the chair in front of him, playing with his phone under that table (the one he thinks you cannot see), or talking to the student beside him about his favorite video game. You are fully aware that he is not paying attention to the engaging lesson that you spent hours planning, that your university professor would rave about, and that has the remainder of your students mystified and happily engaged in deep thought and profound intellectual conversation. When asked to complete a task that he perceives as tedious or monotonous, he becomes visibly frustrated and demands to go the restroom, after all it is an *emergency*!

The same student will not turn in his homework today and probably not any other day. He will open his backpack and it will appear to burst. Crinkled notebook paper and thoughtfully planned assignments will fall to the floor. You will see an old apple core roll across the classroom, and you are sure that you can smell his socks from the entire semester of gym. He will search through mounds of papers and clothes to find the binder that his parents carefully purchased to hold all of his work for all of his classes at the beginning of the semester. They envisioned nice, neat color-coded dividers with his work nicely stored behind each of them. You are fully aware that

DOI: 10.4324/9781003109983-2

Image used under license from Shutterstock.
Sasirin Pamai/Shutterstock.com.

they hoped, this year, he would store the math homework that he needed to complete in the front of the binder and the completed work neatly behind the blue divider with math typed on the label. After all, he was older than the year before and they carefully explained to him that if he just kept that beautiful binder organized, he could quickly locate his work and submit it to the teacher, so that he would not have missing assignments and zeros in a gradebook that made his class average plummet to an F all the years before. He had excitedly agreed, and his parents could tell that he meant it and his motivation was tangible. Nonetheless, it is now November, and the three rings of the beautiful binder are bent and will no longer close. Paper protrudes from the top and sides of the binder, a majority of which looks like drawings probably something to do with the same video game that he was talking about earlier in class. When you ask the students to pass their completed homework forward, he begins frantically searching through the sad binder and digging through the socks in his backpack. You see him forget that he is looking for his homework and start talking to the student beside him, or maybe he did not forget, he just gave up. You know that you will get a call when his parents see his grades. You know they will say that he completed all of his homework, because they checked. They saw it complete. They bought the nice binder!

This same student might have an individualized education program (IEP) or a section 504 plan that was developed by his teachers from last year, along with the principal, the student's parents, the social worker, the school counselor, and the school psychologist. When he was in elementary school, his parents provided documentation from a physician, maybe a psychiatrist, but probably his pediatrician, that he had attention-deficit/hyperactivity disorder (ADHD). The team developed a plan with a long list of accommodations they thought would help him by removing expectations for him to engage in activities that were especially difficult because of his ADHD. The plan included giving him extra time to submit his homework, as he tends to take longer because he is frequently off task; leaving a copy of books at home so that he does not have to find them in his backpack or remember to take them home to complete his homework; prompting from the teacher to remind him to get back on task or to submit his homework; and frequent breaks so that he can get out of his designated area and walk around when he is feeling especially fidgety.

You follow the plan carefully and you notice that when you send the list of missing assignments home to his parents and allow him extra time to submit the work, his grades get better. When you prompt him to get back to work or pay attention, he frowns at you, but casts his eyes to the assignment and picks up his pencil. He may complete the assignment, and when you give him a break, he seems to get less frustrated with assignments. But you wonder what he is learning from these accommodations. You have read the recommendations from others, and you understand that ADHD is a neurodevelopmental disorder, that his behaviors are not caused by laziness and that his intention is not to drive you nuts.

But you question the long-term effects of these strategies to yourself. After all, you are a teacher and you want to teach him the skills that he needs to function independently. You wonder if you could teach him to pay attention, organize his materials, or manage his time. What will happen when he goes to college or gets a job? Will he be able to explain to his boss that he has ADHD and needs extended time? Possibly, but is that really the best that we, as educators, have to offer him? These are the questions that many educators (including the three authors of this book) ponder about students with ADHD—questions that I (Judith R. Harrison) contemplated as a mother of two children with ADHD (now adults), a general and special education teacher, a counselor, a college professor—and the questions that drive my work, and the work of my co-authors. The answer is yes, we can teach those skills to adolescents with ADHD with the evidence-based interventions described in this book.

First, we need to make sure that we are all on the same page about diagnosis. As you probably have heard, many educators believe that ADHD is over diagnosed. Many teachers have been heard to say that the number of students they see in their classes with ADHD increases each year. This is partially an accurate statement, as the trend has consistently increased over time. However, prevalence estimates are a tricky matter, as they are influenced by the type of survey, changes in ADHD criteria, and the number of individuals surveyed. Nonetheless, the prevalence has increased across surveys over time (CDC, 2022). It is possible, and probable, that this is caused by increased awareness of ADHD symptoms by parents, teachers, pediatricians, and others. However, you may have heard individuals state that parents and students seek ADHD diagnoses and use that as an excuse to avoid completing difficult tasks or to increase test scores. This may be true for some people. For this reason, it is vital that a comprehensive evaluation be conducted for each and every student in question.

ADHD is diagnosed by a clinician, based on the presence of specific criteria. The clinician is typically a psychiatrist, psychologist, licensed counselor, or pediatrician. Information for the diagnosis should be obtained from a comprehensive clinical history and interview, rating scales completed by individuals from multiple settings (schools, home) with knowledge of the child, and direct observation of the student's behavior. The American Association of Pediatrics standards (Wolraich et al., 2020) recommend that pediatricians screen children between the ages of 4 and 18 who are struggling academically and behaviorally. Results of the screening should indicate whether DSM-5 criteria (see Figure 1.1) have been met in more than one setting. In addition, pediatricians should screen children and adolescents for comorbid conditions, as many students experience other social, emotional, behavioral, and learning disorders along with ADHD. In fact, approximately 64% of youth with ADHD experience at least one of these comorbidities (CDC, 2022). Pediatricians are encouraged to treat individuals with ADHD as they treat others with a chronic condition, as it is known to continue into adulthood for most individuals.

Three types of ADHD can be diagnosed based on the symptoms the child is experiencing: Predominantly Inattentive presentation ADHD (ADHD-I), Predominantly Hyperactive-Impulsive presentation ADHD (ADHD-HI), or Combined presentation ADHD (ADHD-C). There is no doubt that you can close your eyes and visualize students from each diagnosis. The student who was diagnosed with ADHD-I may remind you of Pooh Bear. She might be a girl and you frequently see her staring out the window. For the physician to have diagnosed her with ADHD-I, he had to have evidence that she demonstrated six or more symptoms of inattention and not six or more symptoms of hyperactivity-impulsivity. What about the student who reminds you of Tigger? You see him frequently bouncing down the hall on his tail. It is likely that he was diagnosed with ADHD-HI, as it is probable that a physician found evidence of six or more symptoms of hyperactivity-impulsivity. It is uncommon for middle school students to meet criteria for ADHD-HI, because at this age most who have hyperactive and impulsive symptoms are also inattentive. And, of course, there is

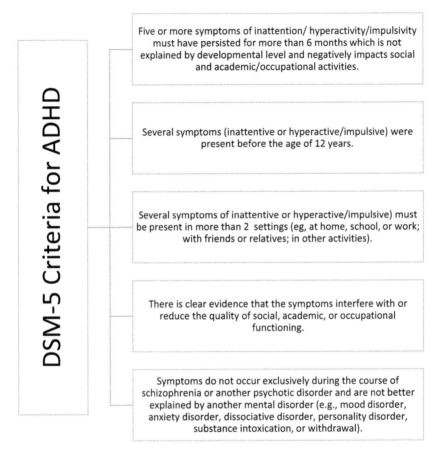

Figure 1.1

Rabbit, cranky frustrated Rabbit. No doubt, this student is bouncing down the hall and struggling to attend to anything for more than a brief moment. He has to deal with all of the symptoms and challenges associated with ADHD. No doubt that he may be cranky.

In the following chapters in Section 1, we will explore ADHD in-depth, beginning with symptomology and areas of impairment in Chapter 2. Our purpose in taking this deep dive is to establish a solid understanding of what is and is not ADHD. Armed with this understanding, you will be able to advocate for evidence-based interventions (those with research to support their use) that are directly related to individual students' strengths and needs. You are likely to have the opportunity to make these decisions on your own in your classroom and on school-based teams.

# Reference List

Center for Disease Control (CDC). (2022). *Attention deficit across the years*. www.cdc.gov/ncbddd/adhd/timeline.html

Wolraich, M. L et al.; Subcommittee on children and adolescents with attention-deficit/hyperactive disorder. (2020). Clinical practice guideline for the diagnosis, evaluation, and treatment of attention-deficit/hyperactivity disorder in children and adolescents. *Pediatrics, 144*(4), e20192528. doi: 10.1542/peds.2019-2528. Erratum in: Pediatrics. Mar; *145*(3): PMID: 31570648; PMCID: PMC7067282.

# Symptomology and Areas of Impairment

Attention-deficit/hyperactivity disorder (ADHD) is one of the most common neurodevelopmental disorders of childhood. "Neurodevelopmental" indicates that the disorder is brain based. In this chapter, you will learn about the basics of ADHD, symptomology, and impairment.

Approximately 7.2% of children and adolescents worldwide have ADHD (Danielson et al., 2018). This probably does not surprise you or most teachers, as it equates to at least one student in every classroom. When observing your classroom, you are likely to notice one or two students who appear to be a bit different than the others. These students are more likely to be boys than girls, as boys are twice as likely to have ADHD than girls.

Although individuals with ADHD are all unique with differing characteristics (see figure 2.1), they demonstrate behaviors associated with inattention and/or hyperactivity/impulsivity (APA, 2013). These behaviors interfere with academic progress, social functioning, interpersonal relationships, and/or acceptable behavior in multiple environments, such as home and school. In the following sections, we describe students who you will likely recognize. Within each description, we identify the criteria for each symptom and area of impairment (APA, 2013). You will notice the

Image used under license from Shutterstock.
Monkey Business Images/Shutterstock.com.

DOI: 10.4324/9781003109983-3

| INATTENTION | HYPERACTIVITY/ IMPULSIVITY |
| --- | --- |
| Makes careless mistakes/lacks attention to detail | Fidgets with or taps hands or feet, squirms in seat |
| Difficulty sustaining attention | Leaves seat in situations when remaining seated is expected |
| Does not seem to listen when spoken directly to | Experiences feelings of restlessness |
| Fails to follow through on tasks and instructions | Has difficulty engaging in quiet, leisurely activities |
| Exhibits poor organization | Talks excessively |
| Loses things necessary for tasks/activities | Blurts out answers |
| Easily distracted (including unrelated thoughts) | Has difficulty waiting their turn |
| Is forgetful in daily activities | Interrupts or intrudes on others |

*Figure 2.1* Characteristics of inattention and hyperactivity/impulsivity.
Image used under license from Shutterstock. Ollie The Designer//Shutterstock.com.

criteria in italics after the description of the student's behavior. It is likely that you have seen these criteria on behavior rating scales that you have completed for your students.

## Inattention

Students with ADHD-I and ADHD-C experience and demonstrate symptoms of inattention. Inattention is defined as a lack of focus on a required activity, item, or event. Youth who are inattentive struggle to initiate attention, maintain attention, and shift attention between activities. Simply initiating attention is not enough. When successfully attending to tasks individuals must avoid distractions, both internal and external. Many distractions exist in educational environments. Students talk and move about. Bells ring. People come to the door. Announcements are made on the loudspeaker. Alarms are sounded. Students get angry and loud. Students get excited and loud. If that is not enough, individual thoughts can be distracting. When is the dance? What is that girl doing? I hope Mom is cooking tacos tonight. As such, when attending to tasks, one must avoid all competing distractions.

In your classroom, you are likely to see a student who is inattentive. She really struggles with beginning a task and focusing on the task until it is completed [*initiating and maintaining attention*]. The scenario always seems to be the same. You tell the student to begin working, she does not. Instead, she stares out the window

Image used under license from Shutterstock. Ollyy/Shutterstock.com.

and plays with her hair [*easily distracted*]. You notice that some other students look away from their work for brief moments, but return to the assigned task quickly, but not this student. She stares off into the distance for much longer.

Finally, you, as the teacher, prompt her to begin her task, as you have done so many times before. She does not respond to your verbal prompt. This is not new, she never listens to you [i.e., *does not seem to listen when spoken to*], so you become frustrated. You tap your finger loudly on her paper and tell her to get started, once again. The student tells you that she has a headache and cannot work for that long [*avoids/dislikes tasks that require mental effort over time*]. You inform her that she has no choice, so she slowly turns to the paper and begins writing. She works for about five minutes and then she asks to go to the nurse; she thinks her head is going to explode. You think to yourself "she probably thinks her head is going to explode if I say one more word." You let her go. She returns with only five minutes left in class and she has not completed her work. You tell her to take it home with her and finish it for homework. You know that she will not return with the completed work; she will lose it before she gets home or on the way to school the next day [*forgetful*]. It is doubtful that she will make it out of the building after school with the work, but if she does, it will be done with many careless errors!

After class, you notice her walking down the hall. The hall looks like a busy flowing highway in a large city. Everyone seems to be walking at about the same speed and talking to the peer beside them, except her. She is walking a bit slower than everyone else is and she is by herself. She stops at her locker, opens the door, and her notebook and gym clothes fall to the floor [*often has trouble organizing tasks and activities*]. You see her slowly taking everything out of her locker looking for her math book [*often loses things necessary for tasks and activities*] and she finds a note from her friend [*is often easily distracted*], forgetting that she was looking for her math book, she reads the note [*often has trouble holding attention on tasks or play activities*]. You call her name and tell her to hurry to class, but she seems to just look through you [*often does not seem to listen when spoken to directly*]. You know that she is thinking about something much more fun than hurrying to class. It is obvious that her inattentive behavior is as much of a problem in the hall as it was in the classroom.

## Hyperactivity/Impulsivity

Students with ADHD-HI and ADHD-C experience and demonstrate symptoms of hyperactivity and impulsivity (APA, 2013). Hyperactivity is defined as movement at a higher rate than what is needed or would be expected in the situation. Hyperactivity in middle and high school students often looks different than that demonstrated by children. For example, younger children who are hyperactive may run when walking is expected, and get out of their seat when remaining seated is expected. Adolescents who are hyperactive are more likely to feel restless, fidget with objects, wiggle their legs, and tap their pencils on desks. Impulsivity is defined as acting without thinking. Adolescents with ADHD often talk in class without permission, blurt out answers to questions in class, interrupt others, and make decisions without much thought. As such, hyperactivity and impulsivity frequently interfere with academic performance.

When you gaze across your classroom, you are probably amazed at how the student diagnosed with ADHD-HI can attend to everyone else, including your behavior but not his own. He is simply bouncy and energetic. When your class is assigned to do independent work, you watch him in his seat. He is staring at

Image used under license from Shutterstock. Aleutie/Shutterstock.com.

his paper and spinning his phone on his desk [*often fidgets with or taps hands or feet or squirms in seat*]. He notices that his pencil needs to be sharpened; that is probably because he broke the lead last period when he was twirling it in the air. He gets up to sharpen his pencil for the tenth time [*often leaves seat in situations when remaining seated is expected*]. On his way back to his desk, he wanders over to a friend and begins to talk to him [*talks excessively*] about the football game the night before. You ask him to go to his seat and he interrupts you [*often interrupts or intrudes on other conversations*] before you finish the sentence, he says "yeah, yeah, I know!" When he gets to his seat, he sits down, and seems to begin his work but instead he throws his pencil at the ceiling to see if he can make it stick. His peers laugh and you ask him to come sit at the front of the room with you. He seems to be always moving and he makes you feel exhausted [*is often on the go, acting as if driven by a motor*].

When he leaves your classroom and is in the hall, the first thing he does is jump for the exit light [*often runs about or climbs in situations where it is not appropriate*]. He taps it with his hand and gives himself a loud congratulatory whoop [*often unable to play or take part in leisure activities quietly*]. You see him weaving in and out between students like a race car on the highway. He barges into the conversation that two peers are having about their plans for the evening and invites himself to the party [*often intrudes*]. They laugh, but quickly tell him that he is not invited. When he gets to the vending machine, he does not appear to see the line of students waiting. He marches right to the front of the line, puts his money in the machine, and takes his snack down the hall [*often has trouble waiting their turn*]. He turns, looks at them, and laughs, finally arriving at his next class where the teacher waits at the door. You see the look on the teacher's face. It seems to say "here we go . . ."

## Areas of Impairment

As you have probably noticed, the impairment of ADHD is more troublesome than the actual symptoms. For example, you worry about the academic performance of your students more than you are concerned about their inability to sit quietly in a chair. Impairment is defined as the cost of symptomology to student daily functioning. Professionals making decisions regarding diagnosis refer to "impairment," as that is the language

Image used under license from Shutterstock. Lidiia Koval/Shutterstock.com.

used in the DSM-V (APA, 2013); however, you will note that many educators prefer the term "challenges," as some do not want to portray individuals with ADHD as having deficits or impairment. As such, we refer to challenges, which represent areas that can be overcome with intervention. For example, being able to sit quietly in a chair during independent work is definitely a challenge for students with ADHD and likely will result in the assignment not being completed and the student making low grades. However, with intervention, the student can learn to complete the required assignment. In this chapter, we describe three broad challenges associated with ADHD: academic, social/interpersonal, and behavioral. Within each of these three broad areas, you will find a figure with associated behaviors linked to potential interventions, and references to chapters that describe those interventions in detail. Furthermore, we provide detailed discussion of each area and possible explanations for those challenges.

## Academic Challenges

Adolescents with ADHD are known to struggle academically (Kent et al., 2011). Academic competence is complex and requires many skills, attitudes, and behaviors. For academic success, students must be motivated, know how to study, and initiate and remain engaged in class work. Students who exhibit competence academically are often positive, value education, and demonstrate behaviors that are conducive to learning. You are likely to be thinking, these are not the characteristics of the students that you know with ADHD, and you are correct, as students with ADHD experience a host of academic impairments (see Figure 2.2).

Successful academic performance is demonstrated by earning passing grades in classes (including rigorous core subjects like English, math, science, social studies/history), passing scores on high stakes/achievement tests, attending school regularly, following school rules and expectations,

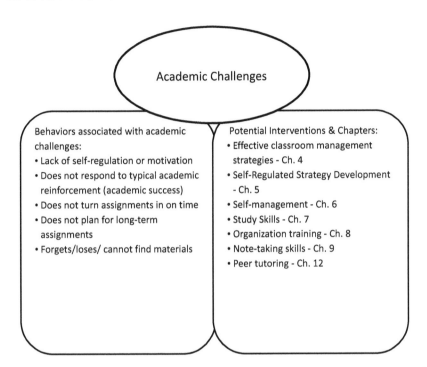

**Academic Challenges**

Behaviors associated with academic challenges:
• Lack of self-regulation or motivation
• Does not respond to typical academic reinforcement (academic success)
• Does not turn assignments in on time
• Does not plan for long-term assignments
• Forgets/loses/ cannot find materials

Potential Interventions & Chapters:
• Effective classroom management strategies - Ch. 4
• Self-Regulated Strategy Development - Ch. 5
• Self-management - Ch. 6
• Study Skills - Ch. 7
• Organization training - Ch. 8
• Note-taking skills - Ch. 9
• Peer tutoring - Ch. 12

*Figure 2.2*

engaging in school activities, and developing strong relationships with teachers. To do this, adolescents must be able to manage secondary environments that are very different from elementary schools. In secondary schools, students must independently organize their work and materials and manage time to navigate the environment. They must understand, remember, and follow the rules and expectations for academic and behavioral performance across multiple teachers, as many as eight in some schools. Although schools have common school-wide expectations, all of us have experienced teachers with more or less stringent expectations. Some teachers allow students to answer questions spontaneously; others expect them to raise their hands and wait to be called on. Furthermore, students must arrive at class on time with all the needed materials, such as books and notebooks. Additionally, assignments require independence and/or collaborative skills. Many assignments are long term, requiring students to organize, plan, and complete multiple parts over time with very little adult direction and feedback. Throw all of this into the mix of the social priorities of adolescents, many of which are achieved in the hallways of middle and high schools, and you have a formula for disaster for adolescents with ADHD.

Students with ADHD may struggle with many of the expectations just described because of the characteristic of ADHD. You have seen these students walking down the halls of schools. Sometimes they have a "deer in the headlight" expression on their faces. You realize that they are trying to remember where they are going, the combination to their locker, where they put their books for the next class, and where they put the homework assignment that has to be turned in. Oh, wait, they remember that they did not do that homework. Then you see complete frustration move across the confused face! You wonder why they do not just open their agenda book to see what needs to be done, and then you realize they lost it many weeks ago. As you can see, academic impairment is problematic to middle and high school students with ADHD. As such, teachers and parents often complain that students with ADHD do not perform academically as they would expect. I am sure that you have heard teachers say, He should not be failing my class. He is so smart and capable of doing the work. If he would just pay attention and do his work, he would be fine. When he answers questions in class, it is obvious that he understands the content.

This is when the "lazy" word is often used, or teachers might use the word "unmotivated" or "oppositional" or "stubborn." There is no doubt that many adolescents with ADHD appear to fit those descriptions. After all, many students with ADHD earn failing grades and are twice as likely than their typically developing peers to drop out of high school. It is clear through research and teacher experience that students with ADHD often forget to complete their homework, submit incomplete assignments, or do not submit any part of the assignment, and lose the materials needed to complete their work, or lose their work altogether. As you

Image used under license from Shutterstock. New Vectors/Shutterstock.com.

may guess, all of this leads to failing grades and at times failing the grade level and even failing to graduate from high school. This can be frustrating to parents, teachers, and even the student, because often the adolescent has the cognitive ability to excel academically but appears to choose not to do just that.

In sum, many adolescents with ADHD are challenged to achieve academically. This is directly related to the academic impairment associated with the disorder. Understanding this connection is necessary for teachers to effectively intervene. This is an area in which researchers have developed and explored the effectiveness of many interventions. There are evidence-based interventions for teachers to implement in their classrooms. In addition to helping students through intervention, this understanding also helps you, as a teacher, have more empathy for the student and for yourself as you struggle to find the answers.

## *Social/Interpersonal Challenges*

When individuals are socially competent, they possess the behaviors needed to engage appropriately in society. Social competence (see Figure 2.3) is a developmental skill that evolves as individuals mature to adapt and meet

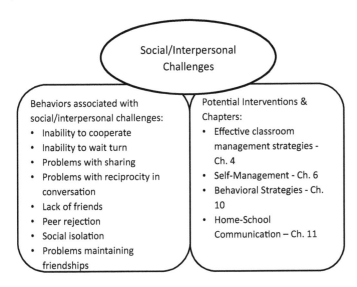

*Figure 2.3*

the demands of their social environment. Individuals who are socially competent consider the perspectives of others, learn from past experiences, and apply that information to present situations. As such, they have the ability to understand the opinions and feelings of others, and have empathy for friends even when they do not agree. Furthermore, they have effective communication skills and tend to demonstrate kind behavior. They regulate their own emotions, be it frustration or exuberance. As you know, this description of social competence is not "the picture of students with ADHD."

Adolescence is the social time! Students begin the process of identifying who they are; they move away from the influence of adults, such as parents and teachers. They rely on friends for guidance in developing their social selves. As we all know and have experienced, this is a tricky period in life that requires competence in interpreting and giving social cues. To effectively manage this developmental stage, students have to learn to behave in a socially appropriate way, allow others to speak and listen to what they are saying, regulate the volume and tone of their voice to fit the situation, engage collaboratively in work and social situations, and refrain from interrupting others. Unfortunately, this is an area in which adolescents with ADHD are known to struggle. In fact, they often struggle with each of these behaviors.

Students with ADHD often struggle in social situations. If you have ever sat and observed students with ADHD in the school cafeteria, you have seen a small sample of their social lives. You may have noticed the different friend groups sitting together. Historically, you see individuals with common interests at the same table. For example, the athletes, scholars, mischievous, popular, and socially awkward students all seated in their individual groups in deep conversation or simply staring at their food,

Image used under license from Shutterstock. Lucky Business/Shutterstock.com.

phones, or the ceiling. Sometimes the students with ADHD have the same characteristics as one of these groups, but other times, you see them floating from table to table. You know the one, the one that does not know where he fits. He moves to the table with the athletes and barges into their conversation. They stare at him blankly and then one of them makes a joke about him and they laugh. He laughs too because he does not realize that the joke was meant to be cruel or he just doesn't know how to respond. He gets up to move on and tries for a fist bump, but they just laugh harder. Our student with ADHD moves on to the table with the scholars and sits down beside his friend from elementary school. He tries to engage in the conversation, talking super loud so that the girls at the popular table can hear him. The girls giggle in a manner that seems to be an embarrassed giggle, not for themselves but for him. The scholars try calmly to explain to him why his hypothesis about the Martians seen by the Mars Rover just cannot be accurate. He gets bored and moves on to the mischievous table. He slaps the first boy's shoulder, as if to say "Hey, dude." The student shoves him to the ground and says "Get out of here, man." Finally, our student lands at the socially awkward table where he finds another classmate with ADHD, but she is less active and more unfocused. She is frantically trying to finish her homework from the day before that is due in the class after lunch. He begins talking to her and she looks up and explains that she must get her work done. Unfortunately, he points out the poster on the wall advertising tryouts for the next one-act play. She becomes giddy at the thought of trying out. They talk about the play, the tryouts, and then they talk about the horse on the poster. From there they move on to discussing the ranch right outside of town that has horses. She tells him how much she likes the white horse, and he tells her about the white pig that his mom just bought. The bell rings, her homework is not done, and he has no idea where his materials are for the next class. But he smiles and meanders on to class jumping at the exit sign, and she realizes that she is going to get a zero in the grade book, but hey what about white donkeys?

Teachers often misidentify these social challenges as simply adolescent behavior; others think that the behaviors are intentionally inappropriate, and, at times, they think the adolescent was not taught how to behave in social situations by his parents. Similar to the peers in the story you just read, teachers often become frustrated with students with ADHD. When students interrupt you, as the teacher, while you are talking or barge into the conversations of their peers, it simply appears that they are not trying to control their own behavior. Frequently, teachers talk about students "only wanting to get their own way" or being selfish. After all, if the student respected you, he would not interrupt you. In fact, if he was listening to what you were saying, he would not interrupt, but he is not listening, instead he is already moving on to the next topic.

On the other hand, you might think that their behavior is purposeful, with a goal of getting attention. The adolescent with ADHD is often known as the "class clown." It appears that they want to make others laugh, because their "friends" laugh at them and encourage their silly or inappropriate behavior. Other times, you think the function of the behavior is avoidance of the work that they are supposed to be doing. Consider the inquiry-based science classroom. Students are placed in groups and are working to develop hypothesis statements. The student with ADHD puts his head down on his desk and refuses to engage in the activity. The others prompt him to participate, but he refuses. They immediately ask you, as the teacher, for help. You try to talk to the student with ADHD about cooperating, but he starts crying, and continues to refuse to be part of the group. As can be seen in each of these situations, students with ADHD are known to struggle with cooperation, which is necessary in all group-based learning commonly found in classrooms today.

## *Behavioral Challenges*

Some adolescents with ADHD are challenged behaviorally, as they often demonstrate behaviors that are unacceptable in school settings (see Figure 2.4).

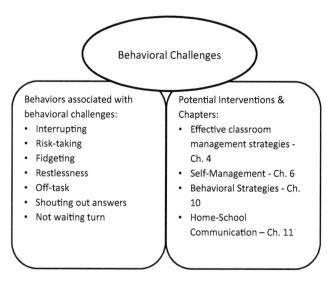

*Figure 2.4*

In most school systems, all students are expected to follow specific behavioral expectations. Students are often expected to quietly listen to teacher instruction and respond only with permission. They are often expected to sit in their chairs or desks for extended periods of time and work independently. In recent years, there has been a move toward instruction of children of all ages that involves more activity. If you walk into classrooms, you will likely see less structure and more conversation than in the past, with students working in small groups, some on the carpet in the corner, some with their desks arranged in circles, and other standing at a table. The students are likely engaging with materials such as textbooks, computers, tablets, manipulatives, and/or science equipment. Nonetheless, there are behavioral expectations within these activities, such as waiting your turn to speak, using materials appropriately, remaining focused and on task, and being cooperative. Adolescents with ADHD struggle to engage in and maintain these behaviors as they experience behavioral impairment.

Behavioral impairment associated with ADHD looks different in adolescence than in childhood. Behavioral impairment of young students is more observable than it is for adolescents. They wiggle in their seats and climb on objects not meant for climbing. They are often seen running around the classroom and jumping over things and people. On the other hand, you have probably not seen as many adolescents jumping over other students or randomly running around the classroom. You have probably seen adolescents with ADHD disrupting the class by fidgeting with manipulatives, leaning backwards in their chairs, interrupting you and their peers, and asking to go to the restroom or nurse every five minutes. You have probably noticed them becoming extremely frustrated when expected to sit for long periods of time and complete tasks they consider less than exciting. Another behavior that seems to be impairing for adolescents with ADHD is their sleep pattern. They tend to stay up late and appear exhausted when expected to get up early for school.

## Summary

Adolescents with ADHD experience symptoms and impairment that often negatively impact their functioning. In this chapter, we described and illustrated inattention, hyperactivity, and impulsivity and how it appears in classroom settings. Furthermore, we described and illustrated the characteristics of academic, social, and behavioral challenges faced by adolescents with ADHD.

# Reference List

American Psychiatric Association. (APA; 2013). *Diagnostic and statistical manual of mental disorders* (5th ed.). American Psychiatric Publishing, Inc.

Danielson, M. L., Bitsko, R. H., Ghandour, R. M., Holbrook, J. R., Kogan, M. D., & Blumberg, S. J. (2018). Prevalence of parent-reported ADHD diagnosis and associated treatment among US children and adolescents, 2016. *Journal of Clinical Child & Adolescent Psychology*, 47(2), 199–212.

Kent, K. M., Pelham, W. E., Molina, B. S. G., Sibley, M. H., Waschbusch, D. A., Yu, J, et al. (2011). The academic experience of male high school students with ADHD. *Journal of Abnormal Child Psychology*, 39, 451–462.

# Interventions

# Effective Classroom Management and Practices

**Ms. Campbell**

Ms. Campbell is a first year Biology teacher in a large urban under-resourced school district. She recently graduated from college and was excited to teach. However, it did not take  her long to realize that five of her twenty students in sophomore biology had ADHD. She is an excellent teacher engaged in inquiry-based instruction, encouraging, and demanding critical thinking skills. Nonetheless the principal described her class as a "zoo". She feels like she is in shock at the end of the class each day. No one prepared her for such behavior. Two of the students were girls with ADHD, who simply stared out the window or off into space a majority of the class. The other three were boys, one repeatedly disrupted class with what he considered funny, one refused to do anything he was asked to do, and one played on his cell phone most of the class. The class is loud during her wonderfully planned lessons and students seemed to be off task a great deal of time. She was frustrated and considering a new career. Maybe she would just go work in a lab somewhere, but that was not her dream. Her dream was to teach all students to love Biology as much as she did. She wanted to reach the "hard to reach" students and give them many opportunities. Luckily, she went to a training on effective teaching and learned about universal instructional strategies, those that are used by effective teachers to teach the whole class.

## Universal Practices

Universal practices, also referred to as foundation skills, level 1, high leverage practices, and tier 1 instruction, are effective practices that are necessary for a well-managed classroom, regardless of content being taught, and that support all student learning and positive outcomes.

DOI: 10.4324/9781003109983-5

25

When implemented often (almost 80% of the time), these practices have the potential to eliminate the need for any other intervention for most students. As such, we encourage teachers to establish universal practices from the beginning of the school year and prior to implementing additional interventions.

In the following sections, we describe several universal practices. Some originate from the high leverage practices (HLP; McLeskey et al., 2017) developed by the Council for Exceptional Children and the CEEDAR Center, and others originated with Positive Behavioral Interventions and Supports (PBIS: www.pbis.org/). Although there are more tier 1 strategies and HLP than we include in the current chapter, we chose to include those that are specific to classroom environments that we consider prerequisites to the interventions in this book. Although beyond the scope of this book, we encourage you to read and explore PBIS tier 1 strategies and HLPs in their entirety.

The first is creating and maintaining a consistent, organized, and respectful learning environment, which includes establishing and encouraging expectations and routines. The second is delivering engaging academic instruction, which means encouraging and demanding student participation through strategies, such as increasing opportunities to respond. The third is participating and encouraging family–school partnerships. At times, it is a bit tricky to build a strong parent–teacher relationship, especially at the secondary school level and with parents who have often gotten negative reports about their child from the school. Each of these will be discussed in depth in the following paragraphs.

At the secondary school level, many educators and parents believe that students should know the expectations and be interested in learning regardless of instructional strategies, and there should be no need to engage with parents, as students should be responsible for their own learning. Unfortunately, this may be true, but adolescents with ADHD struggle to remember and follow expectations, especially when the rule is something that they find difficult, such as waiting their turn to speak. Similarly, as a teacher, you probably have classroom routines, but do not explicitly teach them to your students. For students with ADHD, it is vital that teachers teach and reteach the expectations and routines until students consistently follow them without giving much thought to it. In addition to teaching expectations and routines, teachers must encourage and motivate students to follow the expectations and engage in the routines. All too often, when students transition from elementary to middle school, teachers and parents believe that the students should be self-motivated to follow teacher expectations; however, we encourage you to remember that the expectations of many secondary teachers and schools are very difficult in light of the challenges associated with ADHD. For example, "be responsible" often includes coming to class prepared with all the needed materials, which is very difficult for adolescents who struggle with organization and frequently forget their supplies.

#  Consistent, Organized, Respectful Learning Environment

## Establish Classroom Expectations

The first action that teachers should take is to establish classroom expectations. Although we do not think this is surprising to you, we want to emphasize several characteristics of age-appropriate and culturally responsive expectations. Classroom expectations are the rules that guide behavior and interactions in the classroom. The expectations represent behaviors perceived as important, by the teacher, and necessary to have a highly functioning classroom environment. These expectations differ based on the school, the teacher, and the students. We encourage teachers to meet with the class and develop expectations based on their needs. Allowing students to participate in the development of the expectations increases the likelihood of having mutually respectful teacher–student relationships. This practice also helps teachers develop expectations that value multiple ethnic and cultural perspectives.

Expectations should be observable, measurable, and worded positively. Although expectations are often broad, the specific observable and measurable components are usually subsets of the expectations. For example, consider the common expectations listed in Figure 3.1.

The first is "Be respectful." What exactly does that mean? Does respectful mean different things for different people? No doubt. As such, the teacher added sub-expectations along the lines of raise your hand and wait for permission to talk, listen to your peers, listen to your teacher,

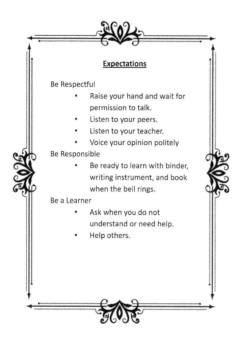

*Figure 3.1* Classroom Expectations.
Image used under license from Shutterstock.
Tartila/Shutterstock.com.

voice your opinion politely. It is important that teachers only include expectations that are important to themselves.

Consider, the expectation to wait your turn to speak. What does that mean exactly? To some teachers that means that the student will raise their hand and wait to be called on to speak. To other teachers, it means that the student will wait until a pause in the conversation to speak; hence, not speaking at the same time as another peer, but not waiting for direct permission to speak. Either way is acceptable, but the teacher must be clear with the student.

In addition to establishing expectations, the teacher must teach and reteach the expectations. We encourage teachers to use a skills training modeling described in Chapter 12 to teach students to engage in desired behaviors. A training model involves defining and describing the expected behavior, modeling and practicing examples and non-examples, providing feedback, and reteaching as needed. Consider Ms. Campbell. She was a young beginning teacher and wanted her students to raise their hands and wait for permission to speak. As such, she began by telling her class that the expectation is to raise their hands and wait for her to call on them to speak. Ms. Campbell described and modeled the behavior. This is one of the most important steps in teaching the rules. Additionally, Ms. Campbell modeled non-examples, such as speaking without raising her hand or speaking while raising her hand. Students tend to enjoy the comical nature of non-examples. After modeling, Ms. Campbell instructed the students to role-play examples and non-examples of following this rule. She offered for this to happen one at a time in front of the class or role-playing in groups of two. Ms. Campbell walked around the classroom as they practiced and provided feedback. She repeated this process frequently after teaching her students the expectations until she was satisfied with the rate of rule following by the entire class. If one expectation becomes a problem, then the teacher reteaches the behavior, role-plays, practices, and provides feedback, as many times as necessary. Although this seems time-consuming, it should only take about five minutes to complete the entire process and can improve following rules in the classroom.

## *Establish Routines*

To maintain order and flow in a classroom, teachers must establish and teach students to follow routines. Classroom routines are procedures for activities that happen daily, or even multiple times a day. This is especially important for adolescents with ADHD who have a tendency to forget monotonous activities, such as submitting their homework to the teacher. One option to help students successfully submit their homework is for teachers to create homework routines, which often begin when they walk into the classroom. For example, Ms. Campbell's beginning of class routine involves students: (1) coming into class before the tardy bell rings; (2) sitting at their assigned desk; (3) taking their homework out of their binders: (4) placing their homework in the assigned bin; (5) returning to their seat; and (6) answering two questions from the whiteboard. Ms. Campbell created a poster (Figure 3.2) with these procedures clearly outlined and practiced completing them every day for the first two weeks of school. If a student does not follow the routine on multiple occasions, the teacher reviews the expectations and has students role-play the activities.

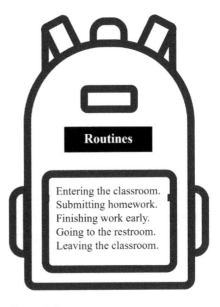

Routines

Entering the classroom.
Submitting homework.
Finishing work early.
Going to the restroom.
Leaving the classroom.

*Figure 3.2*

Image used under license from Shutterstock. Lidiia Koval/Shutterstock.com.

## *Encourage Expectations and Routine*

When students follow established rules and routines, teachers should provide age-appropriate specific feedback in meaningful and caring ways. By establishing, following, and reinforcing expectations of all students within the classroom, teachers will reduce the potential for challenging behavior and increase student engagement. Similarly, when students demonstrate problem behavior that is not in line with the expectations and routines, teachers should provide corrective feedback and reteaching. The assumption should be the student forgot the expectations and rules. It is important to remember the difference between an acquisition problem and a performance problem. If the problem was acquisition, they would have never demonstrated understanding. On the other hand, if they follow the routine sometimes and not others, it is a performance problem. It is important to avoid trying to determine if the student forgot the expectation or purposely disobeyed. The teacher's response should be the same regardless of the reason the student misbehaved. Further, the more one assumes that the student purposely disobeyed, the more frustrated the teacher may become with that student. Thus, it is often helpful to the teacher's mental health to avoid considering intent—just respond appropriately and move on.

Corrective feedback is specific, neutral in tone, and goal directed. It is an important tool for teachers to use to achieve effective classroom behavior management. Studies have shown that when teachers consistently provide appropriate corrective feedback to over half of the student misbehavior in a classroom, there is an overall improvement in student behavior. Student behavior often improves further when responding to over half of the failed expectations but responding to at least half is an important benchmark. Responding to anything over half of the misbehavior leads to student realizing that the teacher is more likely than not to respond to any acting out in class. Contrast that with students who learn that the teacher rarely responds to misbehavior, and it can be clear how important it is to provide appropriate corrective feedback for most misbehavior.

When a student frequently forgets an expectation or routine, the teacher can focus on the specific skill that the student is struggling to follow. For example, one student in Ms. Campbell's class continually forgets to submit his homework. Instead, he slides into his desk and begins talking to his peer about the latest video game. Ms. Campbell's gut reaction is to be annoyed. How many times has she told him to turn in his assignment? However, after a moment of self-talk about how intent does not matter and typical behaviors of students with ADHD, she calls the student to her desk and asks him to tell her and demonstrate the routine. The following day, she pre-corrects his behavior by meeting him at the door and asking him to describe the routine. She continues this practice each day until he automatically follows the routine. On that day, she gives an abundance of positive feedback. Another option is for Ms. Campbell to refer to the steps of the routine posted on the classroom door as students enter the classroom.

## Review Student Section 504 Plans and Individualized Education Programs

One means of demonstrating respect to students as individuals is to follow their individualized plans. Many students with ADHD have section 504 plans or individualized education programs (IEP). It is legally mandated that teachers follow these plans, implementing any intervention or accommodation that is included. Although school districts must provide the documentation of such a plan to teachers, we know of circumstances where this does not occur. As such, we encourage you to reach out to the child study team, the school counselor, and/or the 504 coordinators to determine if any of the students in your classroom have plans.

If a student has a disability that limits one or more major life functioning (29 U.S.C. § 701 et seq.), he is eligible for a section 504 plan through the amendments to the Rehabilitation Act of 1973. Section 504 plans include a list of accommodations and any changes necessary to the general education environment. Students with ADHD are often challenged with learning, which is a major life activity.

If a student meets certain criteria for one or more of the 13 special education categories, he is eligible for an IEP through the Individuals with Disabilities Education Improvement Act (IDEIA, 2004). Students with ADHD might receive services as a student with an Other Health Impairment (OHI) or other conditions, such as learning disabilities or Emotional and Behavioral Disorders (EBD). IEPs are roadmaps for the education of students with disabilities and include specialized supports and services needed

Include interventions in student goals in individualized goals and objectives.

*Given self-management instruction twice per week following the procedures,* the student will maintain attention during independent tasks 70% of five-minute intervals.

Image used under license from Shutterstock.
New Vectors/Shutterstock.com.

to progress academically. These programs include a descriptions of students' present levels of academic achievement and functional performance (PLAAFP), annual goals, procedures for monitoring and reporting progress, any supplementary aids and services, and a statement and justification of the extent to which a student does not participate in general education.

Although neither section 504 nor IEP forms commonly include a place to include interventions, we encourage educators to include evidence-based interventions within the text of the annual goals or benchmarks. In each intervention chapter in this book, we included a programming statement to help develop these.

## Use Strategies to Promote Active Student Engagement

In addition to establishing clear and consistent expectations and routines and abiding by individualized programs, delivering engaging academic instruction has the potential to reduce the need for additional interventions. Engaging academic instruction involves building positive relationships with students, varying activities with numerous opportunities to respond, and connecting learning to students' lives.

### Build Positive Student–Teacher Relationships

The relationship that you have with your students is the foundation for all learning (social, emotional, behavioral, academic). The time that you spend establishing and maintaining relationships will serve you well throughout the year. The most basic step is being honest and genuine. We will explain several specific actions that you can take in the following sections, but if you do not believe what you are saying or doing, students will know. Being disingenuous will harm the relationship. As such, prior to engaging in any of these behaviors, make sure that you know what you are feeling and prepare to be real!

Several easy teacher behaviors can help establish the relationship. Many of these involve communicating to the students that you are interested in them and respect

Image used under license from Shutterstock. Teran Studios/Shutterstock.com.

them. For example, meet students at the classroom door every day with a smile on your face at the beginning of class! Say each students' name. "Hi, Jaiden. Hi Maria. Come on in." Do the same when the students leave the classroom. "Goodbye, Jaiden, Maria." These verbalizations communicate warmth and respect. Show genuine interest in your students. Get to know them. What do they like? What are their interests? Listen when they talk about their families. What do you hear about their culture? You want to not only listen but communicate that you heard them and remember what they tell you! Maintain high expectations while accepting mistakes, made by you and your students. Laugh! Laugh at your own mistakes in front of your students and help students accept theirs. Talk about establishing goals and working to achieve them, even when they are challenging. Use yourself as an example. Give your students choices. Even small choices, like whether they write in pen or pencil, gives the students the chance to have a sense of control and investment in the activities.

Behavior specific praise (BSP) is another means of establishing a positive relationship with your students. BSP is verbal praise. For example, Ms. Campbell might respond to the on-task behavior of one of her frequently off-task students by saying, "Mohan, you did an awesome job staying on task until you completed your math work." Teachers frequently get into the habit of saying, "Good job," "Nice job," or some other phrase. However, at times students do not know what "job" the teacher is talking about or do not take the compliment seriously when delivered this way. With some adolescents, it is best to give behavior-specific praise privately, as some will tell you that it's not cool to be smart or a good student. On the other hand, some students like to be praised in front of their peers. Know your students and do what works best for them.

## *Varying Activities With Numerous Opportunities to Respond*

Another means of keeping students engaged while learning is to have all students respond to instruction simultaneously, instead of asking questions and calling on one student. Several means of accomplishing this goal are used by teachers. For example, Ms. Campbell might give all her students' individual whiteboards and markers and ask them to write one question for their reciprocal teaching groups. She might also give her students note cards with yes on one side and no on the other and ask them to answer basic questions about the reading simultaneously by raising the side of the card they believe answers the question. Adding technology to student response options can be exciting and motivating. For example, using Smart Board® "clickers" in which all students answer questions and each response appears on the smart board is an excellent means of having students respond. The idea is that all students answer a question at once, increasing motivation to attend to the lesson by requiring a response from other students.

Another way to increase opportunities to respond is by including collaborative learning activities that are completed with student partners or groups, such as partner learning, cooperative learning, and/or inquiry-based instruction. Each of these strategies involves active student engagement, learning, and participation. Effective use includes learning goals, clear and concise directions, clear explanations for student roles and responsibilities, and precise measures of student progress.

Partner learning involves two students working together during a lesson. Educators have developed several different structures for partner learning, such as Think-Pair-Share (TPS). TPS involves three steps. First, the teacher asks a question and instructs students to think about the response quietly for a specified period. At this point, the teacher can instruct the students to jot down possible answers with a few words, possibly a bullet list, or to write possible answers in their journals. Second, the teacher puts the students in pairs (either assigned or by student choice) and instructs them to talk about their answers. Third, the pairs share their thoughts and ideas with the entire class.

Cooperative learning is the process of planning instruction around small groups of students who work together. The success of each individual student is dependent on all other students. As such, not only are all students

*Figure 3.2* Cooperative Learning Roles.
Image used under license from Shutterstock. NeuendorfNiclas/Shutterstock.com.

active, but they also learn to work collaboratively while being responsible for their own role. Prior to beginning the activity, teachers assign students to a specific role and explain the expectations (Figure 3.2). It is very important that teachers explain the roles prior to beginning the lesson and provide feedback specific to the responsibilities of the role. For example, if the student role is recorder, the expectation is for the student to keep notes throughout the lesson and then to summarize what was taught. The teacher would read the notes and the summary and provide feedback regarding accuracy. As students become familiar with the expectations throughout the year, they will need less and less teacher direction and feedback.

Another popular option is to use inquiry-based instruction, a method focused on learning through discovery. With inquiry, students are actively engaged in knowledge construction through teacher-developed experiences. Inquiry-based instruction begins with a question that guides the students

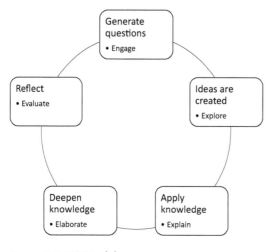

*Figure 3.3* 5-E Model.

through learning, as opposed to explicit instruction in which the teach is the "expert" delivering information to be absorbed by students. The question is designed to motivate students through natural curiosity.

One model of inquiry-based instruction is the 5-E model (Duran & Duran, 2004; Figure 3.3). The teacher "grabs" the students' attention in the engagement phase with a short lesson that clarifies the question, activates prior knowledge, helps students make connections between prior knowledge and the current lesson, and describes how to use the materials. Next, students work in groups in hands-on discovery learning scaffolded by the teacher as needed. After students have explored the concept in depth, in the explanation stage, the teacher provides terms and concepts used. In the elaboration phase, the teacher provides opportunities for the student to generalize what they have discovered and learned to new situations. In this phase, students engage in conversation comparing their ideas. In the final phase, evaluation, students discuss and demonstrate evidence of the changes that occurred in their understanding, beliefs, and skills. Throughout inquiry-based instruction, all students are actively developing and responding to new knowledge and understanding of the content increasing student excitement for learning, engagement, and motivation.

## Connect Learning to Students' Lives in the Anticipatory Set of the Lesson

Connecting learning to a diverse group of students' lives and experiences increases student interest in the lesson, but can be difficult at times. We have heard teachers ask, "How do we do that? We must follow the school adopted curriculum and/or teach to the selected standards." You can do it by connecting students' lives to the curriculum and incorporating the standards.

It all begins with the anticipatory set, the "hook" or the "gotcha." How do you make students excited about learning? You can spike curiosity early in the lesson! You help students make connections with what you are going to teach and their personal and academic prior knowledge, background, interests, and current or future goals. What would pique the interest of your students? What information do they need to understand to have sufficient foundational knowledge for the lesson? What have you already taught or what do they already know that makes the lesson more exciting?

When the content is far from student's lives, you start with a common idea, connect to a more general idea, and then focus all of that on a specific topic. Consider Ms. Campbell, whose goal is to teach students how to develop a hypothesis in biology. The students in her class have no knowledge of hypotheses, have never heard the word, and are not really interested in learning "some random science stuff." To pique their interest, she begins by defining hypotheses and explaining that it is similar to making an educated guess that needs to be investigated. She might start with a think-pair-share, instructing the students to get into groups and develop a list of guesses about how Covid-19 spread in their community. This task allowed them to begin to consider two things that they had prior knowledge of to learn about making hypotheses regarding the effects of Covid-19 on different populations, beginning with their own community. Next, she would have them share their guesses with the class. Then, she would have them make a list of why their guesses were "educated." What evidence do they have to support their guess? This is only the beginning of the lesson in which students will ultimately describe the connection between educated guess, hypotheses, and predictions regarding the differences between the effects of Covid-19 in urban and suburban districts.

## Encourage Family–School Partnerships

In addition to effective classroom practices, to lay the foundation for student progress and achievement, teachers must develop and maintain strong family–school partnerships. These partnerships are grounded in communication, and in celebrating successes and working together to address student challenges. Collaboration involves needs, goals, instruction, interventions, and student progress. With some parents and teachers, it is natural and easy to establish this relationship, but for others it is more difficult.

We are not enemies ...we are on the same team!

Image used under license from Shutterstock. New Vectors/Shutterstock.com.

Effective relationships are established through mutual respect and equitable collaborations. Teachers can show this respect by valuing family and parent values, opinions, and input. Unfortunately, as children move into adolescence and enter secondary schools, relationships between parents and teachers seems to be less common. This is a natural transition as developmentally the goal is for students to become more independent. It is also due to the fact that most secondary school teachers have many more students than elementary school teachers so it is not practical to get to know all parents. Nonetheless, we cannot overemphasize the importance of these relationships for students who are challenged by the school environment, such as those with ADHD. Parents rely on information from teachers regarding adolescent academic, social, and emotional progress. Teachers rely on parents for information regarding significant events at home and to support their efforts at home. For example, students with ADHD frequently have medication changes. Teachers are the most knowledgeable source regarding the effects of new medications on academic (and sometimes social) performance of students but might not even be aware of the medication change. When parents share this type of information, teachers can provide input to help determine the effects of the change. On the other hand, students might not complete and submit their homework and it is unlikely that the student would inform the parent. As such, teachers can reach out to parents to garner their help, which can be very valuable. With a strong relationship, parents and teachers can share information with each other. However, simply informing the other is not enough. Providing support and understanding to the parent of a student who is struggling can help the student and help the parent who may be quite frustrated.

There are a variety of techniques for developing and maintaining teacher–parent relationships (Figure 3.4). The first, and most obvious is to be friendly and positive. Start the meetings with a smile and say the parents' name. Meet with parents before a problem happens. Begin with a positive meeting. Talk to parents about your classroom expectations, routines, and their adolescent's strengths. Discuss goals for the year.

The second is clear communication, which includes communicating with parents in a way that they understand. The most basic is speaking in a language that they understand. This can be difficult as there are often no translators available to facilitate direct communication. Sometimes there are other members of the student's family who can help translate. There is also free software available that can translate written and verbal communication. For a child who is having difficulty, taking the time to find a way to communicate with parents can make a big difference in the success of the student.

Being clear also means being specific. Clearly explain what you are talking about. Do

**Don't Forget**

Undivided attention

Reflect content and feelings

Refrain from judgement

Request clarification

Ask open-ended questions

Paraphrase

Summarize

*Figure 3.4* Developing and Maintaining Teacher-Parent Relationships.
Image used under license from Shutterstock. SlyBrowney/Shutterstock.com.

not talk in circles. Do not use jargon. As educators, we tend to have our own language. Remember how it felt the time you were at a doctor's office and had no idea what he was talking about. Think about the following comments from the perspective of a non-educator, maybe an accountant or construction worker.

> We are very concerned about Randy's progress. He is on level M, he scored in the 34th percentile on the NJASK, and we want to begin the RTI process to determine if he meets the eligibility criteria for an IEP. Please sign here.

We doubt that this would strengthen the parent's relationship with the teacher. The same information can be communicated without our jargon!

> Hi Ms. Harrison. Randy is doing great in math, but seems to be struggling with reading. When we gave him a reading test, he was reading at level M,

between the second and third grade level, which is concerning as he is in sixth grade. We think that some additional assistance might help him; we would like to try some interventions and see if he does better. We need your permission to begin those interventions. What questions do you have?

As the teacher positions herself as the parent's ally and not some distant and cold professional, parents are more likely to feel respected and appreciated and engage in collaboration.

Being clear also involves active listening.

Although we all think that we listen to what is being said, following the steps to active listening is a skill that most have not been taught. Active listening involves giving undivided attention, refraining from judgmental thoughts, reflecting both content and feelings, responding with open-ended questions, requesting clarification, paraphrasing, and summarizing. Giving someone your undivided attention involves ignoring or blocking out everything around you that might be distracting. To achieve this, it helps to schedule meetings, whether in person or via technology or telephone, in a setting where nothing is distracting you. Call when you have no students in your classroom. Shut your classroom door and put a do not disturb sign on it, so that no one will walk in while you are on the call. As you know, teaching involves wearing many hats, and people expect you to drop what you are doing and attend to their needs. Building relationships with parents involves showing respect and undivided attention. When you feel like you have a good understanding of what the parent is telling you, then you can paraphrase or summarize to make sure that you understand their concerns.

While listening, think about the content and feelings being communicated by the parent. Avoid having judgmental or defensive thoughts. For example, Ms. King called her son's teacher to try and understand why he had a zero on an in-class assignment. She said that she was very confused as her son was upset and told her that he had no idea why he earned a zero. He said that there was no work to be done in class on that day and that the teacher was out of the class most of the time. The teacher's first reaction was to be upset because the student accused her of being out of class and not explaining the assignment. She knew this was not true. She also wondered why the parent was just looking at the student's grades two weeks later. This judgment and defensiveness were sure to show up in her comment to the parent, which is unlikely to be helpful. Many parents would have avoided the call for just that reason, fear of judgment. However, this parent had reached out for help, albeit in a challenging manner. As difficult as it may be to refrain from a defensive response, our judgment is less likely to be helpful than our listening, reassurance, and support.

If you do not understand what the parent is telling you, then clarifying or open-ended questions can be helpful. Clarifying questions are just checks for understanding. Ms. King might say, "So, it sounds like you need clarification on the assignment that your son did not complete that day?" You can also ask open-ended questions if you need more information. "Tell me more about what he did not understand." If you believe you understand, then it can be helpful to summarize, be solution focused, and transition to next steps. Paraphrasing and summarizing allow you to make sure that you understand the parent's concern. "Ok. You want to know what assignment your son missed and how he can eliminate the zero in the grade book. Is that correct?" Being solution focused involves solving the problem. Ms. King might ask for the parent's thoughts on the solution. "Do you have ideas for how we can solve this problem" or suggest a solution, "Your son can complete the assignment tonight and submit if for partial credit tomorrow. I will be happy to let you know when he submits the work. Does that sound like an acceptable solution?" It is usually most helpful in the long run if our communication with parents respects the parents' desire that their child be successful and that we are there to work together to help make that happen.

## Make Data-Based Decisions

Effective teachers make instructional and intervention decisions based on data; however, many are not taught what this really means in pre-service or in-service training. Instead "data" has become a buzz word with varying meanings. Data is defined as facts that can be used in calculating, reasoning, or planning. Specific to education, data are individual facts kept by federal, school, and districts on students. More specifically, for this chapter, we focus on the use of class-level and individual students' data related to academic, social, emotional, and behavioral achievement and progress. Specifically, we describe four steps to data-based decision making: collecting, analyzing, and interpreting data and applying the interpretations to decisions.

## *Collect or Review Existing Data*

The first step is to review and/or collect the data that can be used to measure specific student goals. Teachers have access to data collected by the district and collect data for themselves. Records of data outside of the classroom collected by the school help you understand students' histories. For example, you can review cumulative (collected throughout the students' school years) folders, past discipline records, report cards, behavioral assessments, standardized tests, and special education records to get a picture of the student prior to being in your class. Review of these records can tell you about a student's academic and behavioral progress *and* interventions/strategies used. That being said, we realize that not all districts keep all of these data, and some of it is often in a format that is not easy to review and consider. As a result, reviewing all of your students' data is not practical, but there may be important lessons to learn by reviewing the data of some of the students who are having serious problems in your class.

## *Collect Baseline Data and Begin Intervention*

When a student or students are having problems in your class, one of the most important steps is to gather and retain information about the students' current performance level and, specifically, about the problem areas (e.g., homework, classroom behavior). This is typically done through the collection of baseline data on formative assessments. Formative assessments take many forms depending on the content/skill being measured (Figure 3.5). Following is an example from Ms. Cassidy's class. The procedures described are more comprehensive than what may be necessary for the problem in the example, but we used a simple example to help with the clarity of the explanation. These steps may be most useful when you feel like you are at a dead end with a student and need to take a formal and comprehensive approach.

For example, if Ms. Cassidy is interested in beginning a class-wide intervention to teach her students to enter the classroom quietly, submit

| Content/Skill | Formative Assessment Tool | Reported as |
|---|---|---|
| Behavior | Direct observation | Frequency /Event recording |
|   On-task/off-task | | Duration |
|   Engagement | | Latency |
|   Time to begin task | | Intensity |
|   Disruptive behavior | | Rate |
|   Aggressive behavior | | |
|   Social behavior | | |
| Content | Permeant products | Grades |
| /tasks/skills |   Curriculum based | Percent complete |
|   Completion |   measures | Percent correct |
|   Accuracy | Pre-assessment | |
|   Comprehension | Exit tickets | |
|   Retention | Brief quizzes | |
|   Application | Probes | |

*Figure 3.5* Formative Assessment tools for Content/Skills.

their homework, and begin a short task (such as "Do-Nows") at their desks, she could begin by counting the number of students who follow all the procedures without prompting three days in a row and calculate the percentage of students each day. This would give her the rate of routine-following per day (see baseline in Figure 3.6). She could do the same with the number of her students that can develop an accurate hypothesis. Prior to beginning instruction, she could instruct the students to write one hypothesis on a note card. She could grade the accuracy of the hypothesis as the average percent of components of included across the class. This would give her the base rate of accurately written hypotheses in the class.

Next, if the rate of routine following is below her expectation, then she could implement an intervention. She might reteach the routine, have students practice it, and then provide reinforcement to those who follow the procedures of the routine 100% of the time. To determine if the intervention is effective, she could graph the data.

## Analyze, Interpret, and Apply

Next, the teacher could visually analyze, interpret, and apply the data to instruction. Visual analysis of data involves several steps. First, you

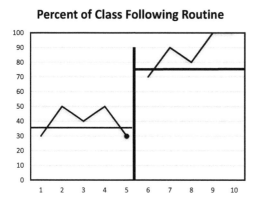

**Percent of Class Following Routine**

*Figure 3.6* Chart for Visual Analysis.

begin by inspecting the data during baseline and intervention. Calculate the average of the data points in baseline and draw a horizontal line across that point in baseline. Is the mean low? Is an intervention needed? Consider the average number of students who enter Ms. Cassidy's classroom and follow all the steps of the routine (40%; Figure 3.6).

Is that enough students following the routine for her class period to be organized and calm? Probably not, right? What about the stability of the baseline data? Are the data stable or do they have too much variability to determine the true percentage of students? The data points are 30%, 50%, 40%, and 30% across five days. No need to collect more data as the percent is pretty consistent. If there had been more variability, then she might have collected more data to make sure the students are really following the routine at a low rate before thinking about spending time on an intervention. What about the trend? Does it appear that the rate is getting higher without an intervention? No, this data seems to suggest that the pattern is not changing. On the other hand, if the data were trending up, Ms. Campbell might want to see if the trend was going to keep moving up without any intervention. Interpreting these three characteristics of the baseline data, could lead Ms. Campbell to be confident that the percentage of students following the routine is below what she expects.

Finally, with the graphed data and a clear picture of student progress, the teacher applies the findings to instructional or intervention decisions. Should the teacher begin intervention or instruction? Is the intervention needed? In the case of Ms. Cassidy, she may decide to intervene.

## Determine Intervention Effectiveness

Ms. Campbell continues to collect, graph, interpret, and apply data after intervention is implemented. The decision to continue, change, or discontinue intervention is based on the data collected after the intervention begins. As you plot student progress on the graph, you continue to visually inspect the data. Making a decision with data after intervention implementation involves visually inspecting progress before intervention and during intervention and comparing progress before and after implementation (Figure 3.6). Consider Ms. Cassidy's class after she implemented the intervention. More students were following all the steps to the routine, as you can see by the increase in average from 40% to 88%. The direction of the data was increasing, indicating that the percentage of students following the routine increased daily. However, the percentage had yet to stabilize, indicating that Ms. Campbell should continue practicing the routine and providing reinforcement to students for following the routine. By inspecting the progress on day five before intervention and on day six after the beginning of the intervention, it appears that the intervention resulted in an immediate change in the percentage of students who followed the routine. Finally, Ms. Campbell could inspect the graph to determine if on any day the student average was the same during baseline and intervention. She would note that is not the case in this situation. From these five properties of the data (Figure 3.7), she may determine that the intervention was helping, and she should continue letting students practice the routine and provide reinforcement when it was done correctly. She will continue until the percentage of students following the routine is the same or equivalent across three or more days, or the direction of student progress goes down, indicating that she has reached the maximum number.

When the average becomes stable across three or more days, Ms. Campbell could stop the intervention and move on to specific students who need help if their

Figure 3.7 Five Properties of Data.
Images used under license from Shutterstock.
fabrika_nasha/Shutterstock.com.

percentage is not at 100%. Which of the students are not following the routine? How can she increase their performance? With the answers to these questions, she would implement an additional intervention and collect individual student data. If the percentage of students following the routine goes down, she may consider changing something about intervention. It is possible that she would add a reinforcer with more value to the students or that she would add a group contingency, in which she split the class into teams and hold a competition won by the team with the highest percentage of students following the routine. The intervention will stop when Ms. Campbell is satisfied with the percentage of students following the routine and the percentage remains fairly stable over time.

## Be Culturally Responsive

Part of effective classroom management and helping students with ADHD involves using techniques that are culturally responsive. Geneva Gay (2002) defined culturally responsive teaching as, "using the cultural characteristics, experiences, and perspectives of ethnically diverse students as conduits for teaching them more effectively" (p. 106).

According to work done by Gloria Ladson-Billings (1995), culturally responsive teaching involves maintaining high academic expectations for all students, being culturally competent, and encouraging sociopolitical consciousness. What does all that mean and how does it look in a classroom? In the following sections we clarify what this can look like in your classroom. As a complete discussion of culturally relevant pedagogy is beyond the scope of this book, we encourage you to always continue studying and learning the latest advice from experts.

Image used under license from Shutterstock. Pressmaster/Shutterstock.com.

### Self-awareness and Cultural Competence

Effective teachers are aware of your own thoughts and cultural biases. As a culturally relevant teacher, it is important to challenge your negative biases about the culture of the students that you teach. Implicit bias is real. You may not be aware of your biases toward cultures other than your own. Stop and think. What are your thoughts about your students' ability to learn? About their parents? About their neighborhood? About their religion? About their language? Be honest with yourself, as many people have discovered their own long-held biases after careful consideration and learning on the topic. Correcting these biases can be very helpful as they can manifest in the way you teach and the way that you act and treat parents and students. Even if you are very aware of these biases and manage them well, thoughtful reflection and learning can improve your ability to value and celebrate the experiences and cultures of your students and recognize their potential.

Improving your awareness of your perceptions of others related to race, ethnicity, sex, gender, poverty, body shape, and other characteristics can help you create a classroom climate where judgment based on these features does not occur and all students feel safe to talk about their cultures and lives outside of school. Teachers can model curiosity, respect, and celebration of cultures that are different than your own. Ask students about themselves. Allow students to challenge cultural norms and discuss openly their thoughts and feelings about incidents happening in the world around them. Really getting to know your students helps with this. It is likely that interacting with students in a genuine and authentic manner will help you challenge stereotypes. Although it can be difficult to talk about these issues sometimes, seek help if you recognize that you are struggling with it.

Effective teachers are culturally competent. The National Education Association (NEA) defines cultural competence as "the ability to successfully teach students who come from cultures other than our own" (p. 2). Cultural competence refers to teacher skills that make students aware that they value their culture and expect them to become fluent in at least one other culture (Van Roekel, 2008). To do this, teachers are sensitive and knowledgeable of other cultures. This includes becoming familiar with the community in which you teach. Really getting to know the community. How do individuals interact in the community? Do you know common colloquialisms, tone, and expectations for eye contact and other behaviors? Do you know what interactions between people look like in the community? Do they exchange pleasantries and small talk for short or long periods of time before getting to the purpose of the interaction? Finally, it is important to consider each student and family within their culture and independent of their culture. A boy who identifies as a female may in some ways resemble the culture of transgender youth, but in other ways be very different than assumed cultural generalities. This gets back to the relationships you have with individual students and getting to know and respect them.

## Expectations, Pedagogy, and Sociopolitical Consciousness

We encourage you to maintain high expectations for all students. Make sure that all your students are fully aware that you expect them to perform academically, behaviorally, and socially, and that you have confidence that they can achieve those expectations. Unfortunately, some teachers communicate, unintentionally, that some students cannot achieve at the same level as their peers. Your expectations can be grounded firmly in your knowledge of the content being taught, your students, and your knowledge of the best culturally responsive pedagogy.

As most teachers, you know the content that you teach, and you are likely to be very passionate about your teaching. After all, it is your area of expertise. Nonetheless, motivating students to learn the content involves making instruction and the environment culturally relevant and inclusive. One way to think about developing culturally relevant classrooms is to ask yourself, metaphorically, is your classroom filled with mirrors where students can see the reflection of themselves, and windows, where they see the lived experiences of those from other cultures (NEA, 2008). When you read this, you probably immediately considered the posters on the walls and the pictures in the books your students read, but mirrors and windows show student much more. When you teach, are all the heroes in history books and in the novels that they read white, or do they see themselves in the characters in history who made a positive difference? Is the content relevant to your students? There is no doubt that you have heard students say, "What does this have to do with me? I will not ever use this stuff. I do not even know what you are talking about!" Culturally relevant teaching is the spirit of the classroom, the conversations of culture, equality, and social justice that permeates all instruction.

Many teachers focus on the mirrors in the classroom but forget to help students see through the window. Help students become aware and celebrate all cultures. When learning something outside of one's culture, bring it into the current context. For example, if you were teaching about the Civil War, you might ask students to think about how someone from the south or someone from the north might feel today in their city. This would help them think through what they were being taught and connect it to their current situations. Similarly, let students share their cultural knowledge and strengths in the classroom. For example, teachers might allow students to respond to instruction using relatable music, as opposed to writing an essay, select a movie and demonstrate how the movie relates to a topic being learned, or use other media to demonstrate their learning. Encourage students to be proud of the native language when it is not English by using their language for presentations and helping others to interpret it.

Sociopolitical consciousness involves exploration of polices, legal mandates, values, and beliefs that influence students, communities, and the world at large. Helping all students explore current situations, why each situation is the way it is, and how it has evolved is at the heart of culturally relevant teaching. Learning to listen and value the opinions of others while maintaining your own values and beliefs is a skill needed by all individuals. Culturally relevant teachers provide a safe space for students to explore current topics without disrespecting anyone else's culture. You must encourage students to become aware of bias and inequity and dismantle inequitable policies and practices. We must teach adolescents to have and use their own voice and challenge inequities and be agents of social change.

## Conclusion

In conclusion, teachers work to establish a classroom that is grounded in many of the universal strategies discussed in this chapter, and that is conducive to learning. This is the foundation for effectively helping your students and is important to achieve in order to increase the likelihood that you can help students with ADHD and other problems with individual interventions like those discussed in the following chapters. We described suggestions for establishing consistent, organized, and respectful learning environments, encouraging family–school partnerships, making data-based decisions, and strategies for ensuring that your teaching is culturally responsive. In the following chapter, we describe interventions to further teach students with ADHD the skills that they need.

# Reference List

Congress, U. S. (1973). Rehabilitation Act. 29 USC § 701 et seq.

Duran, L. B., & Duran, E. (2004). The 5E instructional model: A learning cycle approach for inquiry-based science teaching. *Science Education Review*, *3*(2), 49–58.

Gay, G. (2002). Preparing for culturally responsive teaching. *Journal of Teacher Education*, *53*(2), 106–116.

Individuals With Disabilities Education Act. (2004). 20 USC § 1400.

Ladson-Billings, G. (1995). Toward a theory of culturally relevant pedagogy. *American Educational Research Journal*, *32*(3), 465–491.

McLeskey, J., Barringer, M-D., Billingsley, B., Brownell, M., Jackson, D., Kennedy, M., Lewis, T., Maheady, L., Rodriguez, J., Scheeler, M. C., Winn, J., & Ziegler, D. (2017, January). *High-leverage practices in special education*. Council for Exceptional Children & CEEDAR Center.

Section 504 of the Rehabilitation Act. (1973). 29 USC § 701 et seq.

Van Roekel, D. (2008). *Promoting educators' cultural competence to better serve culturally diverse students*. National Education Agency: Policy Brief.

# Self-Regulated Strategy Development

**Tamika**

Tamika is a 5th grade female student with ADHD. Tamika's follows teacher directions most of the time. She enjoys verbally participating in whole class and group activities. She is bubbly and excited to learn new content. Nonetheless, when required to complete independent writing tasks, she struggles with organization and maintaining attention. As soon as the teacher gives the direction to begin writing, Tamika can be  seen looking around the room at all the posters on the walls. After carefully scanning the room, she attempts to begin writing, but the teacher, Ms. Puente notices she is simply doodling in the margins. When asked what she is doing, she responds by telling her about what she wants to write. Tamika is an elaborate storyteller, but she struggles with getting her thoughts on paper. Ms. Puente frequently discusses ideas with her and prompts her to begin, but she continues to doodle. In addition to struggling to begin writing, she struggles to manage time and complete the task. It is not a secret to Tamika that writing is not as easy for her as it is for the other students in the class, and she is embarrassed and does not believe that she will ever learn. Therefore, she does her best not to draw attention to herself during writing assignments. While Tameka sits quietly, Ms. Puente moves around the classroom working with students who are asking for her assistance. She thinks Tamika does not need her help, because it seems that she is engaged in writing. However, Tamika is sitting quietly in her chair drawing beautiful flowers in the margins of her paper. It is obvious that Tamika has no idea how to even begin the writing process, much less to self-regulate her activities sufficiently to finish the assignment. If intervention does not occur, Tamika is likely to continue to struggle with writing tasks throughout her life. Fortunately, there is a framework Self-Regulated Strategy Development (Graham & Harris, 1985) known to increase the writing performance of students with ADHD that Mr. Saed decided to implement with her.

DOI: 10.4324/9781003109983-6

## Description of SRSD

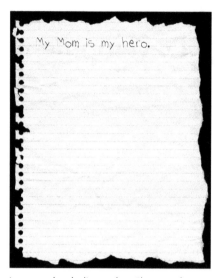

My Mom is my hero.

Image used under license from Shutterstock.
Sarah Kinnel/Shutterstock.com; Tom Murphy.

Self-Regulated Strategy Development (SRSD) is a direct instruction approach used to improve students' academic performance and teach them to regulate their own behavior during the writing process (Harris & Graham, 1985). With SRSD, students like Tamika, who are challenged by writing, learn to independently write stories, opinions, and other types of essays. SRSD involves teaching students specific structured processes, used by skilled writers. As with Tamika, I am sure that you have noticed that students with ADHD struggle to write. The struggle is real, as writing involves attending to task, setting goals, planning actions, organizing thoughts and materials, self-regulating behavior, and remaining goal directed (Harris & Graham, 1996). As you would guess, all of these are components known to be problems for many adolescents with ADHD. It is likely that when Tamika is given a prompt and the instruction to begin writing, she begins to think about the prompt, just as her peers do, but struggles to regulate her attention, thoughts, and time. For example, if Ms. Puente gave the prompt, "Write about a person that you admire and support your opinion." She first thinks of her mother, but then she thinks of her father, but wait what about her grandmother? After quite an internal struggle, she selects her mother and explains with great enthusiasm why she is a hero to Ms. Puente. Unfortunately, she never managed to get more than one sentence on the paper.

SRSD is a learning strategy that will help Tameka complete the task! Results of scientific studies indicate that when SRSD is used to teach students with ADHD, their writing becomes more accurate and the number of words, length, and quality increase, with students including more elements such as supporting details and main ideas (Cramer & Mason, 2014; Jacobson & Reid, 2010; Johnson et al., 2012; Lienemann &

Reid, 2008). This is likely because with SRSD, writing is more concrete and objective. Students are taught specific steps to follow and how to monitor their progress. With a mnemonic that illustrates the steps in hand, the adolescent with ADHD can complete each step, check it off, and feel successful. With this success comes confidence, which leads to more writing. Visual schedules take the mystery out of the writing process that can feel daunting.

## Stages of SRSD

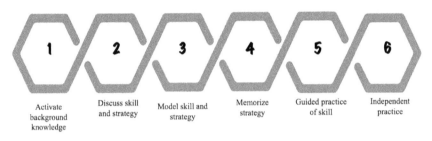

|   |   |   |   |   |   |
|---|---|---|---|---|---|
| 1 | 2 | 3 | 4 | 5 | 6 |
| Activate background knowledge | Discuss skill and strategy | Model skill and strategy | Memorize strategy | Guided practice of skill | Independent practice |

*Figure 4.1* Six steps to SRSD.

SRSD includes six stages (Figure 4.1; Harris et al., 2019) to teach numerous writing tasks in different genres. The first stage involves the teacher activating background knowledge on the type of assigned writing (opinion, story). In this chapter we describe five types of writing (i.e., sentence writing, paragraph, story writing, opinion/persuasive, expository). The mnemonic for each genre can be found near the end of this chapter. The first stage is activating prior knowledge to build anticipation and excitement for the assignment by helping students remember what they already know and how the new lesson is tied to that knowledge. The second stage is an in-depth discussion of the skill and strategy to be taught. This is the stage that builds the foundation for learning and doing. The third stage is modeling the skill and strategy. Teachers demonstrate, in exciting ways, how to use the skill to write the essay, encouraging students to develop their writing. The fourth stage is memorizing the strategy. Students are taught the strategy through a mnemonic device. The fifth stage is guided practice using the skill. Teachers gradually release writing responsibility to the student, differentiating for individual needs. The sixth stage is independent practice when teachers fade all scaffolds and students write independently and build competence for maintenance and generalization.

# Stage 1: Activate Background Knowledge

The first step of SRSD is to activate student background knowledge. For example, Ms. Puente activates Tamika's prior knowledge of opinion essays. She begins by talking about and looking over essays they have read in class. Together, they identify the properties of a good essay in the examples and identify why the author included specific components, such as topic sentences, supporting details, and the conclusion. What was the author trying to communicate? During this stage, the teacher begins the discussion about self-regulation. Ms. Puente could talk to Tamika about using a checklist to monitor her own behavior.

# Stage 2: Discuss Skill and Strategy

Discussing the skill and strategy has four implementation steps: (1) discuss the student's current performance, (2) provide the student with the mnemonic, (3) discuss the purpose, and (4) explain the process of using the strategy.

### Discuss the Student's Current Performance

First the teacher talks about the student's performance. The teacher gives the student the opportunity to talk about how she thinks she is progressing in writing and how she feels about it. It is highly likely that the adolescent with ADHD is struggling to write, and will tell the teacher that she does not like to write. Therefore, the teacher begins to help the student enjoy writing by providing structure to a typically unstructured process. She explains to the student that she is going to teach her some skills that excellent writers use.

### Provide the Student With the Mnemonic

After the discussion, the teacher gives the student the mnemonic on a laminated anchor chart and explains that it will help her learn and remember each component of the skill specific to the sentence, paragraph, or genre (mnemonic examples follow). A mnemonic is a tool, such as a series of letters or words, that helps students remember information. In the case of Tamika, Ms. Puente begins by using the mnemonic, POW TREE, to teach her to write an opinion essay (Figure 4.2).

## Discuss the Purpose

After the teacher provides the student with the mnemonic, they discuss the purpose for the skill and how the mnemonic will help. For example, Ms. Puente tells Tamika that writing opinion essays is important, as they give her the opportunity to formulate and share

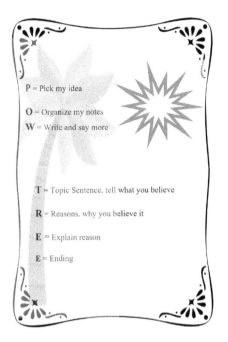

P = Pick my idea

O = Organize my notes

W = Write and say more

T = Topic Sentence, tell what you believe

R = Reasons, why you believe it

E = Explain reason

E = Ending

*Figure 4.2* POW TREE.
Image used under license from Shutterstock. StockSmartStart/Shutterstock; Tartila/ Shutterstock; Frank Heikkinen/Shutterstock.

her opinion. She explains that many great opinion essays have been written by important people and have changed history. They discuss how the mnemonic will help her write, and how she will memorize it. They discuss how she could use the mnemonic to write essays in different settings. Tamika might point out that she often writes opinion essays in history class and can use the mnemonic to guide her. In addition to discussing the use of the mnemonic, the teacher discusses the purpose of self-monitoring within the writing process. The teacher explains that by monitoring her own progress, the student can keep herself on pace and complete the process.

After this brief explanation and discussion, the teacher and student discuss each letter and step of the mnemonic. We encourage teachers to help students make a connection with the mnemonic, so that it is easier for them to remember. For example, Ms. Puente might encourage Tamika to think about the explosion and the tree on the card. Anything that the teacher can do to help the student remember the mnemonic is beneficial. Be creative!

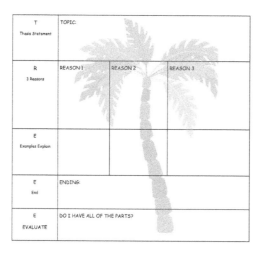

| T Thesis Statement | TOPIC: | | |
| --- | --- | --- | --- |
| R 3 Reasons | REASON 1 | REASON 2 | REASON 3 |
| E Examples Explain | | | |
| E End | ENDING: | | |
| E EVALUATE | DO I HAVE ALL OF THE PARTS? | | |

*Figure 4.3* Graphic organizer with TREEE.
Image used under license from Shutterstock.
StockSmartStart/Shutterstock.

## Explain the Process of Using the Strategy

Next, the teacher trains the student to use the mnemonic starting with the mnemonic anchor chart (Figure 4.2) and the graphic organizer (Figure 4.3) and explains to the student that she will memorize the strategy and use it each time she begins a writing assignment. She explains that using the graphic organizer will help her think about her writing. We have included anchor charts for writing topic sentences, paragraphs, and different genres at the end of the current chapter. The graphic organizer that Tamika will use for POW-TREE is one of the most commonly used organizers.

The teacher explains to the student that she will use the anchor chart until she learns the strategy and then she will be able to use it by herself. The teacher and student agree that the student will refer to the mnemonic each time she writes an opinion essay, making sure that she has followed each part of the tool. Finally, the teacher and student discuss how the student will self-regulate her own writing by giving herself a score and comparing it to her goal. For more in-depth discussion of self-monitoring, see Chapter 5 of this book.

## Stage 3: Model Skill and Strategy

Modeling the skill and strategy involves four implementation steps: (1) reading and critiquing model sentences, paragraphs, and/or papers; (2) modeling each step while "thinking out loud"; (3) teaching students to use their own self-talk (thinking out loud); and (4) modeling self-regulation and scoring.

## Read and Critique Model Sentences, Paragraphs, and/or Papers

Like activating prior knowledge, while discussing the strategy, the teacher and students read and critique opinion essays in other works. The teacher provides models of good and poor essays written at the student's reading level. The two discuss what makes the sentences good or poor. Together they will highlight the properties of the good essays and take notes on the graphic organizer (Figure 4.4) to help the student remember examples of the properties of poor and strong essays.

| Name: Date: Goal: My goal is to write the essay within three class periods with a score of 90% | | | | |
|---|---|---|---|---|
| **Tree** | **Description** | **Possible Points** | **Self** | **Teacher** |
| **T** Thesis Statement | ⇒ States your opinion<br>⇒ Has a catch (engages reader) | 2 | | |
| **R** 3 Reasons | ⇒ Reason 1 in topic sentence<br>⇒ Reason 2 in topic sentence<br>⇒ Reason 3 in topic sentence | 2 | | |
| **E** Examples Explain | ⇒ Reason 1 – explain and provide at least 2 examples<br>⇒ Reason 2 – explain and provide at least 2 examples<br>⇒ Reason 3 – explain and provide at least 2 examples | 3 | | |
| **E** End | ⇒ Reason 1: Ends with concluding sentence and transition<br>⇒ Reason 2: Ends with concluding sentence and transition<br>⇒ Reason 3: Ends with concluding sentence and transition<br>⇒ Ends essay with a concluding message<br>⇒ Essay conclusion ties back to thesis | 5 | | |
| ⇒ Total | | 12 | | |

*Figure 4.4* Graphic Organizer with Scoring Scale.
Image used under license from Shutterstock. Gaslop/Shutterstock.com.

## Model Each Step With Self-talk

Teachers model the entire process and verbally describe what they are doing and thinking. This can occur class-wide, in pairs, or with an individual student. Class-wide, teacher's project what they are writing on a whiteboard or smartboard®. When working individually with a student, the teacher sits at a table and models the writing process on paper. An important component is that as she models and verbalizes what she is doing, she demonstrates enthusiasm and excitement for the topic and for the writing process. She uses language that makes sense to the student and as she models thinking through goal development, she encourages the student to think of her own goals and self-statements (self-prompts).

The entire process is verbalized aloud. For example, Ms. Puente might tell Tamika that she has three heroes, her father, mother, and uncle. She gives several reasons for each and then selects her mother and says, "My goal is to write the topic and three reasons why my mother is my hero on the advanced organizer about my mother as my hero within five minutes of being given the direction to start." She could ask Tamika to pretend to be the teacher and give the direction to begin. To monitor her progress toward her goal, Ms. Puente could set a timer on her watch and stop the timer when she has written the topic sentence and three reasons. Next, Ms. Puente would model writing a thesis sentence with her topic and three topic sentences for her paragraphs.

## Model Self-regulation and Scoring

Next, the teacher models self-regulation and teaches the student to score her own writing. The teacher begins by looking at her self-regulation form and checks that she completed the topic and three reasons in five minutes and says aloud, "I wrote the topic sentence and three reasons." Next, she places checks in the appropriate columns on her self-monitoring form.

## Teach Students to Generate and Use Self-talk

Next, the teacher instructs the student to complete the same process that she just modeled. As the student verbalizes her actions, the teacher provides redirection and reinforcement. For example, Tamika would say, "I wrote a thesis sentence and three topic sentences." As she completes each statement, she would place a check on the self-monitoring form. The teacher and student continue this process until the students demonstrates that she can independently write the sentences.

## Stage 4: Memorize Strategy

In stage 4 the teacher helps students memorize the mnemonic and the coordinating steps. Memorizing the strategy includes two implementation steps: (1) teaching the mnemonic and (2) testing knowledge. The procedures described here can be used throughout each stage, beginning with stage 1.

Teachers use multiple strategies to help students memorize content. In this section, we describe several that are known to be effective; however, you can use any strategy to help the student memorize the mnemonic! Remember that if a strategy does not work for a student, then try another.

The first, and most used, strategy is flash cards. The teacher can make the flash cards for the student or the student can make the flash cards. Allowing the student to be creative while making the cards will help students remember the letters, the corresponding words, and the meaning. Once the cards are made for each letter in the mnemonic, the teacher can pair students together to test each other using the flash cards. In addition to paper flash cards, there are many technology flash cards (e.g., Quizzlet, Cram, Flashcard online, Brainscape) that students can create and use to study with independently.

Another strategy is for the teacher, or the student, to create a memory game. The game consists of individual cards for the letter and meaning of each of letter. In groups of two to four, the students place the cards out on the table and turn over one at a time. When a student gets a pair (i.e., the letter and matching description), the student keeps the cards and gets an additional turn. The student with the most pairs at the end of the game wins. To increase the likelihood of remembering the pairs, the teacher can ask the student to say the letter and description each time a pair is found. Again, there are technology-based memory game options for students to use independently, such as Interacty, Puzzle, and Educaplay. Periodically, teachers test for memory and understanding. As the students memorize and recall the strategy fluidly, the use of memorization techniques is faded. If the student seems to forget the strategy, then the teacher can restart the memorization sessions.

## *Stage 5: Guided Practice*

In stage 5, students are given the opportunity to practice using what they have learned with scaffolding and feedback provided by the teacher. Stage 5 includes two implementation steps: (1) students practicing the writing process with scaffolds and teacher-directed prompts and feedback and (2) fading of scaffolds.

### Practice With Scaffolds

In the current step, teachers assign students a writing task that involves planning, drafting, and revising to be completed with assistance. The teacher provides as much support, in the form of scaffolds, as is needed for students to attain their goals. There are many different types of scaffolds that can be provided to students during this phase. Teachers can provide (1) time for writing in collaborative writing pairs, (2) anchor charts, (3) graphic organizers, and (4) word lists.

In relation to self-regulation, teachers can provide (1) strategy checklists, (2) self-management forms with procedures to achieve initial goals, and (3) personal self-statement sheets to help students regulate goal-directed behavior. Ms. Puente would likely give Tamika the self-monitoring form to help her begin writing and maintaining attention.

### Fade Prompts and Teacher Guidance

In the final step of this phase, the teacher gradually releases all responsibility to the student. Students are taught and encouraged to create their own scaffolds. For example, Tamika could create her own checklist, set her own timer, and reinforce herself for meeting each goal. The rate at which the teacher transfers all responsibility depends on how quickly the student learns the procedures. It is likely that some students with ADHD will need scaffolds for extended periods of time. It is important that students document and graph their own progress, and the teacher and student discuss different ways to use the skills learned. For example, Ms. Puente and Tamika might consider different classes in which Tamika will use her skill in writing opinion papers. This is important, as without prompting, it is unlikely that Tamika would even think about the skills she learned in her history class when she is required to write an essay. Teachers closely monitor student progress during this time and resume scaffolds as needed. The process continues until the student has mastered the skill.

## Stage 6: Independent Practice

The sixth stage involves the student writing independently. During this stage, the teacher provides feedback and support only when asked for assistance. Students are encouraged to use scaffolds they have created for themselves or none. This allows students to move from dependence to independence increasing their "academic self-esteem." Students are encouraged to update their goals and self-management plans, increasing the difficulty, and to document when they use the skill in different environments. Students are encouraged to use their new skill in all of their classes and to self-reinforce the use of the skill. For example, when Tamika writes an opinion essay in one of her classes and follows the steps of POW-TREE, she would make a note in her planner and provide herself with a reinforcer. We encourage teachers to monitor progress and provide booster sessions as needed during this stage.

## Mnemonics for Each Genre

Students are required to write in many genres. In the following figures, we provide five acronyms for writing tasks and genres. Students are taught to write in each genre following the six stages described earlier in this chapter.

**Sentence Writing**

<u>S</u> = Start with a capital letter

<u>W</u> = Written neatly

<u>A</u> = A space between each word

<u>G</u> = Given punctuation at the end

SWAG!

**Paragraph Writing**

<u>P</u> = Pick a topic

<u>L</u> = List your ideas

<u>E</u> = Evaluate your list

<u>A</u> = Activate the paragraph with a topic sentence

<u>S</u> = Supply supporting details

<u>E</u> = End with a concluding sentence

ANY WRITING

<u>P</u> = Pick my idea

<u>O</u> = Organize my notes

<u>W</u> = Write and say more

OPINION WRITING

<u>T</u> = Topic Sentence, tell what you believe

<u>R</u> = Reasons, why you believe it

<u>E</u> = Explain reason

<u>E</u> = Ending

Image used under license from Shutterstock. besunnytoo/Shutterstock.com, Orange Vectors/Shutterstock.com, Littlekidmoment/Shutterstock.com, Gaslop/Shutterstock.com.

# Potential Barriers and Methods of Overcoming the Barriers

There are always some barriers involved when implementing interventions in secondary schools. In this section, we will discuss some barriers to implementation of SRSD with adolescents with ADHD. Further, we provide some options for overcoming those barriers.

## *From Thoughts to Writing*

It is not uncommon for students with ADHD to tell teachers what they would like to write and then simply sit and stare. The struggle to get ideas on paper is real and very complex. Regardless of the reason for this challenge, teachers can individualize prompts and scaffolds. For example, Ms. Puente might allow Tamika to dictate her topic sentence to a teacher or a peer. Using this strategy, the teacher or the peer would write the sentence that Tamika says aloud. Tamika would be responsible for making the essay meet the POW-TREE criteria. Did she pick and describe her idea? Did she organize her notes? Did she write and say more? Specifically, did she include a thesis sentence, three paragraphs for reasons with explanations for her opinion? Did she write an appropriate ending?

For more independence, Ms. Puente might allow Tamika to dictate into a recording device or a computer. If she used a recording device, she could listen with headphones, stop the recorder when she wants, and type or write the sentence. Using this strategy, Tamika moves at her on pace, but has the responsibility of

Image used under license from Shutterstock. Vector/Shutterstock.com.

| Examples of Free Speech-To-Text Programs and Applications |
|---|
| Dragon Professional |
| Dragon Anywhere |
| Otter |
| Verbit |
| Speechmatics |
| Braina |
| Amazon Transcribe |
| Microsoft Auzure |
| Google Gboard* |
| Just Press Record* |
| Speechnotes* |
| Trascribe* |

writing out the essay. On the other hand, if she spoke, using a speech-to-text application or program, her thoughts would automatically be transcribed to the paper. Nonetheless, she would be responsible for the parts of the essay per POW-TREE.

## Handwriting Frustrations

Some students with ADHD struggle with handwriting. Many times, we have heard teachers express concern that the handwriting of students with ADHD is messy and difficult to read. This can be annoying, but more importantly, it can result in students earning lower grades when teachers do not recognize what the students write. It is probably not surprising to you that students with these challenges become very frustrated when asked to write. Unfortunately, this often impacts student ability to demonstrate knowledge and creativity. Therefore, it's important to consider this challenge and provide effective scaffolds.

One scaffold is to allow students to use technological devices. With recent advances, students have access to smart pens, computers, and tablets. SmartPens® are devices that allow the students to write on a tablet and have a digital copy of the file. The program can convert the students handwritten document to text files. Many applications can export the document into a Microsoft Word, Google, Evernote document and others.

Chromebooks, computers, and tablets are commonly used in schools. For example, during the recent pandemic, many schools provided a Chromebook for each of their students. Using the Chromebooks, computers of their own, or tablets, students completed papers online through programs such as Google Docs or Microsoft Office Word. In addition, as already mentioned, students could dictate and others could scribe for them; however, we encourage teachers to use scaffolds that will generalize to other areas of the students' lives and futures. For example, Tamika will need to write many papers in her education and after she graduates from high school.

Furthermore, her handwriting will be a problem when she takes notes in class or for herself. Teaching her to dictate or type notes, will help her complete a range of tasks from writing a grocery list to writing a dissertation!

## Student Engagement

As with any intervention used with adolescents with ADHD, engagement can be a problem. For students to be engaged in any task, they must initiate and maintain attention, and move fluidly from one activity to another. This is a struggle for any student with ADHD.

SRSD has "built-in" strategies to help students regulate their own attention; hence, the "self-regulation" components. However, some adolescents might continue to struggle. As such, there are many interventions in this book that are strictly developed to help students attend to tasks. In Chapter 5, we describe self-management. Combining the procedures of self-management with the self-regulation components of SRSD is likely to be beneficial for students who continue to struggle with attending.

Another means of increasing engagement of students with ADHD is to provide choices throughout the process and consider student interest in all activities. For example, Ms. Puente might give Tamika the five writing prompts in Figure 4.5 when assigning a persuasive essay. This provides an opportunity for choice and creates the probability that Tamika will be able to write something that is of interest to her.

## Missing Instruction

As the lessons of SRSD are taught in stages, it is possible that adolescents with ADHD might miss content. This could happen when students are absent or tardy for school, but it is more likely to occur with students with ADHD when they "zone out" and are not paying attention to what is being taught. For example, during the third stage, Ms. Puente was modeling writing opinion essays and demonstrating self-talk. During the lesson, it started snowing outside. Tamika was enthralled by the snow slowly floating to the ground. She watched several flakes drift and spin in the air gently landing on a leaf right outside the window. After the fifth flake, she realized that Ms. Puente had stopped talking and her classmates were in pairs

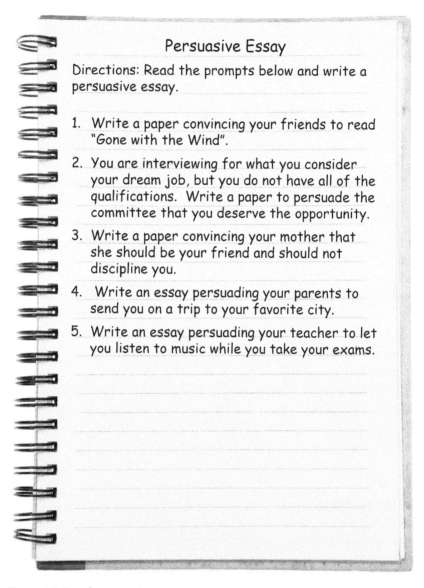

Persuasive Essay

Directions: Read the prompts below and write a persuasive essay.

1. Write a paper convincing your friends to read "Gone with the Wind".

2. You are interviewing for what you consider your dream job, but you do not have all of the qualifications. Write a paper to persuade the committee that you deserve the opportunity.

3. Write a paper convincing your mother that she should be your friend and should not discipline you.

4. Write an essay persuading your parents to send you on a trip to your favorite city.

5. Write an essay persuading your teacher to let you listen to music while you take your exams.

*Figure 4.5* Sample persuasive essay prompts.
Image used under license from Shutterstock. Butterfly Hunter/Shutterstock.com.

working together. When Ms. Puente told the students to begin working with their partners, she was watching snowflake # 4.

When students miss content, it is retaught. We encourage all teachers to use strategies in this book to help students maintain attention. Ultimately our goal is to help students become successful adults with knowledge of strategies to help them overcome challenges. Nonetheless, regardless of the strategies in place, it is likely that they will "zone out" sometimes. When this happens, teachers are responsible for helping them learn the content the student missed. This requires reteaching. Reteaching can be a challenge, as time is a valuable resource in schools. This might be a perfect opportunity for peer tutoring (Chapter 11). With peer tutoring, Ms. Puente can ask Tamika's partner to teach the steps that she missed. Another option is for her to refer Tamika to the visual prompt provided in advance.

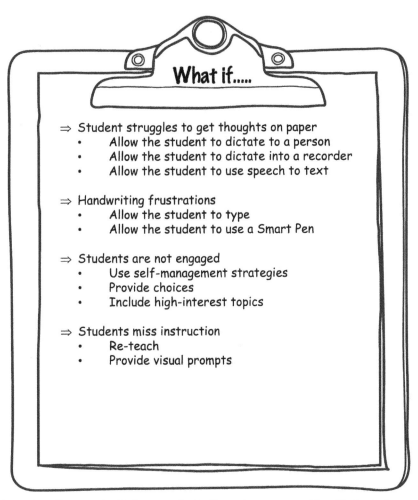

## What if.....

⇒ Student struggles to get thoughts on paper
- Allow the student to dictate to a person
- Allow the student to dictate into a recorder
- Allow the student to use speech to text

⇒ Handwriting frustrations
- Allow the student to type
- Allow the student to use a Smart Pen

⇒ Students are not engaged
- Use self-management strategies
- Provide choices
- Include high-interest topics

⇒ Students miss instruction
- Re-teach
- Provide visual prompts

Image from Shutterstock with license and edited by author. rangsan paidaen/Shutterstock.com.

#  Considerations for Culturally Responsive SRSD

When viewing SRSD through a culturally responsive lens, we encourage you to think about means of increasing student knowledge of professional writers that could serve as positive role models to each child. We have heard many adults from a diverse range of cultures describe never seeing successful people from their own culture. Using SRSD gives teachers the opportunity to provide students with writing examples and prompts that integrate cultures, parts of the world, and diverse authors. Essay writing provides opportunities for teachers to activate students' cultural knowledge. To accomplish this, teachers design writing activities that address the variety of cultures represented in their classrooms

Teachers have the opportunity to expose students to the writing of a diverse group of authors during stage 3 when teachers model "good writing" by exploring the writing of others. Students might be exposed to the writing of Percival Everett when learning to write persuasive essays. For example, Ms. Puente could use the collection of short stories titled "Damned If I Do" when demonstrating the story-writing strategy. The series addresses race and prejudice while simultaneously celebrating the human condition. There are many other options from which teachers can chose. We cannot overemphasize the importance of exposing students to successful writers from their own and other cultures.

# Programming

We strongly encourage teachers to advocate for the inclusion of SRSD on any plan, such as a response to intervention plan, individualized education program (IEP), section 504 plan, and/or any other plan written for an adolescent with ADHD. As you know, research indicates that using SRSD to help students with ADHD learn to write is likely to result in an increase in academic writing skills and self-regulation. Therefore, we provide examples of applicable Common Core Standards and CASEL standard; Tamika's current levels, strengths and weaknesses, and annual goals.

**Common Core Standards**

CCSS.ELA-LITERACY. Write arguments to support claims with clear reasons and relevant evidence.

CCSS.ELA-LITERACY. Write informative/explanatory texts to examine a topic and convey ideas, concepts, and information through the selection, organization, and analysis of relevant content.

CCSS.ELA-LITERACY. Write narratives to develop real or imagined experiences or events using effective technique, relevant descriptive details, and well-structured event sequences.

**CASEL Standards:** Social Emotional Learning Competency: Self-Awareness Sub-competency—recognizing strengths and self-confidence

**Current levels, strengths, and weaknesses:** Tamika is a 7th-grade student. Tamika is earning Cs and Ds in English Language Arts (ELA). Tamika's areas of need include writing and maintaining attention to task. According to Ms. Puente's direct observations, Tamika is engaged with writing tasks about 20% of opportunities. On average, she takes at least ten minutes to write one to three words on her paper. She rarely completes writing tasks within the given time. This results in failing ELA grades. To increase writing achievement and performance, Tamika needs to learn strategies to assist with essay writing and self-regulation.

**Annual Smart Goal:**

- Given SRSD instruction daily following the procedures outlined in [this book], Tamika will write topic sentences with 100% accuracy on four out of five opportunities. Furthermore, she will begin writing within five minutes of being given the instruction to begin.

# Conclusion

SRSD is an explicit instructional intervention. It is also an example of a training intervention (see discussion in Chapter 12) that literature suggests is an effective approach for adolescents with ADHD. Using SRSD, students are taught to utilize scaffolds and supports to write sentences, paragraphs, and essays across genres and to regulate their own behavior and performance. Writing is an important skill for students to master and can be especially challenging for adolescents with ADHD. In this chapter, we discussed six stages and their implementation steps. We discussed student struggles to get thoughts on paper, handwriting frustrations, student engagement, and missing instruction as potential barriers to effective implementation. Furthermore, we stressed the importance of maximizing on the opportunity to expose students to role models across cultures and to capitalize on students' social capital to increase engagement with writing. We strongly encourage you to utilize SRSD with all adolescents with ADHD who struggle to master essay writing across genres.

| Topic Sentence | |
| --- | --- |
| Detail 1 | |
| Detail 2 | |
| Detail 3 | |
| Detail 4 | |
| Conclusion Sentence | |

Appendix

Title:

| Topic Sentence: |
| :-- |
| First, |
| Then, |
| Next, |
| Last, |
| Conclusion Sentence: |

Appendix

Title:

| Opinion: |
| --- |
| Supporting Reason: |
| Supporting Reason: |
| Supporting Reason: |
| Conclusion: |

Appendix

# Reference List

Cramer, A. M., & Mason, L. H. (2014). The effects of strategy instruction for writing and revising persuasive quick writes for middle school students with emotional and behavioral disorders. *Behavioral Disorders, 40*(1), 37–51.

Harris, K. R., & Graham, S. (1985). Improving learning disabled students' composition skills: Self-control strategy training. *Learning Disability Quarterly, 8*(1), 27–36.

Harris, K. R., & Graham, S. (1996). *Making the writing process work: Strategies for composition and self-regulation*. Brookline.

Harris, K. R., Ray, A., Graham, S., & Houston, J. (2019). Answering the challenge: SRSD instruction for close reading of text to write to persuade with 4th and 5th Grade students experiencing writing difficulties. *Reading and Writing, 32*(6), 1459–1482.

Jacobson, L. T., & Reid, R. (2010). Improving the persuasive essay writing of high school students with ADHD. *Exceptional Children, 76*(2), 157–174.

Johnson, J. W., Reid, R., & Mason, L. H. (2012). Improving the reading recall of high school students with ADHD. *Remedial and Special Education, 33*(4), 258–268.

Lienemann, T. O., & Reid, R. (2008). Using self-regulated strategy development to improve expository writing with students with attention deficit hyperactivity disorder. *Exceptional Children, 74*(4), 471–486.

# 5 | Self-Management

---

**Malik**

Malik is a ninth-grade male student with ADHD. Malik is popular with his peers, and he makes them laugh a lot in class and is fun to be around.

However, Malik struggles in class. He repeatedly blurts out answers to questions that his teacher asks, no matter how many times he is reminded. Sometimes his answers are correct and other times, he seems to be off in left field. His teachers and parents are frustrated and feel like they  have worked with him for "years" and he still refuses to pay attention. Daily, they remind him to listen without interrupting and prompt him to get on task. Nonetheless, his behavior only changes in the moment. Give it five minutes and he is back to interrupting or zoning out. Without paying attention, Malik does not hear or remember directions for assignments and/or homework. Without understanding what to do, Malik's report card indicates that he is failing history in seventh grade and earned an "U" in behavior. He was missing many assignments. Although the teachers believe that Malik intentionally avoids assignments, we must note that he, too, is frustrated. He explains that it is not his fault that he does not remember. He can often be heard saying that the teacher did not tell him to do the homework. He continually says that if he has to wait to answer questions, he will not remember what he wanted to say. In his frustration, he often raises his voice, when he exclaims that IT IS NOT MY FAULT! It seems that all involved, the teacher and Malik, are very annoyed and it is likely that if he does not learn strategies to help him maintain attention, he will continue to struggle with similar issues throughout his life....in postsecondary education, his jobs, his social life, and his relationships. Fortunately, Malik can be taught to regulate his attention using self-management strategies.

*Student: ALAM, MALIK*  **Grade:** 7  **Period:** 04/15/22- 05/09/22

| Per. | Course Name | Teacher | Q1 | Q2 | Q3 | Q4 | Teacher Comments | Citz |
|---|---|---|---|---|---|---|---|---|
| 1 | ART | KING, CLINTON | B | | | | | |
| 2 | COMMON CORE MATH 7 | HARRIS, EMMA | C | | | | | |
| 3 | PE SPRING | HERNANDEZ, JOSE | B | | | | | |
| 4 | LANG ARTS 7 | WOODLEY, SUZIE | C | | | | | |
| 5 | TEXAS HISTORY | WRIGHT, MEGAN | F | | | | | U |
| 6 | SCIENCE 7 | SPRING, BRUCE | C | | | | | |

**GPA**
Q1 GPA: 2.50
Cumulative GPA: 2.50

**Terms**
Q1= Quarter 1    Q2= Quarter 2
Q3= Quarter 3    Q4= Quarter 4

**Citizenship**
O= Outstanding    S= Satisfactory
N= Needs Improvement    U= Unsatisfactory

Image used under license from Shutterstock. KPG-Payless2/Shutterstock.com; Alana Harrison.

DOI: 10.4324/9781003109983-7

# Description of Self-Management

Self-management is a strategy that you can use to teach students like Malik to self-regulate their own behavior. Results of scientific studies indicate that self-management training can benefit the assignment accuracy and completion, on-task behavior, appropriate classroom behavior, classroom preparation, and homework behavior of students with ADHD (Gureasko-Moore et al., 2006; Mathes & Bender, 1997). With self-management students learn to monitor and document their own behavior and reward themselves when they have reached a goal (Gureasko-Moore et al., 2006; Shapiro et al., 1998). By teaching students to self-manage, they become aware and begin to understand behaviors that are troublesome to others and that interfere with their progress. As with Malik, many students with ADHD do not recognize these behaviors, as they lose focus and stare off into space thinking of something other than the task at hand. Maybe a nicely placed poster on the wall leads them to think about the school dance on Friday night. Goodness knows it is probably more fun to think about the dance than the 18th-century philosophical movement (the Enlightenment) the history teacher is discussing. While staring off and thinking about something other than what is being taught, student's not only miss valuable content, but they also miss assignment directions. Hence, for many students, this is one reason that they appear to make careless errors and forget to complete their homework.

Illustrated by Alyssa Baran.

As you probably know, when you redirect students, they often look stunned, with a deer in headlights look. They "zoned out" (off task) and were not even aware of it. Think about how many times you have gently stopped a student from tapping his pencil on the desk. Simply putting your hand on the pencil brings about that same "lost" look. That look brings us to the first benefit of teaching students

Image used under license from Shutterstock. New Vectors/Shutterstock.com.

to self-manage their own behavior. Self-management generates student awareness of the problem. When asked to document each time they speak without permission or tap a pencil on their desk, they become aware that they are actually engaging in those behaviors. In our own research, we have counted 50 pencil taps in one minute. When prompted to put his pencil on the table, the student seemed unaware of his own behavior. To say that this is annoying to teachers and peers is an understatement. As such, teaching students to monitor and count the frequency of their pencil tapping focuses their attention on actions that they are not even aware they were doing.

Once students are aware of their own behavior, the less than desirable behaviors are likely to change. The pencil tapping is probably going to decrease as are the number of times that Malik speaks out in class without permission or zones out. In fact, results from research with students with ADHD indicate that teaching self-management is likely to result in increased on-task behavior, assignment accuracy, assignment completion, and productivity, and decreased off-task and disruptive behavior (Harrison et al., 2020a). The goal of self-management is more than simply changing immediate behavior. For youth to be successful independent adolescents, young adults, and even older adults, they must learn to regulate their own behavior. Lack of self-regulation impacts all aspects of one's life, including academic, behavioral, and social. In the following sections, we first describe four stages of self-management and the procedural steps for each stage.

## Stages of Self-management

| 1 | 2 | 3 | 4 |
|---|---|---|---|
| Goal setting | Self-monitoring | Progress monitoring and self-evaluation | Self-reinforcement |

*Figure 5.1* Four Steps to Self-Management.

Self-management includes four broad stages (Figure 5.1). The first is goal setting, the act of the student and teacher collaboratively selecting a target or objective they wish to achieve. It is the process of establishing a behavioral definition of the desired behavior that is observable and measurable. The second stage is self-monitoring, the act of documenting and collecting data as a record of personal behavior. The third stage is self-evaluation, the act of examining the data and determining if the desired behavior is increasing and/or decreasing based on the established goal. The fifth stage is self-reinforcement, the act of rewarding oneself for achieving a goal.

## *Stage 1: Goal Setting*

Goal setting includes three implementation steps, identifying the target behavior and determining baseline, identifying the desired behavior, determining mastery criteria, and selecting the reward.

### Identify Target Behavior and Determine Baseline

The first step is the teacher helping the student identify the problem behavior. For example, Ms. Cassidy, Malik's teacher, guides Malik to understand that not attending to instruction is resulting in his failing grade. Ms. Cassidy asks Malik to think about what might be impacting his grades and annoying his teacher and peers. She asks Malik to think about what he did, how he

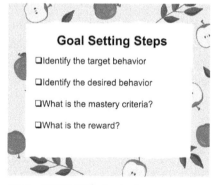

Design PRESENT/Shutterstock.com.

felt, and what he was thinking during class. Malik first reports that he was only thinking about what she was saying or the assignment that he was completing. Ms. Cassidy encourages him to think specifically about the morning when she called his name seven times before he answered. All of a sudden, his eyes seem to light up and he says, "Oh, yeah, I was thinking about the dance on Friday night. Did you know that I have a date? She has the prettiest black hair and brown eyes.

I was thinking about my date and missed everything!

Image used under license from Shutterstock.
New Vectors/Shutterstock.com.

She . . ." At this point, Ms. Cassidy interrupts him saying, "So, the problem seems to be maintaining attention?" Reluctantly, Malik admits that he had not been aware that he stopped listening to what she was saying. Together, Ms. Cassidy and Malik look at his Google Classroom® and explore the effects of not maintaining attention his grades. Malik slowly realizes and admits that zoning out is hurting his grades. Without helping Malik see the impact on his grades, it is likely that he would be less than motivated to change his behavior. It is important to remember that we are asking students to change behavior that they probably enjoy, such as thinking about a date on Friday night, to a behavior that is difficult for them, such as maintaining attention. Student buy-in and motivation are essential!

### Identify Desired Behavior

The second step is the behavior that you would like to see the student demonstrate (desired behavior) instead of the problem behavior. For example, in the case of Malik, Ms. Cassidy would rather see Malik initiate and maintain attention to task instead of zoning out. Although she knows that it will be difficult, Ms. Cassidy and Malik decide together that it would be worth the effort to learn!

### Determine Mastery Criteria

The third step is the teacher and student determining when the student has mastered the desired behavior. This decision is based on the baseline rates of the problem behavior. As such, the teacher must collect baseline data on the behavior. First, the teacher selects the appropriate type of measurement to use. How

Image used under license from Shutterstock.
Monkey Business Images/Shutterstock.com.

often does the student demonstrate the problem behavior (frequency)? How long does the behavior continue (duration)? What is the intensity of the behavior (intensity)? In the case of Malik, Ms. Cassidy noted that he was off task twice daily during her class and remained off task for approximately five minutes each time. When she met with Malik, she showed him the data she had recorded.

### Select the Reward

The next step is to select the reward. For example, Ms. Cassidy and Malik agree that at the end of 20 minutes, if Malik had maintained attention for two out of four five-minute intervals (success criteria), he could take three minutes to play on his phone. Additionally, Ms. Cassidy and Malik discuss that they would increase his goal to 75% and ultimately 100% as he learned to attend to task.

## Stage 2: Self-monitoring

Self-monitoring includes five implementation steps: explaining self-monitoring, selecting mode of self-monitoring, modeling self-monitoring, role-playing, and practicing.

### Explain Self-monitoring

The first step is to describe the rationale and the process of self-monitoring. In the case of Malik, Ms. Cassidy would describe the reason that Malik is going to self-monitor attention to task. Why does it matter to him? What is the motivation for trying to change a behavior that is difficult for him? Ms. Malik will use her knowledge of what is important to Malik to describe the reason. For example, she might help him see the connection between not paying attention and his grades, if grades are important to him. She might help him see the connection between his grades and losing his phone privileges if that is important to him.

### Select a Mode of Self-monitoring

The next step is to determine the method that Malik will use to document and track his behavior. There are at least three methods of self-monitoring: paper-based, game-based, and technology-based. Paper-based self-monitoring is the act of recording one's behavior on a paper form. Technology-based self-monitoring is the act of recording one's behavior on a digital application (app) or on a computer that can sync with a web-based portal to allow teachers to see student progress. Game-based self-monitoring is the act of recording one's behavior on a mobile game, in which student's behavior is the basis of the game. Specifics to using each form of self-monitoring are described later in the chapter in the section titled "Modes of Self-management."

## Model Self-monitoring

The third step in self-monitoring is for the teacher to model self-recording and tracking for the student. Ms. Cassidy might select to model self-monitoring to the entire class or to Malik independently. Ms. Cassidy projects the form, the application, or the website onto the whiteboard. She tells the students that she wants to document and record the length of time that she speaks without allowing students to participate. She adds the goal to the form and demonstrates throughout the lesson. When she documents her behavior, she says, "I spoke without letting you speak for five minutes." This allows students to "watch" her document her own behavior.

## Role-Play

The fourth step in self-monitoring is allowing the student the opportunity to role-play documenting and tracking their own behavior. After modeling, Ms. Cassidy asks Malik to document if he maintained attention during a five-minute interval. After the five minutes, the two discuss the data Malik collected. Was he on task? If so, did he document that he was on task? They would repeat this process until Ms. Cassidy believes that Malik understands the process.

## Practice

The fifth step is to allow Malik to practice documenting his own behavior across time. For example, Ms. Cassidy might set a time for 20 minutes, asking Malik to document whether he was attending to instruction during each five-minute interval. Ms. Cassidy and Malik meet, and she provides feedback to Malik based on the accuracy of his documentation.

# Stage 3: Progress Monitoring and Self-evaluation

## Progress Monitoring

We cannot overemphasize the importance of monitoring the student's progress. Teachers monitor student progress based on the baseline data collected in their class and/or a student's annual goal in an individualized plan. For example, the annual goal for Malik indicates that progress will be monitored five times per week. As such, Ms. Cassidy will directly observe Malik's on-task behavior during independent work each day and document progress. Specifically, she will document the accuracy and completion of his self-monitoring and the change in his on-task behavior. Malik will graph this performance and evaluate progress toward his goal. If he is not progressing, Ms. Cassidy will work with Malik to determine the barriers to progress and select means of overcoming the barriers, develop a plan, and put it in action.

## Self-evaluation

Self-evaluation is the process of documenting and examining progress. One means is by graphing student progress across time, allowing students to see their progress. This in itself is reinforcing to many students. Ms. Cassidy begins to teach Malik to evaluate his own progress by allowing him to decide how he will graph his performance. One of the simplest is for Ms. Cassidy to create a form that automatically graphs the behavior (Figure 5.2).

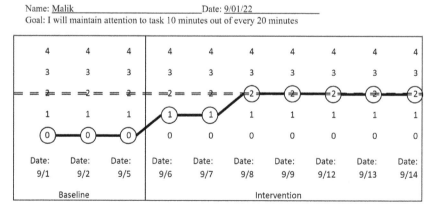

*Figure 5.2* Self-Graphing Form.

Malik is self-managing attention to task one period a day for 20 minutes. He has four opportunities to have been on task. At the end of the history period, Malik circles the number of intervals that he was on task and then connects the circles with straight lines. This process creates a line graph that can easily be viewed to determine if the frequency of on-task intervals is increasing or decreasing. Ms. Cassidy teaches Malik to draw a goal line across all days at "2," so that he has a visual goal to achieve.

Another option is for Malik to graph frequency of engaged intervals is using Microsoft Excel® to create a bar graph. Ms. Cassidy can graph the data or teach Malik to graph the data. First, Ms. Cassidy enters the data into an excel sheet with the rows being dates and columns being the frequency of on-task intervals. Next, she selects "insert" and the 2D column in the icon list. The program will take the data and create the chart on the work-sheet using the column labels. Next, Ms. Cassidy and Malik add a goal line to the graph by drawing a straight line at "2." The teacher and student can format the chart as they want . . . change the font, the colors, and/or axis labels. Once the chart is created, the student can update it daily adding the data as needed.

**Malik On-Task 9/1 - 9/11**

*Figure 5.3* Bar Chart.
Created by author.

### Interpret the Data

The next step is to interpret the graphed data. Ms. Cassidy teaches Malik to compare his performance between days and the goal line. They discuss whether his attention to task was increasing or decreasing. Looking at Figure 5.3, you can see that his attention was increasing across days. Next, they compare his behavior to the goal line and realize that he has mastered his goal five days in a row.

### Draw Actionable Conclusions

The next step is to draw actionable conclusions from the interpretation. As Malik's attention to task is increasing and he met his goal, he and Ms. Cassidy decide to increase his goal for the following week to 75%. If his behavior had been decreasing, they would have made a different decision. In this case, they would follow the problem-solving steps (see Figure 5.4) to determine what needed to be changed.

They began by identifying the problem (i.e., no increase in attention). Next, they would discuss possible reasons for the decrease in behavior and select a possible solution to the problem. For example, they might decide that five minutes was too long and decrease the interval to three minutes. They might decide that Malik was not interested in the reward. In this case, they would

*Figure 5.4* Problem Solving Steps.
Image used under license from Shutterstock.
besunnytoo/Shutterstock.com.

change the reward. The goal of this step is to determine what action to take next based on the data. Once a decision is made, then the change would be made, and progress monitoring would continue.

## Stage 4: Self-reinforcement

The final step is to administer the reward. If Malik met his goal, Ms. Cassidy would allow him to use his phone for three minutes. It is important that the reinforcement be administered immediately in order for this step to maintain or increase the probability of Malik continuing to manage his own behavior.

#  Modes of Self-management

As mentioned in the second step of self-monitoring, there are three possible modes for students to use to record and track their behavior: paper-based, game-based, or technology-based.

## Paper-based Form

Paper-based self-management is the use of a self-monitoring form to record student behavior. If Ms. Cassidy and Malik select paper-based

| Name: Malik | | | |
|---|---|---|---|
| Week of: September 1, 2023 | | | |
| Goal: I will maintain attention to task for ten minutes out of each twenty minutes. | | | |
| **Monday** | | | |
| 11:00 – 11:05 | I paid attention | Yes | (No) |
| 11:05 – 11:10 | I paid attention | Yes | (No) |
| 11:10 – 11:15 | I paid attention | Yes | (No) |
| 11:15 – 11:20 | I paid attention | Yes | (No) |
| **Tuesday** | | | |
| 11:00 – 11:05 | I paid attention | (Yes) | No |
| 11:05 – 11:10 | I paid attention | Yes | (No) |
| 11:10 – 11:15 | I paid attention | Yes | (No) |
| 11:15 – 11:20 | I paid attention | Yes | (No) |
| **Wednesday** | | | |
| 11:00 – 11:05 | I paid attention | (Yes) | No |
| 11:05 – 11:10 | I paid attention | (Yes) | No |
| 11:10 – 11:15 | I paid attention | (Yes) | No |
| 11:15 – 11:20 | I paid attention | (Yes) | No |
| **Thursday** | | | |
| 11:00 – 11:05 | I paid attention | (Yes) | No |
| 11:05 – 11:10 | I paid attention | (Yes) | No |
| 11:10 – 11:15 | I paid attention | (Yes) | No |
| 11:15 – 11:20 | I paid attention | Yes | (No) |
| **Friday** | | | |
| 11:00 – 11:05 | I paid attention | (Yes) | No |
| 11:05 – 11:10 | I paid attention | (Yes) | No |
| 11:10 – 11:15 | I paid attention | (Yes) | No |
| 11:15 – 11:20 | I paid attention | (Yes) | No |

Figure 5.5 Self-Management Form.

self-monitoring, Ms. Cassidy would first develop a form for Malik to use (Figure 5.5). The form would include a sentence stem or question, such as "I paid attention . . ." or "Was I paying attention to my teacher or my task?" and response to the stem or question. For example, if the sentence stem in Malik's form was "I paid attention . . . . " The response to the sentence stem could be yes or no. For some behaviors, such as raising a hand to speak, a frequency count would be appropriate. For example, the stem might be "How many times did I raise my hand to speak in class?" The student could record tally marks or could simply write the number.

## Game-based

Game-based self-management is the use of a digital gamified app, such as EpicWin, for the students to record their behavior. If Ms. Cassidy and Malik select this model of recording, Ms. Cassidy will first teach Malik to use the modified version of EpicWin described by Harrison and colleagues (Harrison et al., 2020a; Harrison et al., 2020b). EpicWin includes a highly visual narrative weaved into gameplay. It was designed as a to-do list for adults and was modified as a self-management app for young adolescents with ADHD. In the app, students indicate that they have completed "quests," earn "loot," and travel along a path with each successful interval.

*Figure 5.6* EpicWin.

Printed with permission from Tak Fung.

The first step is for Malik to download EpicWin (Fung, 2015; Harrison et al., 2020b) on his cell phone (see Figure 5.6). First, he selects an avatar. Second, he enters "on-task" four times into the program as the "quest" to complete. When Ms. Cassidy gives the directive to begin independent work, Malik sets the EpicWin interval for five minutes to vibrate at the end of the time. When the timer vibrates, he either selects the button that he attended to task or not, whichever is the case. At the end of the designated time, Malik will earn "loot" for being on task via the game and possibly level up. As he continues each day, his avatar travels along a path demonstrating success.

## Technology-based

Technology-based self-management, such as I-Connect, is the use of a web-based program to track and record student performance. I-Connect includes a mobile app that teachers can select or add the goals and prompts. Prompts can be set for home, work, school, or in the community. The app prompts the student to record their behavior at designated intervals and provides a graph of student behavior. Teachers and students can view and download the student's progress on the I-Connect website.

If Ms. Cassidy and Malik selected I-Connect, they would download the app from https://iconnect.ku.edu/setting-up-i-connect-in-your-classroom/ and enroll in the web-based system. Next, they would enter a prompt

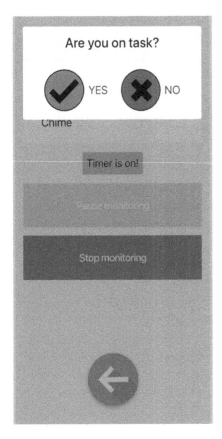

*Figure 5.7* I-Connect.
Printed with permission from Howard Wills.

that could be answered with yes or no. For example, Ms. Cassidy and Malik would enter "Were you paying attention?"

Next, they would identify the interval for the prompt to be displayed. Ms. Cassidy and Malik would enter every five minu tes during the 20 minutes of independent math work.

Next, Malik and Ms. Cassidy would enter the goal and mastery level decided in step 4 and practice using I-connect to document the behavior. Finally, Ms. Cassidy will observe Malik documenting his own behavior. She will provide positive and corrective feedback when needed using specific language. For example, she might say, "Excellent job Malik, I like the way that you noticed that you were off task during the last five minutes and correctly indicated that." Once Malik has demonstrated that he can accurately self-monitor, he will begin to independently record and track his behavior using the app (See Figure 5.7).

# Potential Barriers and Methods of Overcoming the Barriers

It seems there are always barriers to implementing interventions in classrooms. In the current climate of accountability and standardized testing, teachers are required to complete many things within the academic day. Teacher time and other resources are precious commodities; however, it is likely that without intervening on problem behaviors, teachers are spending more time and resources addressing problem behaviors than needed. In this section, we will discuss some known barriers to implementing self-management and provide some options for over-coming those barriers.

## *Time and Resources*

Teaching adolescents with ADHD to manage their own behavior requires time. Time in the academic day and time across the year. As can be clearly seen in the procedures described earlier, teaching students to self-manage can be time intensive at the beginning of the intervention. Teachers must find time to collect baseline data and possibly create forms to self-monitor and/or forms to graph behavior. Although we pro-vide examples in the chapter and other examples can be found on the internet and in commercially available books and websites, we can tell you that we have never found a form that meets all the needs for indi-vidual students or the programs that we were running. As such, teachers may need to create forms if they are not going to use digital tools for self-management. Similarly, if they are going to use digital tools, teachers must find the time to explore the tools and get them ready for use by the student.

The next step that requires teacher time is teaching students to recog-nize and document their own behavior. This requires time for the student and teacher to practice monitoring and documenting the target behavior. After the student learns to document his/her own behavior, the teacher spends time monitoring the fidelity of the process. Did the student follow all of the procedures correctly?

Finally, like many other training interventions (see Chapter 12) one of the keys to success for self-management training is frequent prac-tice with feedback over time. This intervention is not likely to work in just a few days. Improving self-management behavior for students with problems is difficult. The more frequent the feedback and prac-tice (i.e., multiple times per week), the more likely the student will benefit and improve in a relatively short time (e.g., over the course of a month).

Although we will recommend a couple of strategies that might decrease the amount of time required, we encourage teachers to think about using this time to "pay it forward." It is likely that more time will be saved than used when students learn to self-manage. For example, the time that Ms. Cassidy spends responding to Malik's misbehavior is likely much more than the time that she will spend teaching him to self-manage his own behavior.

Nonetheless, there are a couple of strategies to minimize the amount of teacher time. First, teachers can develop a task list for students to follow instead of having to be constantly available to the student. For example, the developers of I-Connect recommend that teachers give students a check-list that includes: (1) turn on/wake up device; (2) navigate to the I-Connect app and click on it; (3) enter our username/password; (4) click on "my monitor"; (5) click on "my school"; (6) click on "start monitoring"; (7) click yes if you are engaging in the target behavior or no if you are not when prompted; (8) click on "end monitoring" when finished.

Another option is to have someone other than the teacher train the student to use self-management. For example, a check in/check out mentor might teach the strategy during morning check in, or a counselor might teach the skill during a counseling session. Similarly, a special education teacher or aid can manage the system and the teacher may be involved in some of the feedback sessions with the student. Although the skill can be taught outside of the classroom, self-management typically happens in the classroom, so the teacher must be familiar with the procedures and what the student was taught.

## Student Cooperation

Over the years, many teachers have told us that students refuse to cooperate with self-management procedures. Students have been heard to say that they do not have a problem paying attention or that they just do not want to participate. Others simply do not write anything on the paper and others mark that they were on task when it was quite obvious that they were not.

Let us begin with by saying it does not really matter if the student is honest in the beginning. The idea is that you are drawing their attention to the behavior. Therefore, it's acceptable to move forward without contradicting the student's rating. However, once the student has become proficient at the process, then teachers can monitor the student's behavior simultaneously and compare and discuss ratings. For example, Ms. Cassidy might rate Malik's behavior while he does. When the 20-minute interval is finished, then the two compare notes and discuss discrepancies. Ms. Cassidy would provide a reward when she and Malik agree on the rating. This would encourage Malik to record accurately.

Additionally, teachers can increase the student's cooperation by using motivational techniques. It is helpful to find something that increases student interest in self-management. For example, students who prefer computer-based instruction might be motivated by I-Connect and students who like video games might be motivated by EpicWin. Giving students a choice of type of self-monitoring can increase cooperation. Being very careful to select mastery criteria based on baseline data so that it will be achievable is also important to motivation. If the student never achieves his goal, then he is likely to become complacent. It is also important to make sure that the student understands the relationship between the target behavior and something that is important to him. For example, Malik is motivated by his grades as his parents reward him for making A's and B's. Therefore, Ms. Cassidy helps Malik see the direct relationship between attending in class and his final grade.

## What if...

⇒ Student is not motivated to learn the strategies.
- Add additional contingencies (negative or positive reinforcement) for students using the strategies. See chapter 11.
- Allow students choice in the assignment and the study strategy.
- Assist students in document success to ensure students experience success when using the strategies.

⇒ Student does not study at home even after learning the strategies.
- Add contingencies.
- Establish a home-communication system and involve parents.

Image used under license from Shutterstock. rangsan paidaen/Shutterstock.com.

## Considerations for Culturally Responsive Self-Management

We encourage you to think about the implications of self-management for varying cultures. For example, some cultures such as Latinx, Chinese, Korean, and Japanese are considered collectivistic, which may make self-management less important for some individuals than for individuals from cultures that are more individualistic, such as the United States, as some consider self-management a westernized notion (Ehrlich et al., 2016).

Within collectivistic cultures, individuals think of their own behavior in relation to a group and demonstrate loyalty to that group. Therefore, working on group goals is more important than individual goals. As such, it might be beneficial to focus on the impact of the Malik's behavior in relation to the class. To accomplish this, the teacher might create a group-monitoring form or enter group goals into the applications. On the other hand, the teacher might simply help the student focus on the impact of his behavior on the group and teach the student to self-manage his own behavior.

Another option is to involve the entire class (or the student's peers) in developing the self-management application. There is no harm in teaching all students to either manage their own behavior or the behavior of a group. We encourage teachers to talk to their students about how they would like to self-manage. The more buy-in from students, the more likely the intervention will be effective.

## Programming

We strongly encourage teachers to advocate for the inclusion of interventions with evidence of effectiveness on any plan written for the student, such as a response to intervention plan, individualized education program (IEP), section 504 plan, and/or any other plan developed for an adolescent with ADHD. As you know, research indicates that self-management can increase academic achievement and decrease disruptive behavior. Therefore, we provide an examples of Malik's current levels, strengths and weaknesses, annual goals, and short-term benchmarks. In addition, we provide a description of self-management that can be included in the accommodations/modifications section of the plan.

---

**CASEL Standards:** Social Emotional Learning Competency: Self-Awareness Sub-competency—recognizing strengths and self-confidence

---

**Current levels, strengths and weaknesses:** Malik is a ninth-grade student. Malik reads on the ninth-grade level and is receiving C's and D's in math, science, and social studies. Malik's areas of need include functional skills related to attending to task. According to Ms. Cassidy's direct observations, Malik is on-task an average of 25% of the time during independent work periods. As he struggles to maintain attention to task, he only completes his work 50% of the time. This results in missing and incomplete assignments lowering his grade considerably. To increase his academic performance, Malik needs to learn to remain engaged and finish his tasks.

---

**Annual Smart Goal:**
- Given self-management instruction twice per week following the procedures outlined in [this book], Malik will maintain attention during independent tasks 75% of five-minute intervals during four consecutive weeks.

---

 # Conclusion

Self-management is an intervention that directly addresses impairment associated with ADHD. To increase lifelong success, students with ADHD must be taught to acknowledge and change their behavior when it is interfering with their goals. In the current chapter, we discussed four stages of self-management and their implementation steps. We discussed time, resources, and student cooperation as potential barriers to effective implementation. Furthermore, we stressed the importance of considering culture in implementation particularly with students from cultures that value groups over individuals. We strongly encourage you to teach all students with ADHD to self-monitor and manage their behavior, as the benefits can be seen academically and behaviorally.

# Reference List

Ehrlich, C., Kendall, E., Parekh, S., & Walters, C. (2016). The impact of culturally responsive self-management interventions on health outcomes for minority populations: A systematic review. *Chronic Illness, 12*(1), 41–57.

Fung, T. (2015). *EpicWin* (AMSI Version 1.67) [Mobile Application Software].

Gureasko-Moore, S., DuPaul, G. J., & White, G. P. (2006). The effects of self-management in general education classrooms on the organizational skills of adolescents with ADHD. *Behavior Modification, 30*(2), 159–183.

Harrison, J. R., Evans, S. W., Baran, A., Khondker, F., Press, K., Wasserman, S., . . . Mohlmann, M. (2020a). Comparison of accommodations and interventions for youth with ADHD: A randomized controlled trial. *Journal of School Psychology, 80*, 15–36. https://doi.org/10.1016/j.jsp.2020.05.001

Harrison, J. R., Kwong, C., Evans, S. W., Peltier, C., & Mathews, L. (2020b). Game-based self-management: Addressing inattention during independent reading and written response. *Journal of Applied School Psychology, 36*(1), 38–61. https://doi.org/10.1080/15377903.2019.1660748

Mathes, M. Y., & Bender, W. N. (1997). The effects of self-monitoring on children with attention-deficit/hyperactivity disorder who are receiving pharmacological interventions. *Remedial and Special Education, 18*(2), 121–128.

Shapiro, E. S., DuPaul, G. J., & Bradley-Klug, K. L. (1998). Self-management as a strategy to improve the classroom behavior of adolescents with ADHD. *Journal of Learning Disabilities, 31*(6), 545–555.

# Study Skills Strategies

**6**

---

**Josiah**

Josiah is a 6th grade student with ADHD. Unlike many adolescents with ADHD, Josiah tends to complete his work in class and turn it in. He works hard to keep his binder organized, so that he can remember to complete and submit all of his work. He was lucky enough to have been taught Organization Skills by his fifth-grade teacher and realized how important it is to submit his work, take notes and maintain attention in class. However, he continually fails his history tests and have his privileges restricted at home. He is not  allowed to play video games or use his phone most of the time. In fact, his mother currently has his phone locked in a filing cabinet in her office. To pass exams, Josiah must study in class and/or at home. He does not like to study with his peers, because he has a hard time remembering facts. When he studies with his peers, they recognize and sometimes comment on his struggle to remember. At home, he begins to study for tests by opening his notes on the computer, but then he remembers that he should check his iMessage's as the icon at the bottom of the computer draws his attention. He clicks it and finds that his friend sent him an invitation to play an online game. What a great idea! He could spend just thirty minutes playing the game and then return to studying. Two hours later his mother tells him that it is time for dinner. He tells her that he has not finished studying. She suggests that he eat and then she will help him study. After dinner, she tries to help him by calling out questions from a study guide and having him answer. She calls a question out, asks him to answer it, and tells him the correct answer. He continues to give the wrong answer and she becomes frustrated with him. She believes, and tells him, that he does not try. Josiah's teacher, Mr. Quong, is also frustrated, but more about his inability to teach Josiah the information. He feels like he is failing his students. Although, he does not reprimand Josiah for his grades, his frustration is apparent and, at times communicates unintentionally to Josiah that he cannot learn the material. In addition to failing History, Josiah's mom and Mr. Quong are concerned that he will not pass the state mandated test at the end of the year. If he does not, then it is possible that he will have to take 6th grade history again. Furthermore, it will reflect poorly on Mr. Quong. Josiah has dealt with this cycle of condescending comments and adult concern for many years and it is especially frustrating to him as he has worked so hard on his organization skills. Finally, Mr. Quong attends a workshop and learns several evidence-based interventions to teach Josiah, and his other students, how to used study and test taking strategies. study. He is excited to return to class and begin to teach the skills.

DOI: 10.4324/9781003109983-8

# Description of Study Skills Strategies

Study skills strategies are a set of techniques designed to help students improve their ability to comprehend, memorize, and retain content for tests and quizzes. In comparison to their typically developing peers, students with ADHD demonstrate poorer working memory, which is associated with inattention, hyperactivity, and impulsivity, and results in academic underachievement. Additionally, 15% to 35% of students with ADHD experience high levels of anxiety. This combination of challenges is a disaster waiting to happen while studying and taking exams. As such, it is essential that we teach adolescents techniques to use when they are studying and taking tests, such as memorization and test-taking strategies. The specific skills in this section can be taught in any order and many may be taught or practiced simultaneously. Students should learn all strategies to be able to select the one that works best for them.

The benefits are numerous. Results from scientific studies indicate that teaching study skills to students with ADHD increases assignment accuracy (Brasch et al., 2008; Moser et al., 2012). At the most basic and obvious level, students will learn the material, which will likely result in increases in their confidence. Similarly important, students will demonstrate their learning on exams and their grades will increase. Imagine the benefits of Josiah's grades increasing. There will be less frustration from him, his mother, and his teacher. Relationship dynamics will change, and he will begin to feel more confident in his academic functioning. Josiah will begin to feel like he belongs at school! Win-win for everyone, right?

In the following sections, we describe the basic stages for teaching students to use study and test-taking strategies (See Figure 6.1). We describe five possible techniques: (1) flash cards; (2) mnemonics (acrostic, Imagery/ Loci Method, acronyms); (3) summarizing; (4) cover, copy, compare; and (5) test-taking strategies.

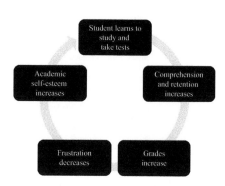

# Stages to Teach All Study Skills Strategies

| 1 | 2 | 3 | 4 | 5 |
|---|---|---|---|---|
| Understand the need | Select a strategy | Develop materials | Teach and practice the strategy | Monitor progress |

*Figure 6.1* Five Steps to Study Skills Strategies.

## Stage 1: Understand the Need

The first stage is to teach students the importance of study skills. In order to learn the strategies, students must understand why they need to study. What is the benefit of studying? What is the benefit of learning the strategies? Earlier, we wrote that the benefits of teaching students to study are many. However, the goal of stage 1 is more than listing the benefits in a simple paragraph or describing them in a few minutes to the student. The goal is to truly help students realize the benefits. To initiate this understanding, you, as the teacher can describe the benefits to the student. In addition, you can ask students to predict future outcomes if they learn to study. You might be surprised by the benefits that students report. For example, Josiah might tell you that his mother and teacher will stop harassing him. Although, we want students to understand that the ultimate benefit of studying is learning, it is doubtful that this will be their first response nor is this outcome likely to motivate many students. In fact, do not be surprised, or overreact, if the student tells you that study strategies are a waste of time. The goal of explaining the benefits to them is not to convince them (although that would be nice), it is to share the potential benefits for them to consider. For many students, the benefits of these strategies may not seem meaningful until they see changes in data and grades over time.

As such, teachers begin by collecting baseline data and showing the student their current progress in a nonjudgmental manner. For example, Mr. Quong shows Josiah his grades in the computer system. Josiah might see three failing grades for the three tests taken in the semester. Mr. Quong tells Josiah that by learning study and test-taking strategies his grades will increase. After each test going forward, Mr. Quong will meet with Josiah and demonstrate the impact of studying by showing him the increase in his test scores. Hopefully, seeing his own progress will persuade Josiah that these strategies are beneficial. It is a good idea to go beyond grades. Mr. Quong and Josiah may discuss the additional benefits, including the lack of harassment that he previously mentioned. This collaborative reflection continues throughout and after the process of teaching and practicing the use of the strategies.

## *Stage 2: Select a Strategy*

After collecting baseline data on student test scores and meeting with the student, the teacher selects the first strategy to teach to the students. Strategies can be introduced simultaneously or one at a time depending on the goals of the teacher and the abilities of the students. For example, Mr. Quong includes vocabulary words on most of his weekly quizzes.

As such, a teacher may teach Josiah how to use flash cards or cover, copy, and compare to study for the quiz. Moreover, he often asks students to write lists, such as the explorers of America in chronological order. Therefore, he will teach Josiah to use mnemonics. Finally, Mr. Quong is aware that his students will have to read passages and answer questions about facts and main ideas on the state standardized exam. Therefore, he often includes such items on unit tests and will teach Josiah to summarize the main idea and identify the facts in the passage. In addition to teaching Josiah to study, he will teach strategies for answering multiple-choice questions, true-false, matching, and essay questions. In the following sections, we describe study and test-taking strategies, many of which are included in the Challenging Horizons Program (CHP), a multimodal intervention discussed in Chapter 12 of this book, developed by Steven W. Evans (co-author of this book). As such, many of the procedures described here originated in the CHP treatment manual (Evans & Langberg, 2011).

Image used under license from Shutterstock. Shpadaruk Aleksei/Shutterstock.com.

## Study Strategies

Image used under license from Shutterstock.
Cmspic/Shutterstock.com.

*Flash cards* are study tools to be used when memorizing content. Flash cards are used to learn information, such as the definition of words or math facts and are typically made on note cards, or other paper. Students read the question/word on one side and the answer on the other side. Students can quiz themselves, or others can hold the question side of the card for the student to see and ask the student to answer. Either way, the student or his/her peer immediately shows the answer and determines if the answer is correct. If the answer is correct, then the students place the card in a pile of "learned words," and if the answer is not correct, then the card is stacked in a pile of "continue to study" words. The student continues this process until he has mastered each card. It is important that the student continue to study the entire stack until all facts are learned.

*Mnemonic devices* are memory tools that help students recall and retain large amounts of information. Mnemonics are especially helpful for learning lists and/or when order is important. Several different types of mnemonics can be used, including (1) acronyms, (2) acrostics, and (3) imagery/loci method. Acronyms are the words or names created by combining letters from words in the list being memorized. Two very common acronyms that students are frequently taught are: (1) PEMDAS to remember the order of operations in mathematics—Parenthesis, Exponents, Multiplication, Division, Addition, Subtraction; and (2) HOME for the Great Lakes—Lake Huron, Lake Ontario, Lake Michigan, and Lake Erie. Students can create their own or teachers can provide the acronym. Students must practice saying or writing the acronym until they have memorized the acronym itself and the intended knowledge.

Acrostics are poems and the first letters of each line spell out a word or message. For example, each line of Edgar Allan Poe's poem spells out the name "Elizabeth" (see Figure 6.2). As with acronyms, students can create their own poems, or they can learn one that the teacher provides for them. Once created the student memorizes the acrostic and the material.

Another mnemonic device is the Loci Method, also known as memory journey, mind palace, or memory palace, which uses imagery to help students remember lists of information. Students are taught to visualize very familiar environments, such as their house, bedroom, or neighborhood, and visualize the information to remember in different spaces.

For example (see Figure 6.3), Mr. Quong was worried about Josiah remembering the people that he learned about for his end-of-course exam. He helped Josiah create a memory palace with all the individuals he had learned about in sixth-grade world history. Josiah developed a memory palace using his house. He imagined walking into his living room and seeing Socrates and Alexander the Great sitting on the couch watching television. He walked to the library

**Elizabeth**

Elizabeth, it surely is most fit
[Logic and common usage so commanding]
In thy own book that first thy name be
  writ,
Zeno and other sages notwithstanding;
And I have other reasons for so doing
Besides my innate love of
  contradiction;
Each poet - if a poet - in pursuing
The muses thro' their bowers of Truth
  or Fiction,
Has studied very little of his part,
Read nothing, written less - in short's
  a fool
Endued with neither soul, nor sense,
  nor art,
Being ignorant of one important rule,
Employed in even the theses of the
  school-
Called - I forget the heathenish Greek
  name
[Called anything, its meaning is the
  same]
"Always write first things uppermost in
  the heart."

-Edgar Allan Poe

*Figure 6.2* Acrostic.
Image used under license from Shutterstock. Tartila/Shutterstock.com; Edgar Allen Poe.

and say Petrarch sitting in a chair reading a book and Shakespeare sitting at the desk also reading. He continued to the office and saw Aristotle sitting at a desk working, then to his bedroom where Plato was sitting at another desk. He moved to the dining room and saw Constantine at one end of the

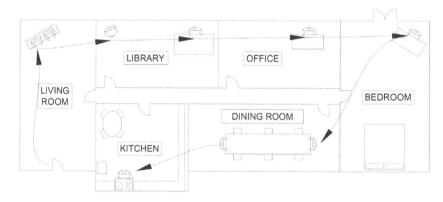

*Figure 6.3* Loci Method/Memory Palace.
Printed with permission from Randy Harrison.

table and Queen Elizabeth I at the other. Moving on to the kitchen, he saw Leonardo Da Vinci standing at the stove cooking. By developing and using the memory castle, the probability of Josiah remembering the people hear had learned about throughout the academic year increased.

*Summarizing* is the process of restating the components of content presented orally in class or read in a textbook. Specifically, the student writes the main idea and supporting details in their own words demonstrating understanding of what they read/heard. A major component of studying involves the ability to summarize material from textbooks, passages, or news-paper/magazine articles. After taking notes in class or from reading the student explains the material to an adult or peer using the notes as a guide. The adult or peer is encouraged to ask the student questions when the explanation is not clear (e.g., student uses too many pronouns in explanation, so it is not clear about who the student is referencing). We recommend that the person listening to the student not simply "correct" the student, but ask questions that lead to inquiry (e.g., looking up information in the textbook) so the student self-corrects any errors. The student may update notes as part of the summarizing process to add clarity or missing information (Figure 6.4).

*Cover, copy, and compare* is the process of the student reading a card (developed by the student or the teacher) with a question and answer, covering it, and then responding. After writing a response, the student compares his answer to that on the card to check for accuracy. Mr. Quong could use this with Josiah when studying any history vocabulary. Josiah would look at a card with the word and definition, then cover the card and write the definition on a separate piece of paper. Next, he would uncover the definition and check to see if he wrote it accurately. If he did then he would move on to the next word, if he did not, then he would repeat the process, read, cover, copy, and compare.

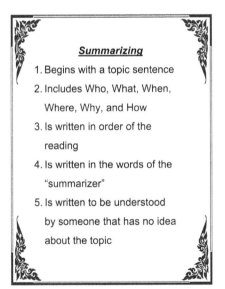

*Figure 6.4* Thoughts For Summarizing.

**Summarizing**
1. Begins with a topic sentence
2. Includes Who, What, When, Where, Why, and How
3. Is written in order of the reading
4. Is written in the words of the "summarizer"
5. Is written to be understood by someone that has no idea about the topic

## Test-taking Strategies

In addition to teaching students how to *study* for tests, it is essential that we teach them how to *take* tests. Test-taking strategies help students remember to read test directions carefully (highlighting important words), think about the test questions and select an approach to answering each different type of question, and plan the amount of time to spend on each question. Typically, there are four types of questions (multiple choice, true-false, matching, and essay) students encounter as adolescents.

    *Multiple choice questions* are test items that include a question or problem stem with a list of possible responses. Typically, students are forced to select one response. Multiple-choice items are commonly used to evaluate knowledge of the material covered in class. Students are taught to follow a systematic process (see Figure 6.5) when answering multiple choice questions.

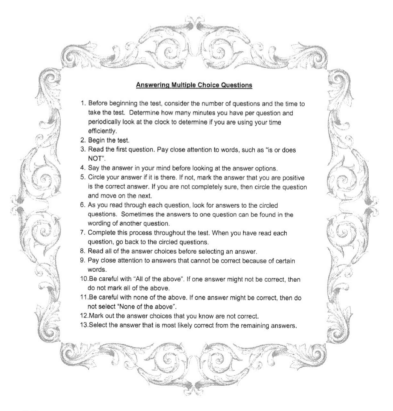

**Answering Multiple Choice Questions**

1. Before beginning the test, consider the number of questions and the time to take the test. Determine how many minutes you have per question and periodically look at the clock to determine if you are using your time efficiently.
2. Begin the test.
3. Read the first question. Pay close attention to words, such as "is or does NOT".
4. Say the answer in your mind before looking at the answer options.
5. Circle your answer if it is there. If not, mark the answer that you are positive is the correct answer. If you are not completely sure, then circle the question and move on the next.
6. As you read through each question, look for answers to the circled questions. Sometimes the answers to one question can be found in the wording of another question.
7. Complete this process throughout the test. When you have read each question, go back to the circled questions.
8. Read all of the answer choices before selecting an answer.
9. Pay close attention to answers that cannot be correct because of certain words.
10. Be careful with "All of the above". If one answer might not be correct, then do not mark all of the above.
11. Be careful with none of the above. If one answer might be correct, then do not select "None of the above".
12. Mark out the answer choices that you know are not correct.
13. Select the answer that is most likely correct from the remaining answers.

*Figure 6.5*

Image used under license from Shutterstock AcantStudio/Shutterstock.com.

*True-false questions (alternative-response)* are test items that include a statement that students must determine is either correct (true) or incorrect (false). True-false items are typically used to test surface-level knowledge; however, depending on the content may require critical thinking. Students can be taught a process (see Figure 6.6) for answering true-false questions.

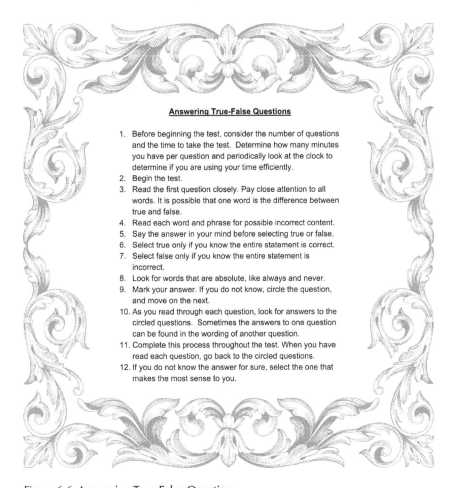

**Answering True-False Questions**

1. Before beginning the test, consider the number of questions and the time to take the test. Determine how many minutes you have per question and periodically look at the clock to determine if you are using your time efficiently.
2. Begin the test.
3. Read the first question closely. Pay close attention to all words. It is possible that one word is the difference between true and false.
4. Read each word and phrase for possible incorrect content.
5. Say the answer in your mind before selecting true or false.
6. Select true only if you know the entire statement is correct.
7. Select false only if you know the entire statement is incorrect.
8. Look for words that are absolute, like always and never.
9. Mark your answer. If you do not know, circle the question, and move on the next.
10. As you read through each question, look for answers to the circled questions. Sometimes the answers to one question can be found in the wording of another question.
11. Complete this process throughout the test. When you have read each question, go back to the circled questions.
12. If you do not know the answer for sure, select the one that makes the most sense to you.

*Figure 6.6* Answering True-False Questions.
Image used under license from Shutterstock AcantStudio/Shutterstock.com.

*Matching questions* are test items that include adjacent lists of test items and answers. Each question is paired with an answer and the student matches the question to the answer. Matching questions are commonly used to test recognition and recall, although can be used to test

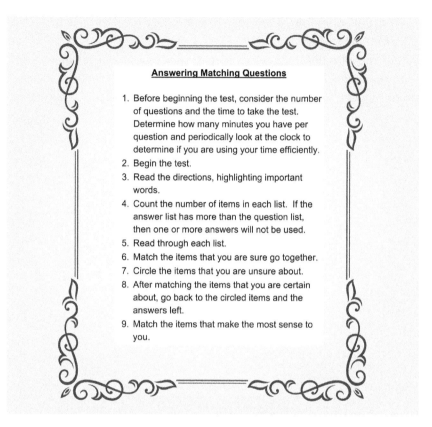

**Answering Matching Questions**

1. Before beginning the test, consider the number of questions and the time to take the test. Determine how many minutes you have per question and periodically look at the clock to determine if you are using your time efficiently.
2. Begin the test.
3. Read the directions, highlighting important words.
4. Count the number of items in each list. If the answer list has more than the question list, then one or more answers will not be used.
5. Read through each list.
6. Match the items that you are sure go together.
7. Circle the items that you are unsure about.
8. After matching the items that you are certain about, go back to the circled items and the answers left.
9. Match the items that make the most sense to you.

*Figure 6.7* Answering Matching Questions.
Image used under license from Shutterstock AcantStudio/Shutterstock.com./ *Shutterstock.com.*

higher-order thinking. Students complete a systematic process (see Figure 6.7) for answering matching questions.

*Essay questions* are test items that are open-ended questions that cannot simply be answered by yes/no. Students answer the question with a written explanation or analysis of one or more sentences. Typically essay questions include directions specific to the length of the required answer. See Chapter 4 for stages to self-regulated strategy development (see Figure 4.1).

Students complete a systematic process (see Figure 6.8) for answering essay questions.

**Answering Essay Questions**

1. Before beginning the test, consider the number of questions and the time to take the test. Determine how many minutes you have per question and periodically look at the clock to determine if you are using your time efficiently.
2. Read the question carefully. If you have need further explanation, ask the teacher.
3. Identify key words in the directions and highlight them and follow directions per word
4. Begin the test by rephrasing the question as an answer.
5. Write an outline to answer the question (introduction, one to three paragraphs with supporting main idea, conclusion.

*Figure 6.8* Answering Essay Questions.
Image used under license from Shutterstock. Anton Dzyna/Shutterstock.

## Stage 3: Develop Materials

Once the strategies are selected, teachers develop the needed materials. The amount of time that it takes to create materials varies based on the teacher. For example, some teachers do not want to spend any time developing strategies. In that instance, teachers can purchase many of the materials that we describe in this section. On the other hand, if you are a teacher who likes to develop materials and finds it relaxing and rewarding, you might spend a great deal of time on the materials. Another option is to allow students to develop their own materials. For example, it is often helpful to have the student prepare flash cards for studying as they have to identify the key words and write a succinct explanation of the meaning or related facts on the back of the card. In addition to saving time, this process often lays the foundation for learning the strategies and content. In the following paragraphs, we

| Describe | List |
|---|---|
| Summarize and retell main idea and details. | Record topics in order. Provide descriptions of each if requested. |
| **Compare and Contrast** | **Summarize** |
| Describe the similarities and differences. | Summarize using steps above. |
| | **Give examples** |
| **Discuss** | Provide examples that relate directly to the question. |
| Discuss the information. | |

Image used under license from Shutterstock
Shpadaruk Aleksei/Shutterstock.

describe materials needed for flash cards, mnemonics, summarization, cover, copy and compare, and test-taking strategies.

## Flash Cards

The materials needed for flash cards include the list of content (e.g., vocabulary words), note cards or other thick paper, writing utensils, scissors, and other materials needed for optional decorations. The teacher or student writes the stem (e.g., vocabulary word, math fact) on one side and the answer (e.g., definition, answer) on the other side. In the early stages it may be helpful for the teacher to write the stems to be sure that the appropriate content is included. The student could write the information on the back of the card. Teachers and students can also draw figures or pictures on one side to help the student remember. Another option is to print the text and/or pictures or cut them out of a magazine. Students can attach them to the note cards.

## Mnemonics

Very minimal materials are needed for mnemonics. The teacher and students will need to identify the content to be learned. We suggest that regardless of whether the teacher or the student creates the mnemonic that it be written on paper, preferably something like note cards or card stock, so the student can refer to it as needed. This applies to acronyms, acrostics, and memory palaces. Again, students can be allowed to create their own card, decorating as desired, so cards or card stock, markers, and other writing utensils are needed. Other materials can be used at teacher and student discretion.

## Summarizing

Even fewer materials are needed for summarizing than the other strategies. Students will need reading materials to summarize, and this is often most helpful if it is sections of a textbook relevant to material currently being taught in one of the student's classes. We suggest that teachers begin with short reading samples and move on to longer readings as students become competent in summarizing. Further, teachers may wish to use multiple means of student responses, such as using marker boards in addition to paper and pencil.

### Cover, Copy, and Compare

Materials for cover, copy, and compare are similar to flash cards. Students will need cards or card stock with the question/problem at the top and the answer on the bottom, on the same side of the paper. Students will need paper and a writing utensil to write the problem and answer and something to cover the answer for comparison.

### Test-taking Strategies

Materials to teach test-taking strategies are sample test questions of various formats. It may be most helpful to use recent quizzes and tests from the student's current classes. Using these tests can enhance the benefits of learning test-taking strategies by also including a review of content that the student may need to know for future tests in a class.

## Stage 4: Teach and Practice the Strategy

Teaching adolescents with ADHD study and test-taking skills can best be accomplished through the skills training steps discussed in Chapter 12.

### Introduce Study and Test-taking Skills

The first step in teaching study skills is to explain the procedures to students. Teachers should prioritize the strategies based on the needs of the class and individual students. For example, if Josiah is struggling to remember the chronological order of the explorers, Mr. Quong will begin by teaching Josiah to use the loci method and create a memory palace. Similarly, Mr. Quong would prioritize the test-taking strategies, selecting the most relevant one to teach first. The teacher follows these procedures introducing one strategy at a time until students have been taught all strategies.

## Model

The second step, which can happen simultaneously or shortly after the teacher explains the intervention, is to model the strategy. The teacher demonstrates the use of the strategy by projecting on the whiteboard or smartboard for the entire class or sitting with small groups or individual students. As the teacher demonstrates, she "thinks aloud" describing each step and her thoughts as she studies (study skills) or answers questions (test taking).

## Rehearsal, Practice, and Feedback

After describing and modeling the strategy, the teacher instructs students to practice the skill through role-play. Students can role-play the strategy in groups, pairs, or individually. The teacher closely monitors student progress providing positive and corrective feedback as needed. Teachers must demonstrate how using the strategies will increase the students test and overall grade. Rehearsing and practicing test-taking skills involves providing the student with practice tests with different types of questions and asking the students to verbally describe the process of answering the type of questions. The teacher assists and provides feedback as the students go through the process. Additionally, when a teacher gives the students a test, she can begin by asking students to verbally describe the steps that they are going to take when answering the questions. Teachers fade these procedures as students master the skill.

## *Stage 5: Monitor Progress*

The final stage in teaching students' study and test-taking skills is to monitor their progress. This can be accomplished in several ways. First, teachers can assess student use of the strategies by asking students to describe the study and test-taking strategies verbally or in writing. Second, teachers can ask students to explain the skill that they used for studying for a test and the evidence that it was an effective strategy. For example, Mr. Quong could ask Josiah to explain the loci method that he used to learn and recall historical figures. Josiah would verbally describe his memory palace and the rooms where each individual was located. Next, he would explain that using the method helped him remember the individuals as demonstrated on his exam. We encourage teachers to provide a verbal and social reinforcer when students demonstrate these skills.

# Modes of Study Skills Instruction

We describe three modes of instructing students how to use study and testing taking strategies, group or individual, peer-based, and computer-based. Teachers can select the mode of delivery that best meets their student needs. We suggest that teachers initially use the teacher-directed mode to ensure that students have a thorough understanding of the strategy. After initial instruction, it is likely that different methods will be used depending on the strategy being taught. For example, some strategies, such as flash cards can easily be practiced in peer pairs, while others, such memory palaces, are very specific to individual students and are best practiced independently. In addition, we encourage teachers to use more than one mode when appropriate while students are learning and practicing the strategies.

## *Teacher-directed Class, Group, or Individual*

The first, and most common, instructional mode is teacher directed for the entire class, groups, or individual students. Following the procedures just described, the teacher provides direct instruction to the whole class, small groups, or individual students.

## *Peer Pairs*

The second mode of study and test-taking skill instruction is allowing students to work in pairs. Students are allowed to work in pairs after they have received initial instruction on the strategy. Once the teacher is confident of student skill, the students take turns guiding the study. For example, when Josiah works with a peer using flash cards, one student holds the cards, showing the student one card at a time. The other student provides the answer to the prompt and the card holder informs the student of the accuracy of his response. It is important that students are taught how to appropriately respond when peers are correct and incorrect. Additionally, we encourage teachers to carefully monitor student attention to task, as students working in pairs are likely to have the opportunity to be distracted and off-task.

## Computer-based

The third mode of instruction is computer-based. With the increases in technology, different computer-based study strategies are being developed daily. Some are designed for students to use independently, and others are designed for class wide studying. For example, we have used Quizlet and Kahoot in our classes. Quizlet is an online study program that is primarily known for its flash cards. Students study independently with the electronic flash cards. In addition, the program includes different modes, such as matching and testing. Quizlet is also available in an application for mobile devices. It is free to use and includes many ready-made study sets. Moreover, teachers and students can make their own set of "flash cards."

Image used under license from Shutterstock. Rawpixel.com/Shutterstock.com.

Kahoot® is a game-based learning platform that allows students to compete against each other in group settings. Teachers create a list of questions that are then projected in front of the class. Students sign in to the game site either with their own name or a pseudonym and respond to the questions on their individual devices (tablet, iPad, cell phone). The game is fun, fast-paced, and motivating. Additionally, teachers can assign an individual version of the game for students to use for studying at home or in the classroom.

## Potential Barriers and Methods of Overcoming the Barriers

There are always barriers to intervention implementations in classrooms. Although learning to study is an essential skill for adolescents, many find the strategies less than exciting to learn. As such, in this section, we discuss motivation and student cooperation at home as barriers. Furthermore, we provide some options for overcoming the barriers.

## Motivation to Learn

Some students are internally motivated to study and learn; however, many students with ADHD may not be motivated by the opportunity to improve learning. When student's view studying as something boring and difficult, they struggle to be motivated to do it. This is especially true when studying for the test is a passive activity, such as re-reading the book or notes. As such, we encourage teachers to make studying fun using the preceding strategies. Help students explore each option and find the one that works best for them. What is most interesting, most exciting, and less passive? Helping students find strategies that work for them is the beginning of helping them want to study!

Encourage parents to help their adolescent study at home. We suggest asking students to study for shorter periods of time across days. Adolescents are not likely to be motivated to be engaged with a strategy if it will take them three hours to learn the content. At this point, the task is overwhelming and daunting. Help them establish long-term strategies for studying. When is the test? How many days do they have to study? How much can they learn each day? With this information, how much time do they need to study in one day? Help them learn to write it down and check off what they have completed. In essence, you are teaching them to monitor their own progress, so combine these strategies with those in Chapter 5 of this book. Remember to provide positive reinforcement to students for studying each day and fade external reinforcement to self-reinforcement. For example, if parents provide a note that they studied for a test with their student using the summarizing technique for at least 20 minutes over the day preceding the test, the student may earn three extra credit points. Ultimately, we want to help them learn to feel rewarded by their achievement, but short-term rewards can help with motivation!

## Student Cooperation at Home

Simply teaching students study strategies is not enough. For greatest impact, students must be able and willing to use the study strategies beyond the school day. Studying, especially at home, is difficult for many adolescents

## Check List

1. Sign in with your ID _____ and password _____ ☑
2. Select your course ☐
3. Select modules ☐
4. Click on the module with this week's date: ☐
5. Click on the module guide and follow the directions for the day's homework ☐
6. When homework is complete, click on the assignment tab. ☐
7. Open the tab with today's date ☐
8. Upload the assignment. ☐

Image used under license from Shutterstock. PixMarket/ Shutterstock.com.

with ADHD. Consider the many distractions in home environments. There are televisions, computers, video games, parents, friends, siblings, pets, and cell phones, amongst a few things that are likely to distract adolescents while studying. Although this is true for all students, home environments are especially distracting for students challenged to avoid distractions, regulate their own behavior, and attend to often monotonous tasks.

We encourage teachers to provide guidance for parents to help them establish homework routines. Adolescents need a quiet and comfortable place to work with all their necessary supplies. Many parents would be glad to tell you that students become distracted looking for writing utensils and paper to complete their tasks. As such, providing a pencil holder and a folder for blank paper and helping students remember to replace supplies as needed will go a long way toward decreasing the amount of time that it takes for the adolescent to complete homework. Similarly, we have seen students spend inordinate amounts of time trying to locate their homework on a computer. This often surprises teachers. After all, the student has worked on Google® Classroom or Canvas (or other web-based programs) the entire year! How could they not remember? It is important to keep in mind that one symptom of ADHD is "forgetfulness or losing items." Unfortunately, this applies to technology also. To help students overcome this barrier, teachers can provide students with a laminated note card with the steps to finding homework files. Another option is to use one of the memory tools previously discussed. For example, Mr. Quong, will help Malik develop a mnemonic device for finding his homework on Canvas®, such as "Sam Saw Success when he Chose to Clear his schedule and Work On Understanding." Applying memory techniques across students' lives will help them complete multiple tasks, such as submitting homework.

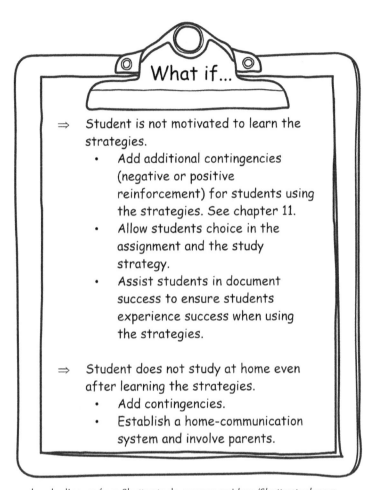

## What if...

⇒ Student is not motivated to learn the strategies.
  • Add additional contingencies (negative or positive reinforcement) for students using the strategies. See chapter 11.
  • Allow students choice in the assignment and the study strategy.
  • Assist students in document success to ensure students experience success when using the strategies.

⇒ Student does not study at home even after learning the strategies.
  • Add contingencies.
  • Establish a home-communication system and involve parents.

Image used under license from Shutterstock. *rangsan paidaen/Shutterstock.com.*

## Considerations for Culturally Responsive Study Skills

As we have mentioned before, there are several tenets of culturally relevant teaching.

Teaching students study skills aligns closely with the goal of high expectations for all students. Although students with ADHD are a heterogenous group with many individual strengths and struggles, a majority can master grade level standards; however, doing what it takes to learn and remember the content is often a problem. As such, maintaining high expectations requires helping students learn and retrieve information using study and test-taking strategies.

Second, study strategies materials should be developed with consideration of the rich and unique cultural wealth, knowledge, and skills of students from varying cultures. The most basic requirement to meet this goal is to include multicultural content. This can be accomplished by working with the students' parents and families to identify adaptations of the strategies that fit within their home context. Specific considerations and adaptations should be given to family routines and resources. Once again, we encourage you to learn about the students' lives. What resources are available? Computers? Tablets? Wi-Fi? Do parents have the time and capability to help with homework? What language is spoken at home? What other responsibilities do adolescents have in the afternoons? Jobs? Siblings? Extracurricular activities? Effectively situating homework into the diverse lives of students helps teachers establish expectations and students learn to achieve them.

## Programming

We strongly encourage teachers to advocate for the inclusion of interventions with evidence of effectiveness on any plan written for the student, such as a response to intervention plan, individualized education program (IEP), section 504 plan, and/or any other plan developed for an adolescent with ADHD. As you know, research indicates that study skills can increase academic impairment and decrease disruptive behavior. Therefore, we provide an examples of Josiah's current levels, strengths and weaknesses, annual goals, and short-term benchmarks. In addition, we provide a description of self-management that can be included in the accommodations/ modifications section of the plan.

**Common Core Standards**

CCSS.ELA-Literacy.CCRA.R.1 Read closely to determine what the text says explicitly and to make logical inferences from it; cite specific textual evidence when writing or speaking to support conclusions drawn from the text.

CCSS.ELA-Literacy.CCRA.R.2 Determine central ideas or themes of a text and analyze their development; summarize the key supporting details and ideas.

**CASEL Standards:** Social Emotional Learning Competency: Self-Awareness
Sub competency—recognizing strengths and self-confidence

**Current levels, strengths and weaknesses:** Josiah is a sixth-grade student. Josiah is organized and takes excellent notes in class when required. Josiah is failing several classes, because he earns passing grades on less than 50% of his exams. Josiah and his mother report that he struggles to study at home. As such, he rarely tries to study. To increase fluency in studying and exam scores, Josiah needs to learn studying skills and test-taking strategies.

**Annual Smart Goal:**
- Given study skills and test-taking strategy instruction three times per week following the procedures outlined in [this book], Josiah will report studying for exams and use test-taking strategies at least 90% of opportunities and score 70% or above on all exam's tasks for each course in one semester.

# Conclusion

In conclusion, in order to learn and demonstrate learning on assessments, students must be able to learn and retain information. This is a struggle for many adolescents with ADHD for multiple reasons including struggles with working memory, inattention, and distractibility. Many research-based strategies are available and covered in this chapter to help students learn and retain information. As educators, it is our responsibility to ensure that students have the skills that they need to succeed!

# Reference List

Brasch, T. L., Williams, R. L., & McLaughlin, T. F. (2008). The effects of a direct instruction flashcard system on multiplication fact mastery by two high school students with ADHD and ODD. *Child & Family Behavior Therapy, 30*(1), 51–59.

Evans, S. W., & Langberg, J. (2011). *The challenging horizons program treatment manual* Unpublished manuscript.

Moser, L. A., Fishley, K. M., Konrad, M., & Hessler, T. (2012). Effects of the copy-cover-compare strategy on acquisition, maintenance, and generalization of spelling sight words for elementary students with attention deficit/hyperactivity disorder. *Child & Family Behavior Therapy, 34*(2), 93–110.

# Organization
# Training

Cedric is a ninth-grade student with ADHD. Cedric is intelligent, out-going, creative and a leader to his peers both in class and on the football field. In class, you would observe Cedric engaged in discussions, interjecting critical and witty comments. His teachers praise his abilities and his class participation. Nonetheless, Cedric struggles to keep his materials organized. His mother states that when she opens Cedric's backpack, if he manages to get home with it, it is likely to burst open with loose papers, lunch leftovers, clothes, and trash. She is happy to tell anyone that the backpack is more likely to be on the floor of a classroom, in his locker in the gym, or in the back of his pickup truck than in the house with all the materials that he needs to complete his homework. In fact, Cedric had to get a part time job to pay for a complete set of textbooks when he left the entire backpack in the truck in the rain. Without needed materials, Cedric rarely submits his homework to his teachers. As such, he is failing History, Algebra, English, and Biology. It is likely that he will have to repeat those courses. Needless to say, Cedric's teachers are frustrated with him. Ms. Prior, his science teacher speaks to Cedric every morning before school. She has become his unofficial mentor and he likes to visit with her. The conversation each morning is similar. They begin by reflecting on the lesson the prior day and what will be covered in class. They move on to a discussion of what is happening on the football team, in the community, or amongst Cedric's peers. Finally, they get around to Cedric' grades. Ms. Prior reminds him that he has failing grades in several of his classes because he does not complete and turn in his homework. She asks what she can do to help. Cedric has no idea what would help him. He talks about the frustration of knowing the content, making an A on tests, and failing classes. Why does he have to do the ridiculous homework if he knows the content? He tells her that he just cannot get home with the materials he needs to do the work and how extremely frustrating the entire situation is for him. Ms. Prior tries to explain to Cedric that he must learn to be organized across his life. Without organization skills, he is going to struggle in every aspect, his social life, college life, work life, and in his relationships. Ms. Prior convinces Cedric to participate in organization training intervention each morning when he meets with her.

Image used under license from Shutterstock. Prostock-studio/Shutterstock.com.

DOI: 10.4324/9781003109983-9

# Description of Organization Training

Organization training (OT) is an intervention to teach adolescents to sort and store paperwork; identify homework; and track, locate, and turn in assignments. The organization training described here has been researched extensively, revealing an association with materials organization and course grades (Evans et al., 2009; Harrison et al., 2020a). With OT, students like Cedric are taught to store their materials and supplies in a manner that makes it easy for them to find homework, pens, paper, and other items when needed.

Organization difficulties are related to inattention. Therefore, challenges with organization are very much a barrier to academic performance for adolescents with ADHD. It is likely that at the beginning of the semester, Cedric had nice, neat binders for each class, well, at least for one day. He probably started each day with a homework sheet given to him by Ms.

Image used under license from Shutterstock. New Vectors/Shutterstock.com.

Prior; she hands the sheet to her students immediately before the bell rings to change classes. The student sitting beside Cedric placed his sheet neatly in her binder and wrote the assignment in her agenda book. Cedric, on the hand, shoved his sheet into his backpack, and began talking to a friend about their plans for afterschool. This scenario repeats in the next three classes. Then he goes to his athletic class. Instead of paper, he shoves dirty socks into his backpack. Given OT, students with behaviors similar to Cedric's actions are taught the organization skills needed for success in secondary schools.

# Stages of Organization Training

| 1 | 2 | 3 | 4 | 5 | 6 | 7 |
|---|---|---|---|---|---|---|
| Preparation | Determine level of organization | Dump and reorganize | Checking, correcting, and contingencies | Fade behavioral contingencies | Guided independence | Independence |

*Figure 7.1* Seven Stages of Organization Training.

Organization training involves seven stages (Figure 7.1). The first is preparing for implementation, the process of determining "who, when, and where." The second phase is assessing the student's level of organization. This is the act of monitoring and recording the student's present performance of the target area, such as binder, bookbag, or locker. The third is area dump and reorganization. Area dump is the process of an adult and student collaboratively removing all materials and items from the target area (binder, bookbag) and reorganizing the area based on the organization checklist (Figure 7.2 and Figure 7.3). The fourth stage is checking, correcting organization mistakes, and establishing rewards, in which the teacher compares the area to the organization checklist and helps the student correct any errors. Additionally, the teacher and student select a reinforcer, a goal, and the percent of organization needed to meet the goal. The fifth stage is fading behavioral contingencies, in which the teacher slowly removes any external reinforcers and encourages the student to motivate himself. The sixth stage is progress monitoring, in which the teacher frequently checks, and the student corrects any organization errors. The seventh stage is independence and matching, in which the student independently organizes his own target area without assistance. Finally, the teacher and student both complete the checklist and compare the ratings.

## *Stage 1: Preparation*

The first stage is when educators decide who is going to implement the intervention, when the intervention will be implemented, and where the intervention will be implemented. These decisions can "make or break" the success of the intervention. This process involves talking to the faculty at the school to determine who is interested and who has sufficient time. Typically, OT is implemented three

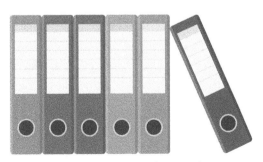

Image used under license from Shutterstock. Modvector/Shutterstock.com.

times per week either during the school day or immediately after school for approximately 30 minutes. Some sessions may last more than 30 minutes. Consider Cedric, Ms. Prior makes arrangements for Cedric' mother to bring him to school 30 minutes early, so that Ms. Prior can work with Cedric in her classroom. Although this is an option for Ms. Prior it may not be a working solution for all. It is vital that the decisions in this phase are made based on educator and student availability and interest.

## Stage 2: Determining Level of Organization

The second stage is measuring the student's percent of organization prior to intervention to establish baseline. The teacher collects the student's bookbag or binder(s) and places a "Y" for yes or "N" for no in the cell that corresponds to the criteria on the organization checklist. For example, before Ms. Prior implements bookbag organization with Cedric, she asks Cedric to bring her his bookbag. She explains that she is going to start an intervention with him, but first she is going to check his bookbag and binder during three consecutive class periods. He continues with his work, and she compares his bookbag and binder to the checklist.

## Stage 3: Area Dump and Reorganization

Image used under license from Shutterstock. New Vectors/Shutterstock.com.

The next stage is area dump and reorganization. In this stage, the teacher and student collaboratively take everything out of the area (e.g., bookbag, binder, locker) and start over with an empty binder, bookbag, or locker. The teacher and student sort the materials by subject discarding what is not needed. This typically includes paper and worksheets; however, it is not surprising to find dirty gym clothes and

## Organization Checklist – Binder.

Open your binder and go down the checklist: for each item, write a Y (for Yes) if you meet the criteria fully for all binders being checked or an N (for No) if you do not meet the criteria fully. When finished, divide the number of Y's by 8 and record this in the last space.

| BINDERS | DATES | | | | | |
|---|---|---|---|---|---|---|
| 1. Do you have the correct binders for today? | | | | | | |
| 2. Are your binders free from loose and irrelevant material (e.g., non-subject related material)? | | | | | | |
| 3. Is your planner present? | | | | | | |
| 4. Is your planner free of loose and irrelevant material? | | | | | | |
| 5. Are each of the cells in your planner complete? Did you document homework to be done and finished? | | | | | | |
| 6. Inside your binders: are there clearly defined locations for storing incomplete assignments? I keep them in _____ "I keep them in _____." | | | | | | |
| 7. Inside your binders: are there clearly defined locations for storing completed assignments (i.e., those assignments ready to be turned in)? "I keep them in _____." | | | | | | |
| 8. Inside the binders: are there clearly defined locations for storing all other class papers (e.g., graded assignments, class notes, class handouts)? "I keep them in _____." | | | | | | |
| 9. Is there a clearly defined central location for recording all long-term projects for each subject? "I record them in _____." | | | | | | |
| 10. Do you have a specific place to keep your homework? I keep it in _____ | | | | | | |
| **What percent of your binder is organized? Divide the number of Y's by 10 and then multiply by 100.** | | | | | | |
| <u>Comments:</u> | | | | | | |

*Figure 7.2* Binder Organization Checklist.

## Organization Checklist
### Book Bag

Open your bookbag and go down the checklist: for each item, write a Y (for Yes) if you meet the criteria fully or an N (for No) if you do not meet the criteria fully. When finished, divide the number of Y's by 8 and record this in the last space.

| | DATES | | | |
|---|---|---|---|---|
| **BOOKBAG** | | | | |
| 1. Do you have the books and materials you need to complete tomorrow's homework? | | | | |
| 2. Is your book bag free from unnecessary clothing? | | | | |
| 3. Is your book bag free from unnecessary materials or materials not placed in appropriate containers/binders, such loose papers and objects, pens, crumpled papers, etc.)? | | | | |
| Percentage of criteria met (# of Ys/3)*100 | | | | |

*Figure 7.3* Book Bag Organization Checklist.

other items. Papers are often wrinkled and even waded into balls. These papers should be straightened out to the best of your ability. As a word of caution, we encourage you to store all materials deemed as "unneeded" for safekeeping. More than once, we have spent time searching through trash cans for worksheets that students, originally, told us were not needed only to find out later that they needed the sheet. Once papers are grouped by subject and date, the student and/or teacher punch holes in each sheet to attach the sheets by three rings in the binder. Loose pencils and pens are placed in a pencil holder or some other container for safe keeping and easy location.

Students can have one three ring binder with dividers or a separate binder for each subject. It depends on teacher and student preference. Either way, the goal is to have all papers attached by all three rings in the binder.

For backpacks and lockers, the student and teacher remove all materials, remove what is deemed as "not needed," and organize what

Image used under license from Shutterstock. ONYXprj./Shutterstock.com.

is needed. For example, when Ms. Prior and Cedric empty his backpack, she finds a sandwich in a baggie covered in mold, a hoodie from the winter even though it is May, loose papers, and random pencils and pens. After dumping it out, she helps him identify what is needed and how to keep the backpack organized. Together, they put loose papers in binders attached by three rings. We find that using the pockets for all papers, tends to result in a mess. Next, she helps him put all of his pens/pencils in a pencil holder.

During this phase, the teacher also reviews the student's planner/ agenda book to explain to the student what is meant by the three items on the organization checklist. If students do not have a planner, then the teacher should help them find one. To receive three "Y's" on the checklist, students must have the planner with them, the planner must be free of irrelevant paper, and the planner must have something written for each subject (homework or "none" if no homework).

## Stage 4: Checking, Correcting, and Contingencies

The third stage is checking, correcting the target area, and awarding contingencies. Teachers continue to work with the student to maintain organization of the targeted areas. At each lesson, the teacher and student compare organization to the checklist and make corrections. For example, Ms. Prior opens Cedric's binder and finds papers only attached by two rings. She marks no in the cell that corresponds to the date and the criteria question. She instructs Cedric to place a "replacement sticker" on

Image used under license from Shutterstock. Alexander Yurkevich/ Shutterstock.com.

the torn hole and attach the sheet by three rings. Cedric frequently tells Ms. Prior that he has loose papers in his binder because the bell rings, and he does not have time to attach the sheet by the three rings. Ms. Prior tells him that she understands but continues to mark the indicator a "N." At this point, she also follows a problem-solving process to help Cedric find a solution. She asks him to brainstorm some solutions. What can he do different? How can he get the binder into order? It is likely that he will make excuses about why he cannot organize his binder. He typically tells her "Nothing. It's your fault!" After all, if she would just give him more time at the end of the period, he would be able to get it done. Instead of arguing she agrees to remind the class five minute before the bell rings to put away their materials.

To increase the likelihood that student will maintain organization between each session, teachers provide behavior specific praise, verbally rewarding student behavior. If praise is not sufficient to motivate students to maintain organization, the student and teacher can agree on criteria for earning the reinforcer. For example, Cedric likes to play computer games in schools. He and Ms. Prior agree that every time he earns 100% on the binder checklist, he can play a game on the computer for 15 minutes. Typically, reinforcement can be delivered on different types of schedules (when the reinforcer is delivered). During this stage, the reinforcement schedule is fixed meaning that Ms. Prior clearly explains that Cedric will be allowed to play computer games the last 15 minutes of class if he meets the established criteria (100%). More information specific to behavioral contingencies and adolescents with ADHD can be found in Chapter 9 of this book.

## Stage 5: Fade Behavioral Contingencies

The fifth stage is fading contingencies. During this phase, the teacher reads the questions on the organization checklist and the student answers the questions verbally with the teacher marking the sheet. When the student demonstrates 100% mastery of the organization criteria for four consecutive days, if behavioral contingencies were being used, the teacher begins to fade the rewards (i.e., behavioral contingencies). Fading the reward is the process of systematically moving from a fixed and consistent reward schedule to a variable interval schedule to no reinforcement at all. This process is gradual. For example, Ms. Prior would provide a great deal of praise for Cedric's progress, emphasizing the connection between binder organization and academic success. She explains that she is going to gradually reduce his reinforcement. She starts with randomly extending the length of time to earn the computer time from every day to random days per week.

If Cedric continues to keep his materials organized, she slowly moves to only verbal reinforcement. When the teacher has faded all behavioral contingencies, stage 6 begins.

## Stage 6: Guided Independence

The sixth stage is guided independence. During this phase, the student completes his/her own organization sheet with the teacher watching and completing a different sheet. When the student completes his/her sheet, the two are compared. If a difference is noted, then the teacher and student discuss it. The student is required to correct the mistake. For example, when Cedric completes his own organization sheet, he indicates that the homework folder only contains homework; however, Ms. Prior finds a random piece of notebook paper with formulas on it in the homework folder. Cedric explains that the sheet is notes from class and Ms. Prior reminds him to attach the sheet in his math binder and change his organization sheet to indicate that his homework folder includes paper other than homework. This process continues daily until Cedric and Ms. Prior's organization sheets match for four consecutive days.

## Stage 7: Independence

The final stage is independence. During this phase, students are given the opportunity to demonstrate their organizational skills. This is the point where the goal of independence should have been reached! The teacher continues to monitor student progress, but not simultaneously. For example, Cedric completes the organization checklist based on his materials independently at home. When he meets with Ms. Prior conducts her own random check and the two match their organization checklists. The two discuss any discrepancies and Cedric makes corrections as needed. This continues weekly unless the student receives two or more "N's" or the teacher and student disagree on more than two occasions. If this occurs, the student moves back to the previous phase or contingencies are reintroduced.

# Modes of Organization Training

## *Paper-based*

The typical mode of organization training is paper-based. Using procedures described extensively in the previous sections of this chapter, teachers can implement paper-based organization training (Figure 7.2 and 7.3).

## *Game-based*

Game-based organization training is the use of a video game, such as Athemos, or a digital gamified app, such as a modified version of EpicWin® (Harrison et al., 2020a; Harrison et al., 2020b), to guide and monitor progress on materials organization.

Image from Brandon Schultz with permission.

Athemos, a new computer-assisted intervention (combined with teacher manual and consultation) being developed by Brandon Schultz and Steven W. Evans, is a video game designed to be used as supplementary rehearsal for adolescents with ADHD to increase material organization, assignment tracking, and note-taking skills (Schultz & Evans, 2021). The game story line is that extraterrestrials have launched asteroids at the earth and the player (student) must disable the aliens' robot drones to gather and interpret intel to determine why the aliens are attacking. Intel (sentence fragments) must be organized into one of four alien characteristics associated with science, language arts, math, or social studies. After intel are organized and the organization can be used to encourage materials organization.

Although Athemos is not available for download at the time of this writing, you can sign up here (www.athemosthegame.org/) to be notified when the game is available for download. Once downloaded, you can teach your students to use the game with a USB game controller.

First, students will create a new user account and then begin playing the game. In Athemos, teachers have a portal that allows them to view information about the number of times students log in, the total time played, and progress. In vivo mentoring is an important part of using Athemos. Teachers mentor students by using the game as a reward and an analogy for their materials organization, assignment tracking, and note-taking. The goal is for teachers to help students see the connection between organizing the intel based on a color scheme in the game and organizing binders based on a color scheme and how using the planner in the game could be used as a planner for school assignments (Schultz & Evans, in progress).

EpicWin is a digital application with a highly visual narrative weaved into gameplay. It was originally developed by Tak Fung (Fung, 2015) and updated by Adrian Parkes (Banshee Apps, 2022) as an app for adults to increase motivation to complete tasks, a gamified to-do list. It was adapted by Harrison et al. (2020a) to be used by middle school adolescents as a self-management app. We encourage teachers to consider using the app as a tool to guide organization training. The stems on the organization checklist can be entered as the quests, or tasks, on the game. For example, Ms. Prior would enter the eight tasks on the binder checklist as quests. During the organization training session, Cedric would document if he had or had not completed the "quest." By completing the quests, Cedric's avatar would earn loot and travel along a path with each successful interval. Cedric's character would "level up" as his percent of organization increases.

# Potential Barriers and Methods of Overcoming the Barriers

It is possible that students will experience barriers to success when being taught to organize their materials. As we are sure you know, this is an area that causes great difficulty for a majority of adolescents with ADHD. Our experiences with secondary students with ADHD lead us to conclude that three events interfere: (1) declining progress, (2) lack of time, (3) and student refusal or lack of motivation.

## *Declining Progress*

The academic progress of adolescents with ADHD is notoriously variable. With organization training, student progress toward consistent organization typically fluctuates up and down, increasing in the fall between the beginning of the school year and winter break and flattening out in the spring semester. This is not surprising as it represents the typical trajectory of academic progress for adolescents with ADHD. Without intervention, both organization and academic progress is likely to decrease between winter break and the end of the academic year. As such, when student progress declines for more than two days, behavioral contingencies may be reintroduced.

## *Student Refusal/Lack of Willingness*

We have all heard students say that they do not need to reorganize their binders, often with an eye roll response from their parents. This typically occurs when students have some sort of "system" that they believe is working, although their teachers and parents report that the student cannot locate his materials to do homework or to submit it to the teacher. We have heard students say that they just forget to bring home materials and it has absolutely nothing to do with their materials organization. In other instances, they have accommodations that remove the expectation for materials organization. For example, sometimes students get "organization assistance" from an adult with the adult organizing and maintaining organization of the student's materials. In other instances, students have "no homework" as the accommodation and/or they are allowed to keep all materials in the classroom. Each of these strategies might eliminate the need for some students to organize their materials in the moment, but they also remove the opportunity to teach a skill needed for independence.

This barrier is difficult to overcome and requires motivating the student to learn the organizational strategies being taught. This might be accomplished with valued contingencies and response cost. A detailed description is provided in Chapter 9. Briefly, when this level of resistance is demonstrated by the student, teachers must calmly and consistently follow through with instruction and behavioral strategies. It is natural for any teacher to want to "give up" on the strategy or to become angry at the student; however, neither behavior will teach the student to organize his/her materials. Instead, spend some time exploring contingencies that are highly important to the student. Talk to student about rewards. If positive contingencies do not work, then response cost (removal of valued privilege or item) might be the only option. The privilege being removed with response cost must be important to the student. We encourage you to end the response cost as soon as possible and re-engage the student with a positive contingency plan.

It is important for students to understand the importance of organizing their materials. This is difficult with students who are resistant and oppositional. One strategy likely to help is therapy technique called motivational interviewing (MI; Miller & Rollnick, 2002). Although an in-depth description of MI is beyond this chapter and beyond the scope of teaching, we will describe the five principles (Figure 7.4) for teacher information.

The first principle is expressing empathy, in which the adult demonstrates understanding of the students' feelings. For example, Cedric tells Ms. Prior that he does not want to change his system for organizing his binder because it would be too confusing. Instead of telling him that he is wrong, she says, "It sounds like you think the new organization is too complicated." Expressing empathy is simply about acknowledging the discomfort and difficulty involved with making the change.

The second principle is developing discrepancy in which the student says that he wants to change his behavior but strives to prove to the teacher that it is not necessary. During this phase, the adult gently helps the student see the gap between where they are and where they want to be. For example, Ms. Prior might help Cedric see the difference between

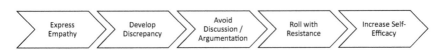

*Figure 7.4* Five Principles of Motivational Interviewing.
Created by author.

developing a system where he can find his homework to submit it and continuing to fail and "be harassed" by his teacher and parents. The idea being to help him see the benefits of changing without insisting or demanding that he acknowledge those benefits.

The third principle is to avoid discussing, augmenting, or trying to persuade the student to change his position as this only encourages the student to defend his position. Instead, the teacher helps the student become find his own answers and solutions throughout the process. For example, Ms. Prior might respond to Cedric, "It seems you're struggling to find a system that allows you to find your homework when it is time to submit it to your teacher. What do you think is the solution?"

The fourth principle is rolling with resistance, in which teachers take into consideration that there is a normal amount of resistance to change. You will notice students resisting learning organization skills when they argue and interrupt you. We have heard many students explain that their materials must be "organized" like they have them, because the teacher or parent said so, they can find things this way, or simply that you cannot tell them to organize their materials "your way." At this point, teachers automatically want to argue and explain to the student why he would be better off if he organized his materials in an *organized manner*. However, this only spirals into more argument. We encourage teachers to increase student control over the situation by beginning questions or responses with, "If you're interested . . ." or "Based on my experience . . ." or "It's your decision, but what do you think about . . . . "

The fifth principle is supporting self-efficacy, in which the teacher allows the student to make some choices on their own. The goal is to increase student confidence. Ultimately, the student has to believe that they can organize their materials, submit their materials, and pass their classes. Acknowledging that it is difficult, but they are making progress contributes to their confidence. For example, Ms. Prior would allow Cedric to determine some of the organization features and would encourage Cedric to keep his binder organized. She would help Cedric see the connection between his binder being organized, his assignment completion, and his improving grades. MI is a more complex than the principles described here; however, these principles are important for teachers to think about when working with a resistant student.

## *Lack of Time*

As with a majority of the interventions for students with ADHD, time (a precious commodity in schools) is needed. Specifically, an average of 30 minutes per session is needed to teach students to organize their materials with more time needed for stage three with less time needed for stage 5 and 6. The sessions can be conducted three to five days per week. For best progress, five days a week is probably needed. We suggest that you consider several options and determine which is feasible in your school. As with Cedric, a teacher can meet with the student before school if the teacher is willing and it is allowed. This is not an option in all schools due to union agreements or state regulations. However, with response to intervention programs, many schools have school professionals meet with students in the morning for mentoring sessions through programs such as Check in/Check out and Check and Connect. OT would fit nicely within those meetings.

Another feasible option is for a school mental health professional, such as a psychologist, counselor, or social worker, to teach the student to organize his/her materials. This is not to imply that these professionals have more available time than teachers, but instead that they are likely to have more time for individual students. Another option might be for school mental health providers to implement the intervention through peer tutoring activities. However, if this is the choice, we cannot overemphasize that the students must be taught to follow the "checking" procedures exactly as designed. More information regarding students working a peer tutors can be found in Chapter 11.

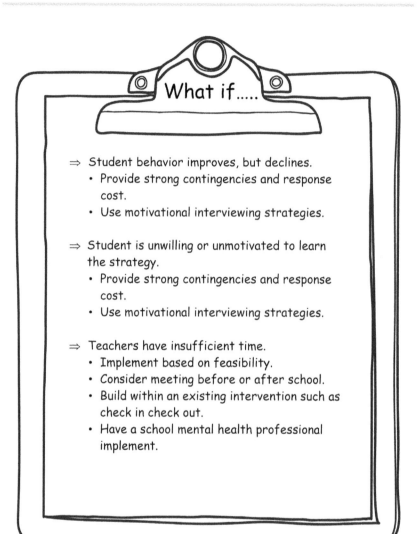

⇒ Student behavior improves, but declines.
  • Provide strong contingencies and response cost.
  • Use motivational interviewing strategies.

⇒ Student is unwilling or unmotivated to learn the strategy.
  • Provide strong contingencies and response cost.
  • Use motivational interviewing strategies.

⇒ Teachers have insufficient time.
  • Implement based on feasibility.
  • Consider meeting before or after school.
  • Build within an existing intervention such as check in check out.
  • Have a school mental health professional implement.

Image used under license from Shutterstock. rangsan paidaen/Shutterstock.com.

## Considerations for Culturally Responsive Organization Training

We encourage you to think about organization training in terms of a culturally responsiveness. Two areas (amongst others) might be considered. First, as you have read, in some cases, contingency management is necessary to motivate students to organize their materials. However, some cultures strongly emphasize respect and obedience and consider reward to be unnecessary and even improper when asking a child to do "what is expected." If this is the case with the student with whom you are working, it might be best to include parents in decisions regarding contingencies. For example, some Latinx parents might prefer response cost over positive praise. If this is the case, then the teacher and parents should clearly explain to the student that they will lose privileges if they do not maintain binder organization. For example, Cedric's mother prefers to remove his computer time after school if his binder is not organized, instead of giving him additional computer time when the binder is organized.

Another consideration is resources. It is important to consider the resources that are needed to implement this intervention and determine if the parent or the school is going to provide the materials. For example, if Cedric is expected to have an individual binder for each of his seven courses, it is possible that that his mother cannot afford to purchase seven new binders. In this case, it is likely that the school has binders that Cedric can use. Another option is to have Cedric use one binder with seven dividers, one for each course. It is important, with all parents, to involve them in the development of the organization system. This allows parents to be involved in the choosing expectations within the context of their own resources and beliefs.

## Programming

We strongly encourage teachers to advocate for the inclusion of interventions with evidence of effectiveness on any plan, written or otherwise, for the student, such as a response to intervention plan, individualized education program (IEP), section 504 plan, and/or any other plan developed for an adolescent with ADHD. As you know, research indicates that organization training can increase binder, bookbag, and locker organization, academic engagement, and academic performance. Therefore, we provide an example of the applicable CASEL standard; Cedric's current levels, strengths, and weaknesses, and annual goals.

**CASEL Standards:** Social Emotional Learning Competency: Self-management Sub competency—organizational skills

**Current levels, strengths, and weaknesses:** Cedric is a ninth-grade student who is intelligent, social, creative, and a leader. Cedric's areas of need include organizing and maintaining organization of his materials and completing and submitting his homework. Often, Cedric will leave his backpack in various places. When he does bring it home, the bag is full of trash and loose paper. This lack of organization makes it exceptionally hard for him to keep up with assignments. Currently, Cedric has failing grades in history, algebra, English, and biology. According to Cedric, everything is overwhelming him. Cedric's science teacher, Ms. Prior, tries to encourage him to stay organized. She has stressed the importance of keeping up with things. Cedric has agreed to meet with Ms. Prior each morning to go through organization training intervention. The intervention is intended to increase Cedric's organization skills and hold him accountable for turning in homework assignments. As of right now, Cedric is only submitting 25% of the homework assignments he is given within a 30-day period. When it comes to organization, Cedric currently has none. These weaknesses need to address to limit long-term bad habits.

**Annual Smart Goal:**
- Given organization training, by the end of the academic year, Cedric will maintain organization of his binder, book bag, and locker independently without prompting and/or behavioral contingencies with 100% accuracy as measured on the organization checklist.
- Given organization training, by the end of the academic year, Cedric will complete and submit 100% of assigned homework as measured by teacher records.

# Conclusion

In this chapter, we described organization training, an intervention that directly addresses several struggles experienced by adolescents with ADHD. Lack of organization directly interferes with the expectations of secondary teachers and schools and negatively impacts academic performance. To increase lifelong success, students with ADHD must be taught to organize materials and manage tasks. In this chapter, we discussed seven stages and their implementation steps. We discussed declining progress, student refusal/lack of willingness, and time as potential barriers to effective implementation. Furthermore, we stressed the importance of considering culture in implementation. We strongly encourage you to teach all students with ADHD to organize their materials and generalize their effects to other aspects of their lives.

# Reference List

Banshee Apps. (2022). *EpicWin* (Version #) [Mobile app]. Publisher/App Store. https://bansheeapps.com/

Evans, S. W. (1999). Mental health services in schools: Utilization, effectiveness, and consent. *Clinical Psychology Review, 19*, 165–178.

Evans, S. W., Schultz, B. K., White, L. C., Brady, C., Sibley, M. H., & Van Eck, K. (2009). A school-based organization intervention for young adolescents with attention-deficit/hyperactivity disorder. *School Mental Health, 1*(2), 78–88.

Fung, T. (2015). *EpicWin* (adapted for AMSI research) (Mobile application software).

Harrison, J. R., Evans, S. W., Baran, A., Khondker, F., Press, K., Noel, D., . . . Mohlmann, M. (2020a). Comparison of accommodations and interventions for youth with ADHD: A randomized controlled trial. *Journal of School Psychology, 80*, 15–36.

Harrison, J. R., Kwong, C., Evans, S. W., Peltier, C., & Mathews, L. (2020b). Game-based self-management: Addressing inattention during independent reading and written response. *Journal of Applied School Psychology, 36*(1), 38–61.

Miller, W. R., & Rollnick, S. (2002). *Motivational interviewing: Preparing people for change* (2nd ed.). The Guilford Press.

Schultz, B. K., & Evans, S. W. (2021, April 15–16). *Game-based strategies for delivering behavioral health programs: Separating fact from fantasy* [conference session]. Southeastern School Behavioral Health Conference, Myrtle Beach, SC, United States.

# Note-taking Instruction

**Muzzammil**

Muzzammil is a ninth-grade student with ADHD. He enjoys social activities and is perceived as a loyal friend by his peers. His parents and teachers describe him as "a good kid". He struggles to maintain attention and avoid distractions while sitting peacefully in all of his classes and completing very few academic assignments. Nonetheless, if you watch carefully, you will see him in the back of the classroom, bothering no one, with his phone in his lap texting his girlfriend or surfing the web while his teachers instruct the class or when he is supposed to be engaged in reading instructional material (articles, textbook). On the rare occasion that that the teacher sees him and asks him to put away his phone, he agreeably puts it in his pocket. This is especially troublesome in his science class. The teacher typically teaches through discussion and has students complete independent and group activities. When the time comes
for Muzzammil to do his independent work or participate in a group activity, he is lost. He does not know what to do and has nothing to contribute. He typically has taken no notes and therefore has nothing to reference the content that was taught and no idea about the directions for the task. Muzzammil's grades are very low and he is failing science. As you can imagine, his parents and teachers are disappointed. It makes no sense to them that such a compliant young man does not complete his school work. His parents have talked to him and taken away privileges. He simply says that he will do better and he does for a week or so, but then the same pattern returns.... not paying attention in class, not completing his work, and failing. This cycle not only impacts his academic success in high school, but if he does not learn strategies to document content taught in class or read in textbooks, he will continue to struggle throughout any instructional or educational endeavors that he attempts. As such, teaching him to take notes from discussions and when reading is vital to his success!

| Student: ALAM, MUZZAMMIL | | | Grade: 7 | | | Period: 04/15/22- 05/09/22 | | | |
|---|---|---|---|---|---|---|---|---|---|
| Per. | Course Name | Teacher | Q1 | Q2 | Q3 | Q4 | Teacher Comments | Citz |
| 1 | ART | KING, CLINTON | D | | | | | U |
| 2 | COMMON CORE MATH 7 | HARRIS, EMMA | F | | | | | U |
| 3 | PE SPRING | HERNANDEZ, JOSE | D | | | | | N |
| 4 | LANG ARTS 7 | WOODLEY, SUZIE | C | | | | | N |
| 5 | TEXAS HISTORY | WRIGHT, MEGAN | F | | | | | U |
| 6 | SCIENCE 7 | SPRING, BRUCE | F | | | | | N |

| GPA | Terms | Citizenship |
|---|---|---|
| Q1 GPA: .667 | Q1= Quarter 1    Q2= Quarter 2 | O= Outstanding    S= Satisfactory |
| Cumulative GPA: .667 | Q3= Quarter 3    Q4= Quarter 4 | N= Needs Improvement    U= Unsatisfactory |

Image used under license from Shutterstock. Rajesh Narayanan/Shutterstock.

DOI: 10.4324/9781003109983-10

# Description of the Note-taking Instruction

Note-taking instruction is a strategy to teach students like Muzzammil to document what is taught to have a record of what was taught during class time, read in learning materials, or learned through experimentation. Given note-taking instruction students also learn to attend to what is being said or read and document the main ideas and details (Evans & Shively, 2019). With accurate and complete notes, students can easily retrieve information (Boyle et al., 2015) needed to complete independent or group tasks. Additionally, when students take and review notes, they are more likely to remember what they were taught and to score higher on tests than if they do not take notes (Kiewra, 1985). This is a highly important skill for adolescents, as beginning in middle school and throughout high school, teachers present about half of the material through lecture and the remaining through hands-on or inquiry-based instruction (Moin et al., 2009). All of this requires retrieval of information, not easily retrieved without some written information.

Results from scientific studies indicate that teaching students to take notes results in increased note completion and accuracy, and bolsters comprehension and on-task behavior (Evans et al., 1995; Harrison et al., 2020). Simply from this description, we are confident that you recognize several reasons why taking notes during class is both helpful and difficult for students with ADHD. Consider Muzzammil sitting quietly in the back of the classroom. It is likely that he truly may intend to attend to class instruction and participate in the class discussion. When the class begins, he retrieves his notebook and pen (assuming he can find them), places them on his desk and looks at the teacher or the classmate who is talking. However, something in the classroom is likely to distract him. Maybe Ms. Rae begins to describe a group project. She instructs the students that they will develop a model to represent the comparison of the needs of animals and . . . (Muzzammil remembers that he forgot to feed April, his dog). He begins to feel a little panicky, as his mother told him that if he forgot one more time, she was going to restrict his activities for the weekend. But he has a date with his girlfriend on Friday night and . . . . As you can see, it is highly unlikely that he will attend to the information that he needs to contribute to a

Image used under license from Shutterstock. New Vectors/Shutterstock.com.

group project. Further, given his limitations with organization it is likely that he will have trouble organizing the information into clear interpretable notes that can be read later.

In this situation, the benefit of learning to take notes for Muzzammil is that it will help him engage in the instruction, concentrate, and attend to what he hears and/or reads. Once he learns to effectively take notes, he will avoid distractions as he concentrates on identifying the main ideas and details of what is being said or read. This process will help him maintain attention because he will be actively engaged in the material. Muzzammil will consistently think about what is important, how to write it quickly and clearly, and how to organize it according to the framework that he learned. This is in contrast to the passive listening and reading that is often exhibited by youth with ADHD. Passive attention to the material exacerbates problems sustaining attention and learning. We have found that adolescents with ADHD who receive daily note-taking training and practice taking notes will master the skill in two weeks to a month. As such, we encourage all middle and high schools to make sure that all students, especially those with ADHD, are given direct instruction in note-taking strategies. This training can occur in the context of a social studies, history, or science class while teaching the necessary material. In the following sections, we describe the five stages of note-taking instruction during discussion-based lessons and four stages when independently reading written material, articles, or other content-related material.

# Stages of Note-taking Instruction for Classroom Discussions

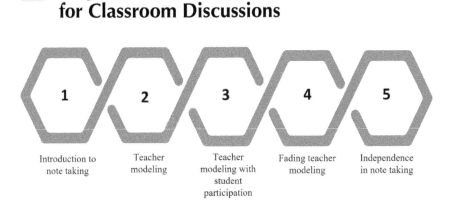

Figure 8.1 Five Stages of Note Taking.

## Stage 1: Introduction to Note Taking

The stages we describe (See Figure 8.1) are modified from those developed by Evans et al. (1995) who based them on the Directed Notetaking Activity developed by Spires and Stone (1989). Evans et al. modified the training program to meet the needs of adolescents with ADHD. The first step is to introduce the student to effective note taking. It is likely that students have developed their own note-taking structure but have never been explicitly taught the skill. In the case of students with ADHD, like Muzzammil, they might not have ever even tried to take notes. Therefore, we begin by exposing students to effective note taking by providing a copy of notes formatted as an outline (Figure 8.2). Notes are organized with a line drawn horizontally at the top of the page and one vertically down the side of the page. The left section is labeled "main idea" and the space to the right of the vertical line is labeled "details." The teacher shares her notes and then teaches the material. While teaching she thinks aloud about what information is important to put in her notes, how to write it efficiently, and how to organize the notes as main ideas and details. Her teaching and thinking aloud correspond to the notes provided to the students at the beginning of class.

## Stage 2: Teacher Modeling

The second stage is modeling effective note taking. This stage lasts for approximately two classes. While the teacher leads a discussion of the content, she

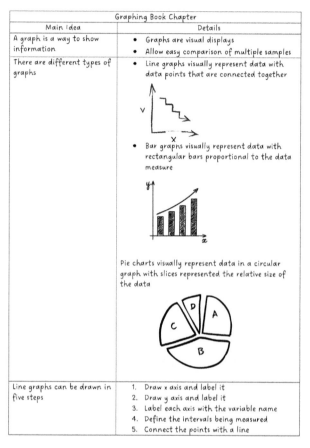

| Graphing Book Chapter | |
|---|---|
| Main Idea | Details |
| A graph is a way to show information | • Graphs are visual displays<br>• Allow easy comparison of multiple samples |
| There are different types of graphs | • Line graphs visually represent data with data points that are connected together<br><br>• Bar graphs visually represent data with rectangular bars proportional to the data measure<br><br>Pie charts visually represent data in a circular graph with slices represented the relative size of the data |
| Line graphs can be drawn in five steps | 1. Draw x axis and label it<br>2. Draw y axis and label it<br>3. Label each axis with the variable name<br>4. Define the intervals being measured<br>5. Connect the points with a line |

*Figure 8.2* Sample Copy of Notes.

Image used under license from Shutterstock. I am Irix/Shutterstock.com; YasnaTen/Shutterstock.com; clickyusho.id/Shutterstock.com.

demonstrates how to document the main ideas and details by projecting her own note taking on a whiteboard, chalkboard, or Smartboard®. As she writes the main idea and details, she discusses how she identified each. For example, she points out to her students that she spoke a little louder when she said, "Animals and plants have needs" and this is the main idea of this portion of the instruction. The teacher may wonder aloud if other phrases should be the main idea but shares her thinking with the class of how she came to choose this phrase as the main idea. Recognizing the topic sentence and voice fluctuations in the teacher helps individuals identify the main idea. She continues to go through a mix of instruction and pausing to think aloud about how to write notes.

## Stage 3: Teacher Modeling With Student Participation

Stage 3 involves the same procedures as stage 2 with one exception. As the teacher writes her own notes for the students to see, she asks students to tell her the main idea and details. When students answer, she either accepts their response and writes it on her notes or guides them to the correct answer. At times, she asks the class if they agree with what the student said and facilitates a conversion about main idea and details during the class. As students independently take notes, their student participation and ownership of the note-taking process increases and the teacher begins to fade the modeling.

## Stage 4: Fade Teacher Modeling

Stage 4 involves further fading teacher modeling. As the teacher presents the information verbally, she slowly stops modeling the note-taking process. She stops projecting her notes and asking students to tell her what she should write a little at a time. This pace and duration of this process is determined by the teacher's perception of student progress. If students continue to struggle to identify the main idea and/or details, the teacher continues to model and reteaches the note-taking process. To measure student mastery of note taking, teachers grade student notes and provides feedback and reteaching as needed. For example, after a week of instruction, Muzzammil continues to miss the main idea. Ms. Rae meets with Muzzammil and guides him through the process of identifying main idea and details on several occasions until she is sure that he has mastered the skill.

## Stage 5: Independence in Note Taking

Stage 5 occurs when the student demonstrates mastery of note taking without teacher guidance. Specifically, when students take notes in Stage 4 that the teacher rates as "good" three times within a two-week period, he is allowed to independently take notes. The exact criteria for "good" is based on teacher opinion. However, we recommend that students document 80 to 90% of what is taught and organizes it accurately on several occasions before being allowed to take notes independently.

# Stages of Note-taking Instruction for Reading Written Material

| Introduction to Taking Notes from Text | Modeling: Identifying Main Idea/Details | Fading Teacher Modeling | Independence |

*Figure 8.3* Four Stages of Note Taking.

## Stage 1: Introduction to Taking Notes From Written Material

The first stage (See Figure 8.3) of teaching students to take notes from written material is to explain to students that taking notes from discussion-based instruction and taking notes from written material are very similar. She tells the students that they will format their note-taking sheet in the same manner as they did with notes from discussion-based instruction with one horizontal and one vertical line. Next, she explains that similar to taking notes from lecture, they will identify main ideas and details.

## Stage 2: Modeling

After teachers have described the procedures for taking notes, they model the process. The teacher begins by giving the students a copy of the reading material and providing them with a note-taking sheet formatted as a "fill in the blank" sheet (see Figure 8.4). Next, the teacher models the procedures by projecting a blank note-taking sheet, for students to see. The teacher can use a computer with projector or Smart Board®. Next, she instructs students to "do as I do" as she models the procedures. She begins by scanning the reading material and identifying the first heading. When the heading is identified she writes that heading as the first main idea. Next, she tells the students that she will identify the details that support this main idea in this first section. She asks herself out loud, "what does the author want me to know?" (or "what might be on the test?") and explains that important details answer that question. Next, she explains that authors often bold and/or italicize words that are important details.

Image used under license from Shutterstock. fizkes/Shutterstock.com.

With each detail that she adds to the notes page, she clearly explains why she thinks what she wrote was noteworthy. As she moves through this process, she begins to ask students to suggest details that support the main idea and to explain why that detail is important. She repeats the process through each section of the reading material. We suggest that teachers start with fairly short passages with more than one main idea with clear headings.

## Stage 3: Fade Teacher Modeling

Similar to fading note taking during discussion-based lessons, the teacher fades modeling across a specified time period. With each new lesson, the teacher transfers more responsibility to the students by asking them to help her identify the main idea and details. They respond and she provides feedback helping them craft their answers. She follows the same procedures with details. Each day she provides note-taking sheets with fewer and fewer main ideas and details included. Furthermore, he slowly removes her verbal input allowing students to provide more and more information. She continues this process gauging how much instruction students need. She reteaches when needed. For example, Muzzammil struggled to identify the details in written materials. He mastered main idea, but then listed everything that was written in the paragraph as details. Ms. Prior re-taught him to identify details with guiding questions, such as "What facts of given to support the main idea?" Once Muzzammil mastered this content, Ms. Prior knew that he was ready to take notes from written material independently.

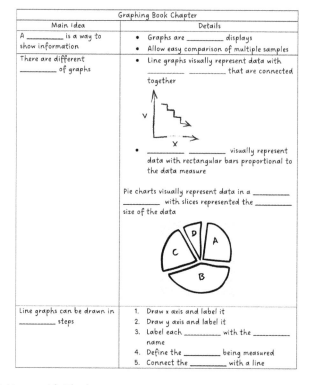

*Figure 8.4* Notes with Blanks.

Image used under license from Shutterstock. I am Irix/Shutterstock.com; YasnaTen/
Shutterstock.com; clickyusho.id/Shutterstock.com.

## Stage 4: Independence

During the independent stage, the teacher passes out reading materials and
instructs students to independently format their note-taking sheet and take
notes. Teachers may provide templates as a scaffold, but it is not likely that
students will need that at this stage. Additionally, teachers must continue to
check students notes to make sure that they make progress. It is not uncommon
for teachers to need to reteach some of the procedures during independence.

## Modes of Note-taking Instruction

Note taking can be conducted through direct and explicit instruction or
through virtual computer-based instruction.

## Teacher Explicit Instruction: Taking Notes on Paper

Image used under license from Shutterstock. ESB Professional/Shutterstock.com.

Explicit instruction is the process just described directly presented by the teacher to teach students to take notes on paper. The teacher gives clear and direct instruction and guides the students through the process of note taking, modeling written notes, until the students demonstrate mastery of the skill. There is not ambiguity of what is expected or what is being taught. Through direct instruction, teachers follow a process of teaching the content, allowing students opportunities to practice the skill, checking for understanding and reteaching when needed. Teachers provide explicit frequent direction and students are given multiple opportunities to practice the skill and get feedback from the teacher.

## Virtual Instruction

Another mode of teaching students to take notes is through computer-based instruction. Many adolescents with ADHD respond well to computer assisted instruction. Many programs, websites, and tips are available to teach students to take notes in a classroom. For example, when we typed "Cornell Note Taking" into the google search bar and indicated that we wanted videos, we got 354,000 hits. Simply giving students with ADHD the opportunity to watch videos on note taking is not typically sufficient to teach them to take notes, but it is excellent supplementary instruction.

## Game-based

Athemos, a new computer assisted intervention (combined with teacher manual and consultation) being developed by Brandon Schultz and Steven W. Evans, is a video game used as supplementary rehearsal for adolescents with ADHD to increase material organization, assignment tracking, and note-taking skills (Schultz & Evans, 2021). The game story line is that

Printed with permission from Brandon Schultz.

extraterrestrials have launched asteroids at the earth and the player (student) must disable the aliens' robot drones to gather and interpret intel to determine why the aliens are attacking. Intel (sentence fragments) must be organized into one of four alien characteristics associated with science, language arts, math, or social studies. After intel are organized into categories, the student identifies main ideas and supporting details, just as in note taking (Figure 8.5).

Although Athemos is not available for download at the time of this writing, you can sign up here (www.athemosthegame.org/) to be notified when the game is available for download. Once downloaded, you can teach your students to use the game with a USB game controller. First, students will create a new user account and then begin playing the game. In Athemos, teachers have a portal that allows them to view information about the number of times students log in to the game, the total time played, and progress. In person mentoring is an important part of using Athemos. Teachers mentor students by using the game as a reward and an analogy for

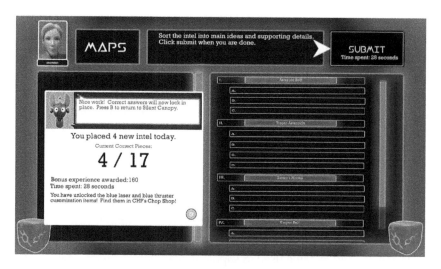

*Figure 8.5* Athemos Intel: Main Idea and Supporting Details.
Printed with permission from Brandon Schultz.

their materials organization, assignment tracking, and note taking. The goal is for teachers to help students see the connection between organizing the intel based on a color scheme in the game and organizing binders based on a color scheme and how using the planner in the game could be used as planned for school assignments (Schultz & Evans, in progress).

## Potential Barriers and Methods of Overcoming the Barriers

### Do It My Way

Students might complain if you ask them to follow a specific format for their notes. For example, Muzzammil told Ms. Prior that he was not going to organize his notes into "main ideas" and "details." He explained that he knew how to take notes, he just did not like to do it. He brought his notebook to her and showed her his notes. They were a mess and when asked to explain what he had written, he could not remember. Nonetheless he insisted that he do it himself. He explained that it would be too much work to try to learn to take notes the way that she taught him. After all, how was he supposed to focus on what she was saying and trying to keep his notes formatted. This is not an uncommon complaint and individuals have written about it on popular websites. Nonetheless, research tells us that if adolescents with ADHD are taught a method and use it consistently then their note-taking ability and academic performance will increase and disruptive behavior will decrease (Evans et al., 1995; Harrison et al., 2020).

That being said, what is important is the student learns and follows a consistent pattern. If Muzzammil chooses to change something about the way that he takes notes, but he manages to get all of the important information on the page in a way that he can read it and use the notes to study, then Ms. Prior might allow the changes. We suggest that she have a conversation with Muzzammil about the similarities and differences between the way that she is teaching him to take notes and "his way." The goal is for him to be comfortable with an efficient and effective means of note taking.

Another option is to provide the student with a template for the notes that includes blank spaces for the student to write the information from the lecture. The teacher explains to the student how to use the scaffold and provides correction feedback and positive praise at the end of the class. When the student

Image used under license from Shutterstock.
Golden Shrimp/Shutterstock.com.

masters using the scaffold, the teacher slowly includes more blank spaces until the student is completing all of the information with no scaffolds.

## Poor Handwriting

Although not unequivocally supported by research, some suspect a direct relationship between poor handwriting and ADHD. As teachers we have recognized many (but not all) students with ADHD have messy handwriting. Nonetheless, this is something to consider when teaching adolescents to take notes. If a student's handwriting is not legible, even for himself, then it is possible that taking notes via a technological device, such as a computer or Chromebook, is the best option. Another option is to allow the student to use an electronic pencil. Using the electronic pencil, the student writes on a tablet and the notes can be saved as handwritten notes or can be translated to a typed document. Prior to using this an option, the teacher and students should make sure that the application "understands" the students handwriting. If not, then this is not a viable option, and the student should be taught to take notes on the computer.

## Understanding Main Ideas

Our experience with students with ADHD is that they tend to achieve accuracy recording details sooner than they learn to accurately identify main ideas. This is especially true when taking notes during class lessons as the main ideas in textbooks are usually bolded making them easy to identify. They often record main ideas in their notes but list them with the details. The conceptual distinction between details and main ideas can be challenging. Persistent practice with feedback will eventually lead to the students gaining this understanding, but it could take longer than a teacher may expect it to for some students.

## *Pace of Instruction*

During note-taking training the pace of instruction is slowed. It takes time to integrate note-taking modeling and instruction into the classroom instruction and this reduces the amount of content that can be covered in a day. There is pressure on many teachers to get through the required material quickly to make sure that everything is covered, and this can make one reluctant to add note-taking training to their instruction. However, if students learn to take useful and accurate notes, then they are more likely to learn the material presented than if they simply sit and passively listen. Learning to take notes can benefit students for years in many classes and in our opinion is well worth the cost of slowing the pace of instruction for a few weeks.

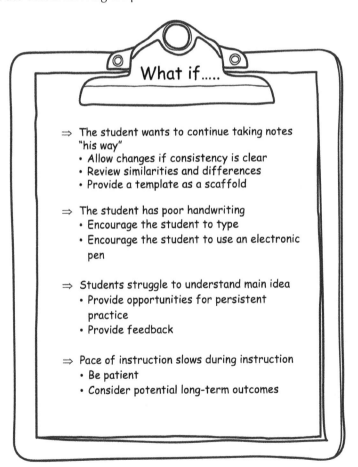

**What if.....**

⇒ The student wants to continue taking notes "his way"
- Allow changes if consistency is clear
- Review similarities and differences
- Provide a template as a scaffold

⇒ The student has poor handwriting
- Encourage the student to type
- Encourage the student to use an electronic pen

⇒ Students struggle to understand main idea
- Provide opportunities for persistent practice
- Provide feedback

⇒ Pace of instruction slows during instruction
- Be patient
- Consider potential long-term outcomes

Image used under license from Shutterstock. rangsan paidaen/Shutterstock.com.

## Considerations for Culturally Responsive Note Taking

Although it does not seem likely that we can provide ideas to make note-taking instruction culturally responsive, we remind you of the first tenet of culturally responsive pedagogy and the value of note taking in classrooms. When Ladson-Billings (1994) observed classrooms of teachers she deemed as effective with African American students, she found that standards were high, and students were expected to work hard. Removing the expectation for students to take notes is unnecessary and potentially harmful. Students who take notes have an advantage over students who do not take notes. Taking notes increases student focus on instruction, provides students with the opportunity to connect the main ideas of the lesson to prior knowledge, and provides a vehicle for student studying. Therefore, we strongly encourage teachers to teach all students to take notes so all students can achieve high standards.

The second tenet is the affirmation of students' cultural competence. To achieve this goal, we encourage teachers to embed cultural diversity in their instruction. As such, the discussion-based lessons and/or written material that students are reading could be related to students' real-life experiences, affirming their culture of origin and teaching students about other cultures.

 ## Programming

We strongly encourage teachers to advocate for the inclusion of interventions with evidence of effectiveness on any plan, written or otherwise, for the student, such as a response to intervention plan, individualized education program (IEP), section 504 plan, and/or any other plan developed for an adolescent with ADHD. As you know, research indicates that note-taking instruction. can increase academic engagement and academic performance. Therefore, we provide an example of the applicable CASEL standard; Muzzammil's current levels, strengths, and weaknesses, and annual goals. We hope these examples will make it easier for you to include note-taking instruction as a component of student's individual goals.

**Common Core Standards:** Reading in Science and Technical Subjects Integration of Knowledge and Ideas

CC.3.5.9–10.I Compare and contrast findings presented in a text to those from other sources, noting when the findings support or contradict previous explanations or accounts.

CC.3.5.11–12.I Synthesize information from a range of sources into a coherent understanding of a process, phenomenon, or concept, resolving confliction information when possible.

**CASEL Standards:** Responsible Decision Making
Sub competency—Identifying problems, analyzing situations, reflecting

**Current levels, strengths, and weaknesses:**
Muzzammil is a ninth-grade student with ADHD. Currently, he has C's and D's in all of his courses with the exception of science which he is failing. Muzzammil's areas of need are paying attention in class and completing assignments/taking notes. According to Muzzammil's science teacher, he is only on task 50% of the time during a 50-minute class period. This means that for 25 minutes, Muzzammil is off-task. His teacher has never seen him take notes in class, and with prompting, there is an approximate one-minute latency period before he will begin the task being asked of him. His inattentiveness and inability to complete assignments has contributed to his failing science grade. To address this situation, Muzzammil needs to be taught strategies to self-regulate his attention. In addition, Muzzammil needs to be taught strategies on how to take proper notes in class.

**Annual Smart Goal:**
- Given note-taking instruction, Muzzammil will take one-page worth of notes for three out of five class periods. If teacher prompting is required, Muzzammil will only take 30 seconds of latency time to complete the task being asked of him.
- Given note-taking instruction, Muzzammil will be on task for 75% of his science period (i.e., 37.5 minutes).

# Conclusion

Note-taking training is an intervention to teach students to engage in systematic note taking during discussion-based lessons and from textbooks. By explicitly teaching students to take notes in a consistent manner, they are more likely to document the information needed to study for quizzes and exams in secondary schools and post-secondary activities. In the current chapter, we discussed four stages of note-taking instruction and steps for implementation. We described students' reluctance to take notes in the prescribed format and poor handwriting as potential obstacles to success. We described how teaching students to take notes is one means of maintaining high expectations for all students. Although difficult to make exciting for most adolescents with ADHD, note-taking skills are needed and will simplify the student's life in educational, vocational, and personal endeavors.

# Reference List

Boyle, J. R., Forchelli, G. A., & Cariss, K. (2015). Note-taking interventions to assist students with disabilities in content area classes. *Preventing School Failure: Alternative Education for Children and Youth, 59*(3), 186–195.

Evans, B. P., & Shively, C. T. (2019). Using the Cornell note-taking system can help eighth grade students alleviate the impact of interruptions while reading at home. *Journal of Inquiry and Action in Education, 10*(1), 1–35.

Evans, S. W., Pelham, W. E., & Grudberg, M. V. (1995). The efficacy of notetaking to improve behavior and comprehension of adolescents with attention deficit hyperactivity disorder. *Exceptionality, 5*, 1–17.

Harrison, J. R., Evans, S. W., Baran, A., Khondker, F., Press, K., Wasserman, S., . . . Mohlmann, M. (2020). Comparison of accommodations and interventions for youth with ADHD: A randomized controlled trial. *Journal of School Psychology, 80*, 15–36.

Kiewra, K. A. (1985). Students' note-taking behaviors and the efficacy of providing the instructor's notes for review. *Contemporary Educational Psychology, 10*(4), 378–386.

Ladson-Billings, G. (1994). *The dreamkeepers*. Jossey-Bass Publishing Co.

Moin, L. J., Magiera, K., & Zigmond, N. (2009). Instructional activities and group work in the US inclusive high school co-taught science class. *International Journal of Science and Mathematics Education, 7*(4), 677–697.

Schultz, B. K., & Evans, S. W. (2021, April 15–16). *Game-based strategies for delivering behavioral health programs: Separating fact from fantasy* [conference session]. Southeastern School Behavioral Health Conference, Myrtle Beach, SC, United States.

Spires, H. A., & Stone, D. P. (1989). The directed notetaking activity: A self-questioning approach. *Journal of Reading, 33*, 36–39.

# Behavioral Strategies

---

**Nora**

Nora does not have many friends. She is described as withdrawn. She likes to read and does well in her science class when the expectation is for her to read quietly. When observing her readings, you can often see her swinging her foot back and forth and twirling whatever she has in her hand, sometimes her hair, sometimes a pencil. These behaviors do not usually interfere with her performance or that of her peers, as she sits in the back corner of the classroom......when she is only reading. You might wonder, why would anyone care if Nora is playing with her hair or her pencil in her science class. It really does not seem to be a problem for anyone except the teacher. However, if you were to observe her while the teacher is providing direct instruction or when the students engaged in group work, you would quickly notice that the behavior is a problem... no one around her, including herself, is getting anything done. Nora and her peers are not attending to the teacher. Instead, they are attending to Nora's wiggling. Much of the time that she is working in a group, both Nora and her peers are off task. She wiggles and fidgets and they complain about her wiggling and fidgeting. Bottom line, her behaviors are disruptive. Nora's teacher, Ms. Rock, implemented self-management training to help Nora notice when she was fidgeting and disrupting the learning or herself and others, but Nora continued to fidget a majority of the time. Additionally, Nora's behavior is interfering with her learning and with her ability to demonstrate what she has learned. She is failing science, and this is likely because of her struggles to attend to the teacher and not her own fidgeting. When she is expected to attend to teacher-directed instruction, she is often seen focusing on her own fidgeting instead of the teacher. When asked a question, Nora looks around the room completely caught off guard and struggles to come up with the correct answer. When asked what she is doing, she responds that she was trying to listen, but the teacher was boring her "out of her mind". Ms. Rock is very frustrated, she describes the behavior as intentional, disrespectful, and intrusive. She frequently calls Nora's name and tells her to STOP fidgeting and pay attention. It appears that Nora does not hear Ms. Rock, or she is simply noncompliant, as she continues the behavior. Eventually, Ms. Rock sends Nora to the hall to complete a worksheet so that she does not disturb the class during instruction. If effective intervention is not provided, Nora might struggle throughout middle and high school ultimately struggling to graduate from high school on time. Fortunately, years of study have led to effective behavioral interventions that teachers can use to shape her behavior when added to self-management

DOI: 10.4324/9781003109983-11

# Description of the Behavioral Strategies

In relation to teachers and students, behavioral strategies are the application of external reinforcement or punishment given to students contingent upon (based on) student behavior. The purpose is to "shape" student behavior through reward or punishment. Behavioral strategies are not new. No doubt, you know about B.F. Skinner, the father of behaviorism. Nonetheless, the bottom line then and now is that all behavior is and can be shaped by environmental stimuli. For example, can Ms. Rock successfully encourage Nora to not tap her foot on the floor? Your first thought is probably . . . no, she has ADHD. Although that is what most of us were taught, it is not necessarily the case. Research tells us that implementing behavioral strategies with students with ADHD is likely to result in decreased disruptive behavior, especially when combined with other strategies such as self-management and when consequences (positive or negative) are immediate and consistent.

Results of scientific studies indicates that with behavioral strategies, students with ADHD are less disruptive and more engaged with instruction and tasks (Harrison et al., 2019). Disruptive behaviors are a hallmark of ADHD. Some indicators of hyperactivity speak directly to the disruptive behavior of students with ADHD . . . "has difficulty remaining in seat when sitting is expected" or "often fidgets with . . . ." When students are out of their seats in a classroom when that is not the expectation, they are likely to disrupt learning. When students fidget, they are likely to be disruptive. Furthermore, impulsivity is often associated with disruptive behavior . . . "often calls out without permission." Behavioral strategies can be used to increase the length of time that a student attends to task and/or to redirect their attention to task when they "zone" out. As you can see, deciding on the target behavior to be changed and the replacement behavior to be taught are important steps in the process.

Image used under license from Shutterstock. New Vectors/Shutterstock.com.

In the following sections, we begin with a brief discussion of the basics of behavioral strategies (positive reinforcement, negative

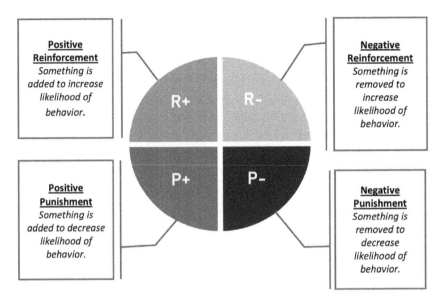

Positive Reinforcement
Something is added to increase likelihood of behavior.

R+

R-

Negative Reinforcement
Something is removed to increase likelihood of behavior.

Positive Punishment
Something is added to decrease likelihood of behavior.

P+

P-

Negative Punishment
Something is removed to decrease likelihood of behavior.

*Figure 9.1* Basics of Behavioral Strategies.

reinforcement, positive punishment, negative punishment). Most effective behavioral programs are based on positive reinforcement; however, it is important to understand all four (see Figure 9.1). Next we describe these four strategies and the steps for implementation within three frameworks.

## Components of Behavioral Strategies

There is no doubt that you have heard about reinforcement, as most teachers have in one context or another. When we reinforce student behavior (through positive or negative reinforcement), we increase the likelihood that the behavior will happen again. We use positive reinforcement when we allow students to earn something (attention, items, time to engage in fun activities) for engaging in the desired behavior. For example, Ms. Rock might agree that Nora could earn time drawing in her art book that she really enjoys, if she will sit at her desk with her hands still without disrupting others.

Negative reinforcement occurs when we remove something to increase the likelihood that a behavior will increase. With negative reinforcement, we remove something that the student finds undesirable contingent upon student behavior. For example, Ms. Rock might agree to let Nora read about the content being taught instead of engaging in a portion of the class discussion if she sits without disrupting herself or the students around her for ten minutes. In this case, Ms. Rock is removing the part of the requirement to sit and listen to instruction that Nora considers boring. The principle is that Nora's negative behaviors will decrease to avoid something that she does not like to do. It is important to remember that use of the "reinforcer" will not increase the behavior if it is not something the student wants and as such is not truly a reinforcer.

Contrarily, punishment is when your actions are designed to increase the likelihood that the behavior will *not* happen again! Positive punishment is when you give the student something that is likely to decrease the likelihood that the behavior will repeat. For example, teachers might verbally reprimand students to decrease negative behavior. Negative punishment is when we take something away with the idea of decreasing the desired behavior. Negative punishment is at the root of many behavioral techniques with which you are familiar such as time out, "grounding" (when we make an adolescent stay home instead of being with friends) or taking away a cell phone. Similar to reinforcement, punishment does not decrease the behavior if the "punisher" is actually something that a student desires. For example, if a student would rather be at home than at school, assigning out-of-school suspension would actually be a reinforcer and not a punisher. This means that the undesirable behavior is more likely to occur again if the student is assigned to out-of-school suspension and prefers that compared to being in school.

## Stages for All Behavioral Frameworks

| 1 | 2 | 3 | 4 | 5 |
|---|---|---|---|---|
| Goal Setting | Select a behavioral framework | Develop a plan and materials | Teach the desired behavior and use of strategy | Monitor progress |

*Figure 9.2* Five Stages of Behavioral Strategies.

There are many frameworks that could be used to implement behavioral strategies. Here we describe five stages for implementing behavioral interventions. In stage 2, we describe three frameworks (basic contingency management, behavioral contracts, token economy). Regardless of the framework that you select to use when implementing behavioral strategies, you can follow the five stages listed in Figure 9.2 and described here. The first stage is setting a goal. The second stage is for the teacher to determine which framework she prefers, and the next stage is to develop a plan. The fourth stage is to explain the plan to the student. No behavioral strategy is going to work if the student does not know how to engage in the desired behavior. Additionally, students must understand the procedures for the framework, and they must be followed consistently.

## *Stage 1: Goal Setting*

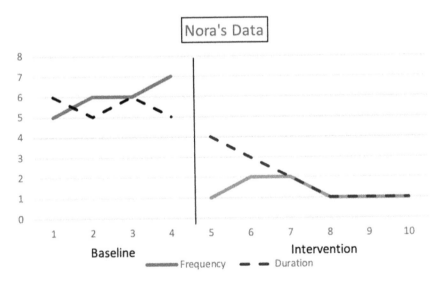

Figure 9.3 Line Graph for Visual Analysis.

The first stage, goal setting, is when the teacher identifies the target behavior and determines how often that behavior occurs (frequency), how long the behavior lasts (duration), the time between when a direction is given and the student begins the task (latency), and/or the strength of the emotion behind the behavior (intensity) prior to any intervention. How often is Nora disruptive? When is she disruptive and how long do the disruptions continue? How intense is her behavior? When looking at the line graph in Figure 9.3, it appears that on average Nora is disruptive six times during the class for an average of five minutes.

When deciding the goal, Nora would meet with Ms. Rock who would show her the line graph. Together, they would consider the average of the behavior and then determine the first goal. They look at the current frequency and duration of the disruptive behavior. With this information they set a goal for decreasing the behavior.

In addition to determining the goal, Ms. Rock and Nora would select a replacement behavior and set a goal for demonstrating the replacement behavior. To select a replacement behavior, we encourage teachers to consider the A-B-C sequence (Figure 9.4). What happens before the problem behavior that makes the behavior more likely to occur (antecedent)? What happens after the behavior that makes the behavior more likely to occur (consequence)?

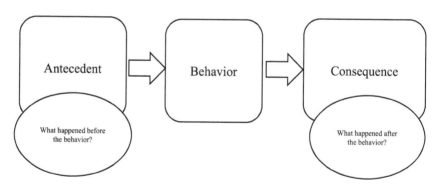

*Figure 9.4* What Happened Before and After.

The first consideration in the A-B-C sequence is the target or problem behavior. What is the behavior that needs to be changed? In the case of Nora, the problem/target behavior is disrupting her teacher and peers. The next to consider, is the antecedent. What typically happens before the target behavior (antecedent)? Nora was instructed to sit quietly and attend to the teacher and/or her peers. Finally, what typically happens after the behavior (consequence)? She avoids attending to instruction until Ms. Rock and her peers call her name and tell her to stop fidgeting. As such, the teacher selects a replacement behavior that allows Nora to avoid (escape) the requirement to sit quietly without being disruptive for a limited period of time (request a break) and gain appropriate attention of her peers. To increase the behavior of using the break card, Ms. Rock can use positive reinforcement or punishment. In addition to increasing Nora's use of the break card, to decrease Nora's disruptive behavior, Ms. Rock can use negative reinforcement or punishment. Each option is demonstrated the behavioral frameworks in the next section.

## Stage 2: Select a Behavioral Framework

Once the target behavior and the replacement behavior have been selected, Ms. Rock decides which framework she would like to use. Would it be better to implement basic contingency management, using positive or negative reinforcement or positive or negative punishment, a behavioral contract, or a token economy system?

### Basic Contingency Management

Contingency management is a system in which the teacher provides or withholds something in response to the target or desired behavior. For example, Nora is taught that when she feels like she needs to fidget and cannot sit any longer without being disruptive, she should place a break card on her desk and draw on her note pad for five minutes returning to work when that time is up. To encourage this behavior, Ms. Rock could verbally provide reinforcement when Nora uses it. She might say, "Great job using the break card, Nora." She might also allow Nora to play a game during science time on Friday (removing the expectation to sit quietly in her seat on Friday) if she uses her card consistently Monday through Thursday. To discourage the disruptive fidgety behavior, Ms. Rock could move Nora's desk away from her peers for a specified period of time.

### Behavioral Contracts

Behavioral contracts are a written contract between an adolescent and teacher (and others if desired) that clearly explains the responsibilities of the adolescent and teacher including the expected behavior of the student and the response by the teacher. In essence, behavioral contracts are a means of "organizing" contingencies. Contracts with students typically begin with the name of all parties involved. At times, individuals other than the student and teacher will be included and "bound" by the contract. For example, Ms. Rock might write a contract with Nora and the school counselor and/ or Nora's parents. The contract could include the names and signatures of the teacher, student, counselor, and parent if involved. It might specify the replacement behavior (ask for a break, sit without disrupting peers), the expected frequency (3x/day), and the length of the contract (one week). Additionally, it would include details about the reinforcer or punisher. So, it might say . . .

> We, Nora, Ms. Rock, and Ms. O'Donnell (counselor) agree that if (or when) Nora sits quietly in her seat during science class with less than one disruption for five consecutive days, she will be allowed to spend thirty minutes of her science class with Ms. O'Donnell playing a game.
> Signed

### Token Economy Systems

Token economies (TE) are a reinforcement framework in which tokens are awarded for demonstration of the replacement behavior. Earned tokens are used to "purchase" a primary reinforcer. For example, Ms. Rock might develop a TE system for Nora, in which she earns tokens (tangible tokens, points) (i.e., positive reinforcement) when she asks for a break and refrains from disrupting her peers and she loses points for disrupting the class (response cost) (i.e., negative punishment). Ms. Rock and Nora agree on the number of tokens needed to trade for the primary reinforcer, such as time to draw in her art book.

## Stage 3: Develop a Plan and Materials

### Develop a Plan

Once the framework has been selected, the teacher develops a plan for implementation. During this step, the teacher determines more of the specifics . . . the nuts and bolts for implementing the system. First, the contingency schedule should be established. Contingency schedules are the rules used to give or remove reinforcers or punishers.

If Ms. Rock is using basic contingency management, how many times can Nora request a break in the class period and continue to be allowed to draw? If Ms. Rock is using a behavioral contract or token system, how many times does Nora have to use her card to ask for a break without being disruptive to earn a reinforcer? How long does she have to sit without being disruptive to earn the reinforcer? How many times does she have to be disruptive to lose a token? Regardless of the framework used, these expectations are established and communicated with the student prior to beginning the system

Next, the teacher determines the criteria for reinforcement or punishment. How many times does Nora have to demonstrate the replacement behavior to earn the reinforcer? How many times does Nora have to demonstrate the target behavior to have something taken away? The answer is in the numbers. Look at Nora's baseline behavior in Figure 9.3. The data indicate that, on average she is disruptive six times for about five minutes each. The first set of criteria for earning a reinforcer might be three times or less for no more than five minutes each. The criteria for moving Nora's desk away from her peers might be four times or more or any number of disruptions that last five minutes or more. How much improvement can you expect over a specified period? It's important for the reinforcer to be attainable. Think about yourself. Would you continue going to work every day if there was no way for you to meet the criteria for your paycheck? When working with students, the decision can be subjective. We recommend that you err on the side of caution. Once the criteria are met, then you begin shaping the behavior by increasing the time between reinforcers, continuing to pay close attention to the data and changing the criteria as needed.

Finally, you decide what reinforcer or punisher the student will earn. In other words, what would the student like to earn or lose that would be sufficiently motivating to increase replacement behavior and decrease the target behavior? What would the student earn or lose that would be likely to decrease the behavior? There are many ways to decide what might be valuable to the student. Consequences typically fall into one of four categories: (1) edible, (2) tangible, (3) activity, and (4) social. The most common used reinforcers are tangible or edible reinforcers. For example, some students like to work for snacks. It is important to understand the school rules about giving students snacks and to follow those rules closely. Another option is to allow students to work for tangible items. Options for tangible items for small children are easier to find than for adolescents. For example, young children will work for fairly inexpensive items, such as stickers or push

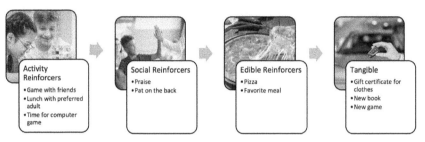

Image used under license from Shutterstock. Mongkolchon Akesin/Shutterstock.com; Drazen Zigic/Shutterstock.com; www.petrovvladimir.ru/Shutterstock.com; ORION PRODUCTION/ Shutterstock.com.

pop bubbles. Although, we have had some adolescents who continue to like to earn stickers, it might be rare. Some other items that we have had adolescents work for include hair accessories, trading cards, and other small items. The last two categories, activity, and social reinforcers, contain the items that secondary students may be most likely to want to earn and less likely to want to lose. Activity reinforcers are when teachers allow students to participate in their preferred activities, such as playing a game with peers, the teacher, or both, working with the custodian, having lunch with the principal, designing a class bulletin board, or decorating for a school dance.

Although all of these are potential reinforcers, this is an area in which teachers often "get it wrong." In order for the "reinforcer to be reinforcing" it must be motivating to the student. In other words, it must be something that the student wants to earn. You can determine what students would like to earn by asking them. This sounds fairly straightforward; however, simply asking them an open-ended question, "What would you like to work for?", often results in a blank stare or an unrealistic request, such as a video game console or a vacation day. If these are the types of responses that you get from your students, then try using an interest survey. Interest surveys (Figure 9.5) ask the students about their interests. For example, some adolescents like to earn collectable cards, such as baseball or Pokémon® cards, and others would tell you that is a ridiculous idea!

Another means of increasing motivation is to add a bit of suspense to the reinforcer by having students work for mystery motivators. In this case, the teacher includes several reinforcers on a wheel, behind "doors," or any other means of making the reinforcer a secret. When the student earns the reward, they are allowed to spin the wheel (Figure 9.9) or open the door to

## Interest Survey

1.  When you have free time, what do you like to do?

2.  What are your hobbies?

3.  Do you like to watch movies?  What is your favorite?

4.  Do you like to play video games?  What is your favorite?

5.  Do you like to read?  What is your favorite book?

6.  What is your favorite food?

7.  What do you like to do on snow days?

8.  Do you like sports?  What is your favorite?

9.  What is your favorite internet site?

10. Do you like to listen to music? What is your favorite?

11. What is your favorite subject at school?

12. Who is your favorite adult at school?

13. If you were going to play a game in school, who would you select as your partner?

14. What is your favorite language?

15. If you could travel anywhere, where would you go?  Why?

16. How many pets do you have?  What are they?

*Figure 9.5* Interest Survey.

Reinforcer Wheel.

Image used under license from Shutterstock.
Dzm1try/Shutterstock.com.

see what they have earned. In this case, every option should be motivating to the student! Another option that we have used is the delivery of the reinforcer through an auction. In this case, students earn and save their points or tokens until a pre-specified date and then participate in an auction of several items to earn the reinforcer.

## Develop Materials

Behavioral interventions often require the development of materials, which can be fun for some teachers! On the other hand, materials can be purchased commercially or through Teachers Pay Teachers (TPT). TPT is a website where teachers post and sell educational materials that they have developed. We encourage teachers to consider the developmental level of the students when creating or selecting the format for the contract or token system. We must reiterate that teachers and student often consider these strategies only appropriate for elementary students. One solution to this perception is the type and look of the materials within each framework. As such, we encourage you to carefully design age-appropriate materials.

When teachers elect to use behavior contracts, they can create an electronic or paper version. The document looks very similar (but simpler) to a legal contract. It should include (1) the student's name; (2) the teacher's name; (3) the name of other educators involved in the contract (e.g., counselor, principal, assistant principal); (4) the desired behavior; (5) criteria for earning or losing something; and (6) signatures of all involved.

If the teacher chooses to use a token economy, then the teacher must develop or purchase the materials that serve as reinforcement. For token economies there is a need to create tokens. In elementary schools, tokens are often marbles, tickets, or poker chips. Depending on the maturity level, choice, and interests of the students involved, physical tokens may or may not be appropriate. One of the authors of this text (Harrison) used tickets that are available in rolls (Figure 9.6) as tokens with middle school students. Another (Soares) used "money" added to a checking account as tokens. Tokens do not have to be physical items. They can be points given on a point sheet. If this is the choice,

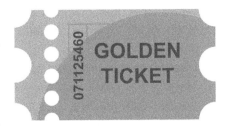

*Figure 9.6*

Images from Shutterstock with license. Image used under license from Shutterstock. Hendra079/Shutterstock.com.

then the teacher must create the point sheet or purchase one (Figure 9.7). Once, the teacher decides what tokens will be used, he/she develops or selects the secondary reinforcers. Based on knowledge of the student, student requests, or preference assessments, the teacher and student select the reinforcers.

| Nora's Daily Point Sheet | | | |
|---|---|---|---|
| Directions: Please mark each box with a 0 for no or a 1 for yes. | | | |
| | I requested a break when needed. | I did not disrupt my peers with my fidgeting. | I requested a break using my break card. | I got on task when break was over. |
| ELA | | | | |
| Science | | | | |
| History | | | | |
| Math | | | | |

*Figure 9.7*

## Stage 4: Teach the Desired Behavior and Use of the Strategy

Before using a behavioral strategy with a student with ADHD, the student must understand the replacement behavior. Many believe, and have told us over the years, that secondary students should know "how to behave" in class. It is highly likely that students know how we want them to behave, but that does not mean that they always remember or choose to perform those behaviors. It is important to consider the symptoms and impairment associated with ADHD. That being said, many performances deficits can be changed with practice. As such, when asking students to engage in behaviors that are different than their own norm, we go through the step of behavioral skills training, either with the whole class, a small group, or the individual student.

To teach the desired behavior and use of the strategy you can follow the training approach described in in Chapter 12. First, teachers describe the behavior and then show the students what it looks like. Ms. Rock could sit quietly at her desk. While she is demonstrating the behaviors, she describes what she is doing . . . "you can see that my hands are not moving, and I am not disrupting anyone around me." She might go on to say, "I put this card on the next to indicate that I want a break to be able to use my hands to draw." Next, the students practice the behavior. Students can work in pairs discussing what the desired behavior does and does not look like. This sounds like an elementary task, but students enjoy it if it is presented in a relaxed and fun manner. It is acceptable for them to be silly while engaging in practice activities. Remember that it is likely that Nora's peers will appreciate her new behaviors, which are not distracting to them. Finally, the students practice the skill during instruction and the teacher provides feedback. Just like academic skills, these behaviors might need to be retaught, practiced, and reinforced over time. Similarly, before implementation, the teacher teaches the student about the framework (basic contingency management, behavioral contract, or token economy) following the same procedures.

## Stage 5: Monitor Progress

Similar to the collection of baseline data during the goal setting process, progress toward mastery must be monitored, graphed, and shared with the student. Data for progress monitoring is easily available when using a behavioral contract. The teacher simply transfers the outcome for the period being monitored onto a table. The teacher visually analyzes student progress to determine if the intervention should be modified or changed. A teacher may convert the data into a graph to make it easier to see changes. These data can help the teacher decides if the intervention should be continued, changed, or stopped. If the student is making consistent progress toward the goal, then the intervention continues. If the student is not making progress to the goal after at least one week, then the intervention may be changed. If the student has mastered the goal, then the teacher decides to either change the criteria or stop the intervention.

The teacher considers the level, trend, variability, immediacy of effect, and overlap between baseline and intervention. For example, looking at Figure 9.3, you first look at the level (average). If you look at baseline, without calculating anything, it appears that the average frequency and duration of disruptive behavior was six times for five minutes. Also, you will notice a positive trend in baseline for frequency, but a decreasing trend during intervention. You also notice that on the final day during baseline, Nora was disruptive seven times. Compare that to the first day of intervention and you will see that there was an immediate effect. Nora was only disruptive one time while using the contingency management intervention. You also notice that there are no days in baseline that were the same during intervention. In other words, there was no overlap between frequency in baseline and intervention. From these data, it is obvious that the intervention was working. As such, the teacher has two choices. Ms. Rock can either stop the intervention or change the mastery criteria. Maybe she wants Nora to sit for ten minutes without disrupting herself or her peers or maybe she is satisfied that Nora has learned to sit quietly for five minutes. If she elects to stop all intervention, then she continues to collect data for at least two weeks and if the behavior returns, then she begins intervention implementation again and repeats the cycle.

## Modes of Behavioral Strategies

### Paper-based

Paper-based behavioral strategies are the traditional form of token economies and contracts. They are hand-written on paper or typed on the

*Figure 9.8*

Printed with permission from Tak Fung.

computer and printed. As such, students and teachers have a point card or contract that they can hold in their hands and write on with a pencil. For example, Ms. Rock and Nora signed a contract handwritten on a piece of notebook paper. On the paper token form, Ms. Rock uses a pencil to place a check mark on her token point sheet when she requests a break. Ms. Rock erases a mark when she did not use her card to ask for a break and was disruptive.

## Game-based

Game-based behavioral strategies are implemented through technology. For example, EpicWin described and studied by Harrison and colleagues (2020a, 2020b) and currently being updated by Banshee apps and Judith Harrison was originally developed as a to-do list game. Used this way, adolescents and their teachers could list the desired behaviors in the game. When students completed the desired behavior, they earn "loot" and travel along a path. The first step is for Malik to download EpicWin (Fung, 2015; Harrison et al., 2020b) on his cell phone (Figure 9.8). The student selects an avatar and enters the desired behavior. When the student engages in the desired behavior, the teacher (or the student) indicates on the app that the student successful engaged in the desired behavior. The student then earns loot via the game and possibly levels up. The adolescent can share loot earned on his Facebook® or Twitter® making it more fun. As the student continues to earn his points by engaging in the desired behavior, his avatar travels along a path.

## Potential Barriers and Methods of Overcoming the Barriers

Researchers and teachers alike acknowledge barriers to using behavior strategies. At times, it is difficult to "get it right." For example, problems may occur with selection and/or awarding of the contingencies or with the expected time to see a change in behavior. In the following sections, we describe some potential barriers and means of overcoming them.

## Resources

As we are sure that you have noticed, lack of resources is a common barrier to many interventions implemented by teachers in schools. We all know that teacher salaries are not the best and that teachers often spend their hard-earned money on teaching supplies. As such, we want to encourage you to not purchase reinforcers for several reasons. The first being that you should not have to do that. The second is that it is likely that adolescents will respond to social or activity interventions at least as positively as they might to tangible reinforcers. For example, Nora may be more likely to remain engaged without disrupting her peers if she was working for time to socialize rather than if she was working for a piece of chewing gum or some other tangible item. It is important to note that items that adolescents often find rewarding are beyond the scope of school budgets, such as video games. Nonetheless, there are adolescents who want to work for inexpensive tangible items, such as stickers or personal hygiene items. In our careers, we have known adolescents who wanted to earn a sonic toothbrush, deodorant, shampoo, and other similar items. In these cases, it is possible to find individuals or businesses who would be willing to donate items. For example, Nora might want to work for an electric toothbrush, in which case, Ms. Rock might approach the local dentist to see if she would be willing to donate some to the school.

## Teacher Perceptions

Another barrier that we have witnessed is the effect of teacher attitude on the success of the intervention. At times, teachers might feel as if providing a reward to a student for following classroom rules is not appropriate. Some believe that all students should engage in compliant behavior because that is the "right thing to do." We agree that rule-following behaviors are important; however, it is unlikely that you would be willing to do your job without a salary. All behavior can be affected by something that is rewarding. Some students are excited and motivated by the thought of learning something new and this may be true for students with ADHD; however, that does not mean that they are excited to work hard to learn to attend, to ignore distractions or to avoid being disruptive. These are difficult tasks simply by the nature of ADHD. As such, there are times when external contingencies are necessary.

Image used under license from Shutterstock. Sudowoodo/Shutterstock.com.

Another perception that is a barrier to successful implementation is the idea that providing positive reinforcement to a student is bribery and that is inappropriate. A reinforcer is "something that strengthens a behavior" and a bribe is "money or any other valuable considerations given or promised with a view to corrupting the behavior of a person" (dictionary.com). When we use reinforcers, either with our students, our own children, our significant others, or anyone else, the goal is to improve. The goal is not to persuade them to engage in corrupt behavior. We all love positive reinforcement!

Another potential barrier that is difficult for some individuals to get past is the issue of "fairness." When faced with a behavior plan that includes behavior strategies, we have heard educators complain that if one student is allowed to work for a reinforcer, then all students should receive the same opportunity. For example, if Nora receives to spend time playing a game with Ms. O'Donnell for sitting quietly and refraining for disrupting other students, then all the students in the class should have the same opportunity. Our response to this comment is that "fair is not equal" (Curwin & Mendler, 1988). Being fair is important; however, being fair means that we treat each individual students, as just that, an individual student by meeting their individual needs. Some students need external reinforcement, and some do not.

## *Time*

As with most interventions in this book, time can be an issue. The time spent planning and preparing for implementation is likely to be no more than the time that a teacher spends redirecting and responding to the problem behavior. However, the time spent upfront can be overwhelming. For example, if Ms. Rock decided to use a token economy system with Nora, she would spend time up front planning and preparing which can be time-consuming, but typically only has to be done once or twice. However, the distribution of primary reinforcers has to happen on a daily basis and probably several times within each day. Teachers can find this daunting. Acknowledging student behavior consistently seems to be the most troublesome. In our practice, we found that adolescents with ADHD can be disruptive more than 50 times within five minutes. If Ms. Rock was trying to write a tally mark on a piece of paper every time that Nora became disruptive, she might find it difficult to work with other students during independent work time.

In this case, we suggest that the teacher select either a single item scale or a multi-item scale. Using either allows the teacher to simply rate the student behavior at the end of a specific period of time. For example, using the single item scale in Figure 9.9, Ms. Rock could rate the approximate frequency of Nora's behavior at the end of the science class. Doing this would diminish the time spent tallying behaviors and can be a reasonable replacement for counting behaviors (Briesch et al., 2010).

Student: Nora

Date: 09/01/22

**On a scale from one for five with one being Never and five being always, how often did the student request a break using the break card?**

- Never
- Almost Never
- Sometimes
- Almost always
- Always

*Figure 9.9*

---

> ### Nora's Checklist
>
> **On a scale from one for five with one being "never" and five being "always",**
>
> 1. How often did the student request a break using the break card?
>    - Never
>    - Almost Never
>    - Sometimes
>    - Almost always
>    - Always
> 2. How often did the student disrupt her peers or herself?
>    - Never
>    - Almost Never
>    - Sometimes
>    - Almost always
>    - Always
> 3. How often did the student to task when the break was over?
>    - Never
>    - Almost Never
>    - Sometimes
>    - Almost always
>    - Always

*Figure 9.10*

Additionally, Figure 9.10 shows a multi-item scale, where multiple expectations are rated. A multi-item scale is a Likert-type scale with more than one target behavior or replacement behavior for teachers to rate. Each target behavior is rated based on anchors that reflect student performance. For example, in Figure 9.10, Ms. Rock rates how often Nora requests a break using her cards as never, almost never, sometimes, almost always. the benefit is that Ms. Rock does not have to count the occurrence of the behaviors, a task frequently perceived as daunting by many teachers.

Another option the teacher has is to complete frequency counts with concrete items. For example, she could put a hand full of paper clips in her right pocket. Each time that Nora was disruptive, she would move one paper clip from the right pocket to the left. Either way, it is of utmost importance that Ms. Rock describes the behavior in such a way that anyone else could come into her classroom and recognize the behavior clearly enough to count each occurrence.

Time often interferes with implementation fidelity (implementing the intervention as designed). With minimal time and a lot of responsibilities, teachers might elect to remove a step or forget to complete a step. Each step that we discussed is important and skipping some of those steps is likely to decrease the effectiveness of the strategy. We cannot overemphasize the significance of following each step. Consider Nora. If Ms. Rock decided that Nora should know how to place the card on her desk without instruction, Nora might also skip the card by taking her drawing book out of her desk and begin drawing without using the card and getting permission. This not likely to receive a favorable response from Ms. Rock. Similarly, if Ms. Rock forgot to tell Nora when she would earn the secondary reinforcement, then Nora is less likely to be motivated to work for it. As with all interventions developed and validated, each step is important and contributes to the overall success or failure of the intervention.

## Lack of Motivation

We have frequently heard teachers say, "this isn't working" when using behavior strategies with a student with ADHD. Sometimes this is said after a few days and sometimes after a week or two. It can be difficult to know how long an intervention should be provided before you can expect it to make a difference. A day is not long enough, and two weeks is likely to be too long. If it has been more than three or four days and no behavioral progress has been made, then we suggest the teacher consider what should be changed about the system. One frequent issue is the desirability of the reinforcer. Does the student care about the reinforcer? Is the student willing to work for the reinforcer? If not, then it should be changed. We suggest that you begin by simply asking the student. It is possible that the student changed their mind since you first agreed on the reinforcer. Maybe it was not what they expected! If the student does not give you any suggestions for a more effective reinforcer, then more investigation is required. Maybe start over with a reinforcer checklist. Another option is to observe and listen to the student. What are they interested in? What do they talk about? Listen carefully and plan accordingly!

One other possible explanation is the length of time between reinforcers. The "correct" amount of time between demonstration of the behavior and delivery of the secondary reinforcer is sometimes a mystery.

Our best advice is when collecting baseline data on the behavior prior to implementing the intervention is to pay close attention to the amount of time between the behavioral occurrences. Once this time is established, then we encourage you to schedule the delivery of the reinforcer shortly before the next behavior is likely to occur.

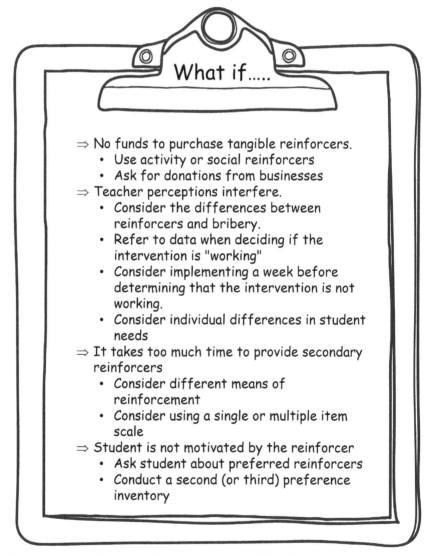

What if.....

⇒ No funds to purchase tangible reinforcers.
- Use activity or social reinforcers
- Ask for donations from businesses

⇒ Teacher perceptions interfere.
- Consider the differences between reinforcers and bribery.
- Refer to data when deciding if the intervention is "working"
- Consider implementing a week before determining that the intervention is not working.
- Consider individual differences in student needs

⇒ It takes too much time to provide secondary reinforcers
- Consider different means of reinforcement
- Consider using a single or multiple item scale

⇒ Student is not motivated by the reinforcer
- Ask student about preferred reinforcers
- Conduct a second (or third) preference inventory

Image used under license from Shutterstock. rangsan paidaen/Shutterstock.com.

#  Considerations for Culturally Responsive Behavioral Strategies

We encourage you to think about the cultural implications for behavioral interventions. One consideration is the issue of rewarding appropriate behavior as discussed earlier in relation to teachers. Some cultures typically favor authoritarian over authoritative discipline in comparison to other cultures (Lansford et al., 2011). Authoritarian discipline is based on adult control with clear expectations, high standards, and consistent punishment with limited warmth and responsiveness, whereas an authoritative discipline is based on adult control with overall warmth and responsiveness (Baumrind, 1971). As such, it is important to discuss cultural acceptability and humility (family is the "expert" in relation to their child and culture) when developing systems for students. These discussions should be held with students and families. Interventions are not likely to be effective if they are not accepted within the culture. Discussions of how to adapt the intervention are appropriate. For example, it is possible that Nora's mother might suggest that Nora earn more practical social or activity items instead of tangible items. Maybe she would like to see Nora work for free or computer time with educational activities, as opposed to earning tangible items, such as a snack. As such, we encourage teachers to understand and collaborate with families.

# Programming

We strongly encourage teachers to advocate for the inclusion of interventions with evidence of effectiveness on any plan written for the student, such as a response to intervention plan, individualized education program (IEP), section 504 plan, and/or any other plan developed for an adolescent with ADHD. As you know, research indicates that behavioral strategies can increase academic impairment and decrease disruptive behavior. Therefore, we provide an examples of Nora's current levels, strengths and weaknesses, annual goals, and short-term benchmarks. In addition, we provide a description of behavioral strategies that can be included in the accommodations/modifications section of the plan.

**CASEL Standards**: Social Emotional Learning Competency: Self-Management Sub competency—Exhibiting Self-Discipline and Self-Motivation

**Current levels, strengths, and weaknesses**: Nora is an eighth-grade student who struggles with ADHD. She does relatively well in her English course with the exception of reading. During reading, she has a tendency to disrupt her peers with random movements. While this has not proved detrimental to her reading proficiency, it has in Nora's science class. Unfortunately, Nora is failing science. This can be attributed to her fidgeting. She struggles to pay attention to her teacher and proclaims that the class is "boring" when asked about her behavior. After direct observation, it was discovered that Nora is frequently off task science during her science class. Nora's science teacher is under the impression that her behavior is intentional. While it can be speculated that Nora's behavior is caused by her ADHD, her science teacher should work to implement behavioral strategies in her classroom that could help with Nora's attentiveness.

**Annual Smart Goal**:
• Given teacher implementation of behavioral strategies in the classroom, Nora will only be off task for 10 minutes out of every 50-minute period.

#  Conclusion

Behavioral strategies are extremely effective with children with ADHD, although there are unique challenges using them with adolescents. Nevertheless, when used carefully they can be effective. Using an effective balance of reinforcement and punishment to increase replacement behaviors and decrease target behaviors can help students succeed. In this chapter, we discussed five stages and their implementation steps and three commonly used frameworks (basic behavioral strategies, behavioral contracts, token economy systems). We discussed four barriers and potential means of overcoming those barriers. Furthermore, we emphasized the importance of considering cultural values around behavior and collaborating closely with families.

# Reference List

Baumrind, D. (1971). Current patterns of parental authority. *Developmental Psychology. 4*, 1–103.

Briesch, A. M., Chafouleas, S. M., & Riley-Tillman, T. C. (2010). Generalizability and dependability of behavior assessment methods to estimate academic engagement: A comparison of systematic direct observation and direct behavior rating. *School Psychology Review, 39*(3), 408–421.

Curwin, R. L., & Mendler, A. N. (1988). *Discipline with dignity*. ASCD.

Dictionary.com. (n.d.). www.dictionary.com.

Fung, T. (2015). *EpicWin* (adapted for AMSI research) (Mobile application software).

Harrison, J. R., Evans, S. W., Baran, A., Khondker, F., Press, K., Noel, D., . . . Mohlmann, M. (2020a). Comparison of accommodations and interventions for youth with ADHD: A randomized controlled trial. *Journal of School Psychology, 80*, 15–36.

Harrison, J. R., Kwong, C., Evans, S. W., Peltier, C., & Mathews, L. (2020b). Game-based self-management: Addressing inattention during independent reading and written response. *Journal of Applied School Psychology, 36*(1), 38–61.

Harrison, J. R., Soares, D. A., Rudzinski, S., & Johnson, R. (2019). Attention deficit hyperactivity disorders and classroom-based interventions: Evidence-based status, effectiveness, and moderators of effects in single-case design research. *Review of Educational Research, 89*(4), 569–611.

Lansford, J. E., Bornstein, M. H., Dodge, K. A., Skinner, A. T., Putnick, D. L., & Deater-Deckard, K. (2011). Attributions and attitudes of mothers and fathers in the United States. *Parenting Science and Practice, 11*, 199–213.

# Home–School Communication
## Daily Report Card

### Cannon

Cannon is a sixth-grade student. He is a funny student who is well-liked by his peers. His classmates always want to sit with him at lunch, and he loves having conversations with those around him. However, Cannon is currently struggling in Ms. Joaunice's English/Language Arts (ELA) class. During instructional time, Ms. Joaunice asks many questions providing tons of opportunities to respond and promote student engagement. Cannon is always eager to answer the questions. Unfortunately, he forgets that he is not the only student in the class and consistently blurts out  the answers to the questions, annoying his peers and his teacher. Ms. Joaunice reminds Cannon daily that the expectation is to raise his hand and wait to be called on. Unfortunately, he seems to never hear those directions. Additionally, many times, when she does not acknowledge his response or asks him to wait his turn, he becomes frustrated and throws objects, such as his pencil and pen around the room. He has thrown pencils and books on the floor proclaiming that Ms. Joaunice is not fair, or Ms. Joaunice hates him. On several occasions, once he calmed down, Cannon engaged himself with paper airplane making instead of listening to the teacher. Once the airplanes were made, he threw them across the tops of his classmates towards the back of the room. During these instances, Cannon's classmates were distracted, and his teacher was frustrated. When it comes time to do individual work, Cannon finishes his assignment quickly. Upon finishing his work, he again disrupts the class. He often gets out of his seat and walks around the room. He looks over the shoulders of his peers while they are completing assignments. When asked about his behavior, Cannon explains that he just forgets to raise his hand and that Ms. Joaunice is mean and thinks that he is doing it on purpose. He exclaims, "She hates me! Every time I do the least little thing like answering a question out loud, she gripes at me. I mean, what does she expect me to do when she asks me a question? Ignore her and do not answer it even when I know that correct answer? I knew the answer and no one else did. She just thinks that I am annoying so she's hateful to me!" Ms. Joaunice sends Cannon to the hall to "recompose himself" where he chats with all of the teachers and students walking by him! Cannon and Ms. Joaunice must come to a mutual understanding before Cannon's behavior permanently affects his academic performance. This can be done through Home-School Communication (HSC). Using HSC, Ms. Joaunice and Cannon's parents work together to clearly describe the expectations and provide reinforcement when he complies. This will provide the opportunity for all involved to be on the same page and take some of what Cannon perceives as teacher judgement out of the equation.

DOI: 10.4324/9781003109983-12

# Description of Home–School Communication Strategies

Home–School Communication (HSC) is a strategy used to motivate students, like Cannon, to increase self-regulation through collaboration between parents, teachers, and the students. The three individuals work as a team to increase the probability of the desired behavior. HSC requires that everyone on the team clearly understands the problem behavior and baseline rates of the behavior, the desired behavior, and the reinforcer. As you are no doubt aware, common computer programs are used to communicate student progress to parents and students. For example, using Schoology or Microsoft® TEAMS (or others), Cannon's mother can view the assignments that he has submitted or *not* submitted daily. These can be very helpful to parents interested in monitoring progress; however, our experience is that there is a great deal of variability in how well teachers keep the information accurate and current.

Unfortunately, many such programs do not include a mode of communicating behavior progress. Additionally, they do not often include a space for writing goals for the student, other than missing assignments. One mode of HSC, that is discussed in the remainder of this chapter provides such information, is a Daily Report Card (DRC). With DRC students are given a written document, verbal direction, and frequent redirection that helps them understand the expectations and reinforcers for meeting those expectations (Owens et al., 2012). By establishing rules and reinforcers that are known by all involved, students can be encouraged and motivated to achieve their goal through self-regulation. As with Cannon, many students with ADHD need clarity and frequent reminders, which are easily provided with DRC.

As can be seen with Cannon's behavior, students with ADHD often claim to be unaware of what they are doing that does not meet the expectations of the class. Whether they are being honest or not when making their claims is irrelevant. One of our goals, as teachers, is to help students learn and demonstrate socially appropriate behavior. Results of scientific studies indicate that the use of DRC increases appropriate classroom functioning, goal attainment, and academic productivity and decreases disruptive behavior for young adolescents with ADHD when compared to typical classroom practices (Fabiano et al., 2010). Nonetheless, as a word of caution, DRC might not be the most appropriate intervention for older adolescents. As such, we strongly encourage you to ensure that any DRC you use is developed in an age-appropriate manner. That being said, when using an age-appropriate DRC, Cannon is likely to raise his hand to speak, Ms. Joaunice will report the progress on Cannon's daily report, he will receive positive reinforcement from home and school, and his behavior will continue to improve.

## Stages of HSC

| 1 | 2 | 3 | 4 |
|---|---|---|---|
| Collaborative goal setting | Develop form of communication | Teach students desired behavior | Report and provide feedback |

*Figure 10.1*

## Stage 1: Collaborative Goal Setting

Collaborative goal setting includes four implementation steps (See Figure 10.1): (1) identifying target behavior and identifying baseline rates of the behavior, (2) identifying desired behavior, (3) selecting mastery criteria, and (4) selecting the reinforcer.

Raise my hand!

Image used under license from Shutterstock. New Vectors/Shutterstock.com.

**Identify Target Behavior and Determining Baseline**

The first step in collaboratively setting goals is to identify the target behavior and determine baseline. It is likely that by the time the teacher has determined the need for intervention, she has an idea of which behavior to target. At times, teachers are faced with multiple behaviors that they would like to target and must prioritize and select one. For example, Ms. Joaunice is concerned about Cannon yelling out answers to questions without raising his hand, throwing objects when he is frustrated, and walking around the classroom disturbing other students when he has finished his work. Using HSC system, the first step to selecting the target behavior is a conversation with the parent. Therefore, Ms. Joaunice would meet with Cannon's parent, Mr. Quantell and describe the HSC being proposed and begin the process by agreeing on the first behavior to be targeted. They probably agree to target throwing objects as this was the most disruptive (a potentially unsafe) of Cannon's behaviors.

## Identify Desired Behavior and Determining Baseline

Once the target behavior is selected, the team determines the desired behavior or the behavior they would like to see instead of the target behavior. For example, Ms. Joaunice would like Cannon to raise his hand to answer questions instead of blurting out the answer. It is important that teachers consider the reason for the desired behavior. Why does it matter to her that Cannon raises his hand instead of simply answering the question? Ms. Joaunice believes that teaching Cannon to raise his hand is necessary for several reasons. When students raise their hand in class to speak, they give the teacher the opportunity to make sure that all students in the class have the opportunity to respond to questions. When Cannon speaks out, he takes the opportunity away from other students. In addition, by raising his hand, Cannon learns effective conversation skills, by waiting for others to speak and listening to their responses. Many teachers contend that asking students to raise their hand decreases classroom chaos! Explaining the rationale for the desired behavior to the student and parents helps the student to be motivated to engage in the behavior.

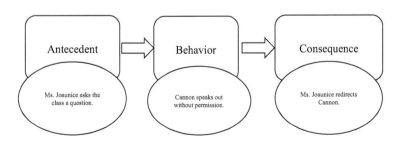

After establishing the desired behavior, the teacher determines the baseline of the behavior to identify the "how often and/or how long" a behavior typically occurs. Understanding how often, how much, or how long a student typically engages in the problem behavior is necessary to determine if the behavior is a really a problem. When combined with future behavioral measurement, this data will allow the teacher, parent, and student to clearly determine if the behavior is changing and if the HSC is impacting student behavior. For example, Ms. Joaunice reported that Cannon ALWAYs screams out the answer to her questions in class, but what does "always" mean in relation to this behavior. A more effective way of describing the behavior is to count the number of times that he answers questions without raising his hand (problem behavior) and the frequency of the times that he raised his hand to answer a question (target behavior). Before she begins her lesson, Ms. Joaunice, puts red marbles in her right pocket. When Cannon speaks out without raising his hand, Ms. Joaunice moves a red marble from her right pocket to her left pocket. Ms. Joaunice does this very discretely and does not tell Cannon what she is doing. She continues with the lesson while she is collecting baseline data. At the end of the day, she writes down how many times Cannon spoke without permission based on the number of marbles in her left pocket. Ms. Joaunice does this for five days in a row and determines that Cannon speaks out without permission an average of seven times during a 50-minute class period per day (Figure 10.2).

### Set Expectations and Selecting Reinforcers

After baseline data is collected, Ms. Joaunice, Cannon, and his mother (Ms. Quantell) meet to discuss his behavior. The three decide that, due to frequency of disruptions, the behavior is definitely a problem and likely to be very disruptive in class. As such, they look at the baseline data together and write a goal for his HSC. The goal must be achievable. If not, then why should Cannon even try? It is not likely that he will speak without permission zero times a day after the HSC is first used, but it is possible that the frequency of disruptions might decrease by one or two at the beginning. As such, a positive goal is set for Cannon to speak out fewer than five times per day. As Cannon masters the goal, the

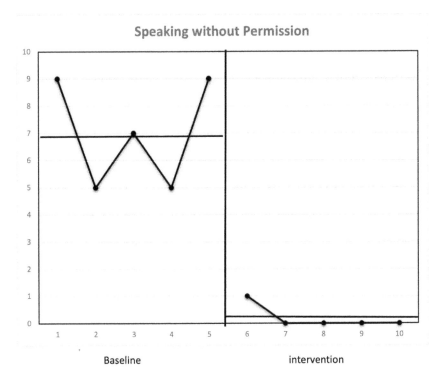

*Figure 10.2* Graph for Visual Analysis.

expectations will increase. If Cannon continues to struggle to meet the goal, the goal will be decreased so that he will experience success, which in turn increases motivation.

Once the goal is established, the three (student, teacher, parent) select potential reinforcers and make a list. Selecting reinforcers often involves asking the adolescent what he/she would like to earn. This can simply be done verbally or using a student interest survey. It is important to select reinforcers that the student wants to earn. Finally, you decide what reinforcer the student will earn.

Think about the question, what would the student like to earn that would motivate him/her to engage in the desired behavior? You can select reinforcers from one or more of four categories: (1) edible, (2) tangible, (3) activity, and (4) social reinforcers. Interestingly, we often think of reinforcers as edible or tangible items, these are our (the authors of this book) least two favorites. We encourage you to try to use activity or social reinforcers, as adolescents tend to be very social individuals. Nonetheless, let's examine edible and tangible reinforcers first. Pizza is a common edible reinforcer used in schools. We suspect that this occurred because students like it and it historically has been easily delivered to schools. In our current climate of food delivery, you could get almost anything delivered. As such, if you are going to use snacks for reinforcers, we encourage you to use healthy snacks and to encourage parents to use the same at home.

Similar to edible reinforcers, it is often difficult to find tangible items that are reinforcing for adolescents and affordable for teachers! No doubt, some adolescents would work for a new Xbox®, but teachers are not likely to be able to buy every student a new gaming system! This is true for parents, as well. With students with ADHD, it is important to select items that are immediate reinforcers, as opposed to large items that require many days of demonstrating the appropriate behavior to earn. It is important to know your student, as you select tangible reinforcers. For example, we have known adolescents who would work for electric toothbrushes, hairbrushes, and trading cards.

Similarly, social reinforcers or social feedback (positive comments, smiles, acceptance, praise) can be strong motivators for adolescents; however, teachers and parents must think carefully about how to effectively use this type of reinforcer. During adolescence, students begin to separate themselves from their families and attend more to peers. You have likely noticed that secondary students are keenly aware of how they are perceived by their peers and attend closely to how their peer group responds to their actions. Teachers often find it difficult to shape the behavior of students such as Cannon, who receives natural reinforcement from his peers for being funny. As such, teachers and parents must find a way to use social reinforcers in their HSC. How can Ms. Joaunice provide social reinforcement for Cannon? Ms. Joaunice could meet with Cannon each morning. The two could think of one joke that he could tell each day at a specific time given that he did not "entertain" his peers the remainder of the day. Another option would be to give Cannon a responsibility that would give him the opportunity to engage with peers and potentially earn him peer praise, such as passing out papers. Regardless of the method, Ms. Joaunice must find a social reinforcer that is as reinforcing as the target behaviors.

Activity reinforcers are typically the most reinforcing for adolescents. Activity reinforcers allow the student to earn the privilege of engaging in their preferred activities, such as playing a game with peers, the teacher, or both, working with the custodian, having lunch with the principal, designing a class bulletin board, or decorating for a school dance. Activity reinforcers are frequently selected by parents as reinforcers. Think of the times that you have heard a student say that they have to earn a passing grade on a test in order to be able to go out on the weekend or to play Xbox with their friends online. Activity reinforcers are strong motivators for adolescents! See Chapter 9 of this book for further information about selecting reinforcers.

## *Stage 2: Develop Form of Communication*

Once the goals are agreed upon, the teacher will select a mode of HSC and develop the form to deliver student progress data. In the current age of technology, the most effective means of communication is through a digital document or program through which the teacher documents progress toward the goal on a consistent schedule, typically daily or weekly. As you would expect, daily is more effective, especially for students with ADHD who require frequent and timely reinforcement. If digital communication is not an option or if the teacher decides that she would rather use a paper-based form, then she would communicate with the parent to make sure that the parent is expecting the form on the day that it will be sent home. As youth with ADHD are known to be forgetful, the parent must be prepared and willing to ask for the form at the expected time.

No doubt teachers can think of several ways to communicate with parents in writing or digitally and any and all will serve the purpose of communicating student progress toward a goal for parent acknowledgment, feedback, and reinforcement. Regardless of the form taken, it is important that the form includes the goal and the progress toward this goal and that teachers are consistent with completing and sending the communication home. We encourage you to avoid anectodical summaries. The purpose is to help the student move toward the goal, which is observable and measurable. When we, as teachers, start writing anecdotal information as data or communication, we tend to include information that reflects more of an opinion, attitude, or feeling than student progress toward a goal. For example, if Ms. Joaunice wrote "once again, Cannon forgot to raise his hand before screaming out the answer disrupting the entire class and depriving his classmates the opportunity to answer questions," then the parent would not be able to identify the number of times that Cannon raised or did not raise his hand, which is the goal. In addition, it is likely that such communication interferes with effective communication with parents. As parents of adolescents with ADHD, they have likely become tired of reading such negative feedback from other adults.

## Stage 3: Teach Students Desired Behavior

Once goals are written and forms are created, students must be taught the desired behavior. Many teachers and parents would quickly tell you that the student knows what is expected and simply elects not to demonstrate that behavior. Nonetheless, each time we initiate a new goal with a student, we begin with TEACHING, just as we would with academic content. We recommend that you follow the four procedures of behavior skills training (describe, demonstrate, role-play, practice).

The first step is to describe the behavior verbally to the student. Teachers would meet with the adolescent in private to describe the behavior. In the case of Cannon or any adolescent, this step seems a bit silly for some of the behaviors, such as raising his hand to speak.

Nonetheless, it is important that the student and teacher are on the same page about exactly what that means. Does Cannon have to raise his hand to speak every time? What if no one else has their hand raised, why can't he just tell her the answer? Ms. Joaunice would explain that he has to raise his hand, even if no one else raises their hand, because it is possible that other students might still be thinking. After all, wait time is not a friend of students with ADHD. In addition to answering the student's questions, the description of "raising hand" would probably sound like: Cannon, the expectation for this class is that you raise your hand to speak. So, you have something to say during the lesson or when you want to answer a question that I have asked, please raise your hand, and wait. While you are waiting, please sit quietly. I might call on you or

I might call on another student. If you have something pressing to say and I did not call on you, please jot a note to yourself on the notepad on your desk, so that you can tell me after the lesson. Ms. Joaunice would show Cannon the home–school communication form that includes the goals. She would tell him where she would indicate whether he demonstrated the behavior or not.

Image used under license from Shutterstock. Lidiia Koval/ Shutterstock.com.

Next, Ms. Joaunice and Cannon would role-play raising his hand. Teachers would meet with the adolescent in private to role-play the behavior. First, Ms. Joaunice would instruct Cannon to be the teacher. While he is role-playing being the teacher, she will raise her hand and wait quietly. She can also demonstrate non-examples of the behavior and scream out the answer to the question without waiting. Next, Ms. Joaunice would be the teacher and Cannon would demonstrate that he understands the behavior. Adolescent often find this step to be silly. Our recommendation is for you to "go with the silliness" and enjoy the roll plays. Many students really like to demonstrate the non-example and that is okay, as long as they identify the behavior as just that. After role-playing, Mrs. Joaunice would demonstrate how she will document on the HSC form at the end of the day.

Although each of the first three steps are completed in private, step three takes place in the classroom. During this step, the student practices the behavior. Ms. Joaunice would meet with Cannon to practice. She would also begin the class reminding the students of the expectation. Ms. Joaunice would give multiple opportunities for Cannon and other students to raise their hand to speak. When the students raise their hand as expected, she would verbally reinforce their behavior. We encourage teachers to practice this skill with all students and not single out the adolescent with ADHD. When any student forgets the expectation and answers a question or speaks without permission, the teacher redirects being very specific, "Barbara, remember to raise your hand and wait for me to call on you." The practice sessions continue until everyone in the class has mastered the skill.

## *Stage 4: Report and Provide Feedback*

The final stage begins after the teacher and student have role-played the desired behavior and the teacher is confident that the student understands the expectation. In this stage, the teacher begins to report student progress to the parent on the selected format. First the teacher notified the parent that the intervention will begin on a specific date and provides a reminder of the reinforcers that will be delivered at home or at school.

After the reminder is sent the teacher begins completing the home–school communication form on a daily basis (regardless of whether the parent sees it daily or weekly) and the teacher/parent begin providing the reinforcer as the student demonstrates the behavior. We cannot over-emphasis the importance of consistency. If the form is not complete, the parent does not review the form, or the student is not allowed the reinforcer, then the behavior is not likely to change. One method to increase the likelihood that the form gets home is to encourage parents to create three levels of privileges for every evening. The high level is for when the form indicates that the student was successful achieving the goal. The second level is for when the student is not successful with the goal but does bring the form home. The lowest level is for when the student does not bring home the form. A system like this is likely to increase consistency and encourage the student to bring the form home every day.

# Modes of Home–School Communication

Several modes of HSC are available for teachers to use. In the following section, we describe four methods of communication, web-based tools, email, shared document (google form), and paper form.

## *Web-based Tools*

Web-based tools for DRC, such as Daily Report Card Online (DRCO) developed by Dr. Julie Owens and colleagues at the Center for Intervention

Research in Schools (CIRS) at Ohio University, are very convenient, effective, and supportive of teacher needs. DRCO can be found at https://dailyreportcardonline.com/#what-is-a-drc. The program provides the opportunity for teachers to create a DRC for individual students in need of intervention. Using the DRCO, teachers complete a survey that produces a report indicating whether the student is a good match for the DRC intervention. The program "wizard" helps the teacher select target behaviors and determine which should be targeted first, complete baseline data collection, and set the first goal. With this information, the DRC is created. Teachers can use any mobile device to collect data related to the target behavior directly into the DRC. The DRCO produces a graph of student daily performance (Figure 10.3) along with recommendations for when to change the DRC. At the end of the day, the teacher can meet with the student review his/her progress toward the reinforcer from a reward menu. Finally, the teacher prints the DRC and sends it home to the parent.

*Figure 10.3* DRCO Graph of Daily Performance.
Printed with permission from Julie Owens.

## *Email*

Another method is to communicate with parents through email. If this is the selected mode of communication, it is important that a template (with

As you remember our goal is for Cannon to raise his hand and wait to be called on FIVE times per class. Today he raised his hand _____ (number of) times and as such earned/did not earn his _____ (reinforcer) to be delivered at home and/or _____ (reinforcer) to be delivered at school.

Thank you for your collaboration!
Ms. Joaunice

*Figure 10.4* Daily Report Via Email.
Image used under license from Shutterstock. Net Vector/Shutterstock.com.

few words) is developed and used consistently. The template would include the goal and the progress toward the goal that occurred during the designated time (Figure 10.4).

## *Shared Document*

A second means of digital communication would be to create a shared document between the parent and the teacher. For example, Ms. Joaunice might create a google sheet that is shared between the parent and the teacher (Figure 10.5). This would require the parent to view it on the designated date. If this is a problem, then a digital reminder could be set for the teacher to remember to complete the form and send an email to the parent indicating that the form is complete. This process could be simplified with RemindApp®, a messaging application frequently used by teachers to remind students to complete specific tasks, or a similar application.

## *Paper Form*

Finally, teachers always have the option of sending an HSC form on the designated date home with the student. Historically, students with ADHD have struggled to get the form in their backpack, remember to get the parent to sign it, put it back into their backpack, and submit it to the teacher. As you can see from this cycle of events, there are many steps that could be forgotten and a paper form that could be misplaced. That being said, for some teachers, it is the easiest to do. If the form is to report progress for one day, then it could be like Figure 10.6, or a week like Figure 10.7. As with the other forms of communication, the form is simple and contains the goal and the achievement for each reporting period. Again, minimal anecdotical information is needed for this intervention.

# Cannon's Home School Communication Form

Dear Ms. Queen,

1. Today Cannon raised his hand

   *Check all that apply.*

   ☐ 1
   ☐ 2
   ☐ 3
   ☐ 4
   ☐ 5
   ☐ 6
   ☐ 7
   ☐ 8
   ☐ 9
   ☐ 10

2. Therefore he

   *Mark only one oval.*

   ◯ Earned
   ◯ Did not earn

3. His home reinforcer (name reinforcer)

   _____

4. His school reinforcer (name reinforcer)

   _____

*Figure 10.5* Google Form Daily Communication.

## Daily Report Card

**Student Name: Cannon**

**Goal: Cannon will speak out without permission less than five times per class period.**

| Period | Subject | # of speak outs without permission | Notes |
|--------|---------|-----------------------------------|-------|
| 1 | | | |
| 2 | | | |
| 3 | | | |
| 4 | | | |
| 5 | | | |
| 6 | | | |
| 7 | | | |
| 8 | | | |

*Figure 10.6* Paper-Based Daily Report Card.

Image used under license from Shutterstock. Oilrladin/Shutterstock.com.

| Weekly Report Card | | | | | | | |
|---|---|---|---|---|---|---|---|
| Student Name: Cannon | | | | | | | |
| Goal:  Cannon will speak out without permission less than five times per class period. | | | | | | | |
| Period | Subject | # of speak outs without permission | | | | | Notes |
| | | M | T | W | T | F | |
| 1 | | | | | | | |
| 2 | | | | | | | |
| 3 | | | | | | | |
| 4 | | | | | | | |
| 5 | | | | | | | |
| 6 | | | | | | | |
| 7 | | | | | | | |
| 8 | | | | | | | |

*Figure 10.7*  Paper-Based Weekly Report Card.
Image used under license from Shutterstock. Oilrladin/Shutterstock.com.

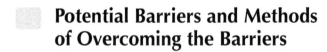 # Potential Barriers and Methods of Overcoming the Barriers

Barriers to the implementation and effectiveness of HSC tend to center on challenges specific to teachers, parents, and students.

## *Time*

One barrier frequently encountered by teachers in middle and high schools is the number of students that they teach daily. Many secondary teachers encounter more than 100 students a day. Additionally, typically many are only with students from 50 to 80 minutes. As such, we encourage teachers to focus on barrier that is directly impacting the teacher's ability to teach, the student ability to make academic progress, and the remainder of the students in the class to learn and complete their assignments. For example, Ms. Joaunice could create a DRC focusing on Cannon's disruptive behavior. She could include the goals of raising his hand to speak and waiting to be called on. She could also include a goal of keeping his materials on his desk. These behaviors are valuable to the teacher, Cannon, and the class and are fairly easy to track. Using a program such as the DRCO to track the behavior and print the DRC would minimize time used. Furthermore, we encourage teachers to remember that even though they teach many students, we suspect that there are only a few that need this level of intervention.

As noted throughout this book, time is a commodity for teachers and schedules are frequently fluid. For example, school days are often interrupted by fire drills, safety drills, assemblies, and/or other programs. Adolescents with ADHD can be pulled from class for unscheduled events, such as meetings with teachers, counselors, or administrators. In addition, teachers are often pulled from class to attend meetings or other events. We encourage teachers to simplify measurement and documentation in an effort to decrease the amount of time required. For example, Cannon's HSC includes a goal that he will speak out without permission no more than five times in a 50-minute class period. Ms. Joaunice elects to carry a clipboard with her and write down each time Cannon speaks out without permission. She could simplify these procedures by counting behavior by moving paper clips from one pocket to the next without carrying the clipboard. This is just one example of simplifying measurement. When you realize that you are struggling with consistency, then consider all options for increasing the opportunity for you to follow the plan as written. If you cannot determine the exact barrier or barriers, meet with a colleague or supervisor to work through the problem-solving steps to identify the problem and select strategies to overcome them!

## Collaboration With Parents of Adolescents Can Be Difficult

The perceived lack of collaboration with parents is an issue with HSC that is well documented in studies of DBR. Researchers and educators alike have described "issues" with parent consistency that interfere with the effectiveness of the program. When this occurs, it is best to communicate with the parents. Instead of simply declaring that you cannot use HSC because the parent "refuses" to cooperate. Communicating with the parent involves listening to the parents' problems with implementation and follow through without judgment. It is possible that they do not understand the expectations for their involvement. Maybe they did not understand that they were responsible for viewing the HSC and providing the agreed upon reinforcer to the student. It is also possible that they forget to look at the HSC every day (if this is the expectation). Parents time is often overloaded as well. How can you help them remember? How can you decrease the expectation? Speak the parent candidly without judgment to determine the answers to these questions. Would it be helpful to set up a reminder on a RemindApp® or would it be more helpful to change the HSC to be weekly requiring the parents to review it and provide reinforcers once a week instead of once a day? Go through the problem-solving steps to help parents determine the barriers and adapt the plan to overcome the barriers. Collaborating with parents involves being true partners working together to overcome barriers without judgment.

## Adolescents Are Not Cooperative

A common barrier to the effective implementation of DRC is the cooperation of adolescents. We have adolescents mention that use of DRC is silly and childish. The answer is within the reinforcer or punisher being used by the parent. Identifying an effective reinforcer is often a challenge for students this age. As previously mentioned, it is important to consider what the student values. For example, while stickers are often effective for young children, this is not often the case for adolescents. You and the parent should begin with a discussion of what is important to the student. Once the DRC is developed and implemented for at least two weeks, if you find that the behavior is not changing, then we suggest you consider the value of the selected reinforcer. The DRC is likely to become less "silly," if access to video games, phones, or cars is part are used as a consequence. The same is true if the reinforcer loses its value over time. The easiest action to take to determine if the reinforcer has lost its value or has no value to begin with is to talk to the student and the parent. The student will likely to be happy to tell you if they do not want to work for the reinforcer that you selected, even if they indicated that they would work for the reinforcer in

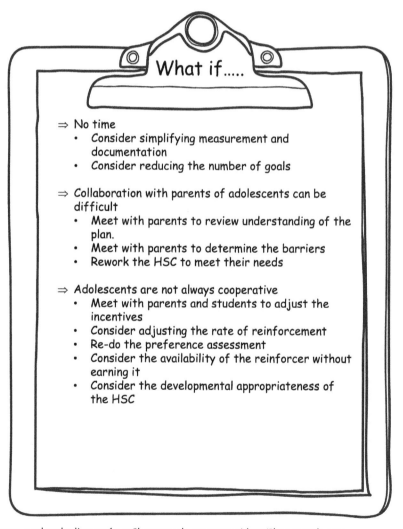

**What if.....**

⇒ No time
  • Consider simplifying measurement and documentation
  • Consider reducing the number of goals

⇒ Collaboration with parents of adolescents can be difficult
  • Meet with parents to review understanding of the plan.
  • Meet with parents to determine the barriers
  • Rework the HSC to meet their needs

⇒ Adolescents are not always cooperative
  • Meet with parents and students to adjust the incentives
  • Consider adjusting the rate of reinforcement
  • Re-do the preference assessment
  • Consider the availability of the reinforcer without earning it
  • Consider the developmental appropriateness of the HSC

Image used under license from Shutterstock. rangsan paidaen/Shutterstock.com.

the past. Along the same lines, it might be helpful to do another preference assessment (see example) that is designed specifically for adolescents. It is very important that you maintain the integrity of the HSC by including the parent and student in any conversation involving changing the HSC.

Another consideration is satiation. Satiation refers to the student getting tired of the reinforcer. For example, if a student is working to earn school supplies, such as pencils or pens. It is possible that writing utensils will soon lose their value. After all, how many pens and pencils do you need? In another instance, if a student is working to earn an hour of computer time, it is possible that the student will get tired of computer time. To overcome satiation, teachers can vary the reinforcer across time. Maybe the student works for pens and pencils one week and notebooks with their favorite sports team or player, or specifically attractive design on the front of the notebook.

## Considerations for Culturally Responsive HSC

We cannot overemphasize the importance of being culturally responsive when you are developing and implementing HSC systems for adolescents with ADHD. This communication can be complex on several levels. First, we encourage you to consider the cultural perspective of misbehavior and disability. For example, there is a strong focus on respect and obedience within Latinx cultures. As such, approaching the HSC from the perspective of white culture that emphasizes assertiveness, independence, and self-determination is not likely to be popular with some parents. As such, educators must build strong rapport with parents that is reflected in strong collaborators in the development of the DRC. Parent opinion and values must be heard and reflected in the DRC.

In relation to the perspective of disability, it is important that we consider cultural perspectives. For example, in some cultures there is a great deal of stigma associated with disability. As such, it is possible that some parents will be very reluctant to consider that their children have ADHD. They might be less than cooperative with HSC systems, if they do not want their child "labeled." As such, it might be beneficial to approach the parent without discussion of disability. The overall idea of HSC is for parents and teachers to work together to help students learn and engage in appropriate behavior in school. Speak to the parent about how you can work collaboratively and truly consider their input. As educations, we sometimes consider ourselves "checking the boxes." Check, we worked with the parent and not really allowing parents to have input. This attitude is not likely to increase the effectiveness of the DRC.

Educators must be cautious about overgeneralizing some knowledge of parents' values and beliefs. It is important to remember that you cannot ascribe your understanding of specific cultural beliefs to individual families. It is possible that the family that you are working with does not have the same beliefs. All families are unique. The answer is to listen carefully and understand what is being said. Your goal is to hear everything and not to listen with the idea of formulating a response. What is the parent telling you? What are you learning about the family as the parent speaks that is important to your communication with them? Trying to convince the parent that they are "wrong" is not appropriate or helpful to the student.

Further, we encourage you to be considerate of the cultural implications, norms, and expectations for communication. Communication with parents happens at two phases of the process. The first is the development of the HSC, which is a meeting. When meeting with the parents and students to develop the HSC, the teacher should communicate in the parents' first language and make sure that the parent understands what is being said and the agreed upon procedures. It is possible that an interpreter will be needed for this meeting. It is our responsibility to build rapport with the parent and make the parent feel comfortable enough to ask questions and share their feelings.

For example, in many cultures, parents expect their children to follow expectations without additional incentives. It is difficult for them to accept that adolescents with ADHD might need additional reinforcers to engage in behaviors that are difficult for them. As such, we encourage teachers to listen carefully and help parents select incentives that are acceptable to them and motivating for the student. For example, Cannon's parents might be more willing to allow Cannon 30 minutes of time on Xbox Live® than to agree to purchase a brand-new system. Teachers have the knowledge and skill to help parents make a selection that is feasible and acceptable to them. If we ignore parents' values and ideas, then it is not likely that the HSC will be followed as designed. In other words, parents are not likely to follow through if the incentive is unrealistic in their perspective.

Similarly, the HSC should be in the parents' first language. Teachers and parents might develop the document so that it is written in both English and the parents' first language. This seems logical, but we have seen many educators communicate with parents in English, when the parents do not read or speak English fluently. Therefore, it is vital to translate the HSC into the parents' language. If the teacher does not speak or write that language, then we suggest asking someone that does to help translate. Additionally, it is important to use an appropriate reading level. The average American reads at the seventh or eighth grade level. As such, the HSC form should be at this level or below. This should not be a problem, because the form should include goals with few words and performance in numerical form. For HSC to be effective, it is imperative that all truly work together!

# Programming

We strongly encourage teachers to advocate for the inclusion of interventions with evidence of effectiveness on any plan written for the student, such as a response to intervention plan, individualized education program (IEP), section 504 plan, and/or any other plan developed for an adolescent with ADHD. As you know, research indicates that HSC can increase academic success and decrease disruptive behavior. Therefore, we provide an example of Cannon's current levels, strengths and weaknesses, annual goals, and short-term benchmarks. In addition, we provide a description of home–school communication that can be included in the accommodations/modifications section of the plan.

---

**CASEL Standards:** Social Emotional Learning Competency: Self-Management
Sub competency—Exhibiting self-discipline and motivation.

---

**Current levels, strengths, and weaknesses:** Cannon is a sixth-grade student who is experiencing behavioral difficulties in Ms. Joaunice's ELA class. Cannon calls out answers when questions are asked of the class instead of raising his hand. He throws objects, which has become a great distraction to his peers. When it comes to completing assignments, Cannon races through them with relative ease causing him to be bored. This results in him getting up and walking around the room when others are trying to work. Ms. Joaunice utilized frequency recording to calculate how many times on average Cannon blurts out when the class is asked a question. On average, Cannon blurts seven times per class period. When it comes to him throwing objects, he threw an item five times out of every 50-minute class period. While Cannon's teacher believes that this behavior is a direct result of his advanced understanding of the content, Ms. Joaunice still needs to address the behavior. Through conversations with Cannon's parents, Ms. Joaunice found that he demonstrates some of these same behaviors at home. As such, Ms. Joaunice and the parents agree that home–school communication can help in addressing Cannon's misbehavior.

---

**Annual Smart Goal:**
- With the implementation of home–school communication, Cannon will speak out without permission less than two times per class period.
- With the implementation of home–school communication, Cannon's will not throw objects during ELA instruction.

---

# Conclusion

Home–school communication is an intervention that helps students learn to engage in behavior in the classroom that contributes to the learning of self and others. Through daily or weekly communication with parents, students earn reinforcers at home and school increasing the likelihood that the student will repeat the desired behavior and refrain from engaging in the target behavior. In the current chapter, we discussed four stages HOSC and their implementation steps. We discussed, stigma, willingness, and resources as barriers to effective implementation. Furthermore, we emphasized the importance of being culturally responsive to increase rapport with parents and in turn increase student learning. Although we frequently think of HSC as only important in elementary schools, we strongly encourage you to work closely with parents of all students at the secondary level.

# Reference List

Fabiano, G. A., Vujnovic, R. K., Pelham, W. E., Waschbusch, D. A., Massetti, G. M., Pariseau, M. E., . . . Volker, M. (2010). Enhancing the effectiveness of special education programming for children with attention deficit hyperactivity disorder using a daily report card. *School Psychology Review, 39*(2), 219–239.

Owens, J. S., Holdaway, A. S., Zoromski, A. K., Evans, S. W., Himawan, L. K., Girio-Herrera, E., & Murphy, C. E. (2012). Incremental benefits of a daily report card intervention over time for youth with disruptive behavior. *Behavior Therapy, 43*(4), 848–861.

# Peer Tutoring

### Jaiden

Jaiden is a ninth-grade student who struggles to pay attention in all, or at least most, situations. He especially struggles to attend to his Algebra teacher, his classwork, and his homework. He struggles to attend to the coach in meetings and even during football games when he is playing. He also struggles to attend to the directions that his mother gives him to complete his daily chores. Jaiden is frustrated, as are his peers, teachers, and parents! Nonetheless, Jaiden continues to be the starting quarterback for the junior varsity football team at his high school. His challenge to attend has interfered  with his academic performance, specifically in Algebra, and his ability to play football. If any of his grades are below a C, he is not permitted to practice or play. Regardless, every day in Algebra, Jaiden opens his phone to use his calculator. Instead of using the the calculator his mother bought him, he downloaded a scientific calculator to his phone. However, once his opens his phone, he finds himself on Tiktok®, Instagram ®, or Snapchat®. After all, it is there and he plans to just check it quickly to see what is happening with his peers and in the world, but he gets lost in the phone until Ms. Renette asks what he is doing. He quickly responds that he is using his calculator, to which she responds that he has not written anything on the paper in a good twenty minutes. At this point, he becomes frustrated and starts shuffling his feet loudly and tossing his pencil up and down. His peers become distracted, and Ms. Renette becomes agitated. This cycle has resulted Jaiden earning a very low passing grade in Algebra putting him at risk of failing. His failing grade will result in him being benched from the football team. A fate that his parents nor his teacher want to see. According to Ms. Renette, Jaiden's inattentive behavior happens daily in her class. She reports that he just cannot seem to ever pay attention. Ms. Renette is becoming complacent in the situation, as she does not want to cause further trouble with the coach or Jaiden's parents. She feels as if she is continually reprimanding Jaiden which has limited her ability in forming a relationship with the student. She understands that Algebra is not Jaiden's favorite subject. However, they are at an impasse, as he has to learn the Algebra content. When asked about his inattentive behavior, Jaiden says that it is not about being distracted or about his phone. He explains that he is just bad at math and has always struggled with the subject. When Jaiden' parents offered to provide tutoring, he gets flustered and screams that Algebra is not necessary because he it is not needed in the NFL, where he is headed! This situation has left everyone exhausted as they feel like there is no hope. Fortunately, Ms. Renette learned about Peer Tutoring. Through peer tutoring, she can enlist the help of Jaiden' peers, increase learning, bringing up his Algebra grade, and increasing his chance of continuing to play football, but maybe not his career in the NFL!

DOI: 10.4324/9781003109983-13

#  Description of Peer Tutoring

Peer tutoring is a teaching strategy in which peers serve as private teachers for individuals or small groups of students, such as Jaiden, who are struggling with academic content and/or attending to instruction and tasks in whole group settings with large numbers of students. By teaching peers to provide instruction, adolescents with ADHD are likely to be more comfortable asking questions, explaining what they do not understand, and listing to a peer further explain the content and answer their questions. In addition, students are more likely to be motivated to attend to a task when a peer is redirecting them or prompting them to return to the task than when they perceive a teacher as pestering them. The ultimate goal is not only for the student to learn the content and practice the skill, but for them to be confident in themselves and their ability to learn the content.

As with Jaiden, by the time children with ADHD become adolescents, they often doubt their ability to learn, even when the challenge is not with learning, but the ability to attend long enough to absorb the information or to practice long enough for the facts to become automatic. Consider all of the times that Jaiden has looked at his phone to open his calculator and instead opened social media; you can only image the instruction that was missed in the current academic year, not taking into account the content that was missed in prior years.

In addition to Jaiden serving as the tutee, it is beneficial for him to serve as the tutor. Students who are tutors tend to develop confidence and independent skills. Furthermore, the acts of preparing to and being the teacher often results in learning as the tutor has to be prepared to teach the content (Goodlad & Hirst, 1990). In this situation, it is possible that the tutee might need to redirect Jaiden (who is the tutor) back to task, but we suspect it will be less often that you would

Image used under license from Shutterstock. Studio Romantic/Shutterstock.com.

expect. Although minimal research has been conducted with adolescents with ADHD, prior research indicates that peer tutoring with and without students with disabilities has resulted in increased academic performance (Robinson et al., 2005). Furthermore, research with students with ADHD has demonstrated increases in prosocial behavior, attention to task, and decreases in task irrelevant behavior (Bowman-Perrott et al., 2014; DuPaul & Henningson, 1993). Frequently and consistently utilizing peer tutoring as a classroom strategy, creates a positive classroom climate where students are engaged, communicating, and self-confident through semi-social and structured activities.

## Stages of Peer Tutoring

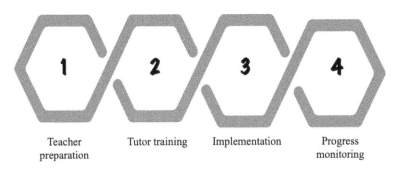

| 1 | 2 | 3 | 4 |
| Teacher preparation | Tutor training | Implementation | Progress monitoring |

*Figure 11.1* Four Stages of Peer Tutoring.

Peer tutoring includes four stages (See Figure 11.1). In the following sections, we describe these steps specific to the one tutor and one tutee (who needs assistance with learning or social goals). Modifications to those steps are included in the Modes of Peer Tutoring section later in the chapter. The first step is teacher preparation. Teacher preparation is the act of getting ready to implement peer tutoring prior to beginning the lesson. We cannot overstate the importance of having a plan and materials prepared prior to implementation. The second step is training the tutors. To be tutors, students have to be taught several very important skills, such as giving corrective feedback. Without this instruction, the lesson is not likely to go very smoothly. The third step, once preparations have been made and tutors have been trained, is implementation, in which the tutor teaches the lesson to the tutee.

The final stage is progress monitoring, in which the teacher monitors both the effectiveness of the tutor–tutee pair and tutee progress toward the academic or social goal.

## *Stage 1: Teacher Preparation*

The first step in peer tutoring is for the teacher to develop a plan and prepare materials. The teacher first determines the learning goals for the lesson. For example, Ms. Renette might plan a lesson with peer tutoring for students to reteach students to solve quadratic equations in one variable. She would begin by deciding if she should use directive or indirective tutoring. Directive tutoring is similar to explicit or direct instruction, in which the teacher describes and explains the concept and how to find the correct solution to problems. Non-direct teaching is similar to inquiry-based instruction, in that the tutor guides the student to discover the correct solution to the problem by asking open-ended questions. In the current situation, it is likely that Ms. Renette would select direct instruction. As such, she would write a lesson plan for the tutor to follow and develop problems for the tutee to solve. The student could respond to the problems through several mediums. Maybe the teacher would like evidence of the work and would assign a worksheet or some form of digital document, such as a Google form or a Google document. On the other hand, she might allow the students to work on a whiteboard, either individual or a large classroom whiteboard, and have the tutor document the correct problems on the worksheet or the computer. If the teacher simply wants the team to work together without documenting correct responses, she might just allow them to use an erasable document (whiteboard, laminated sheet, individual chalkboard).

Image used under license from Shutterstock. New Africa/Shutterstock.com.

Next, the teacher would develop a fidelity checklist (Figure 11.2) for the peer tutor to follow and select tutors and tutees. The sheet would include the reason for the tutoring lesson, the problems the student is having with the content, the objectives of the lesson, steps that the tutor

PEER TUTOR CHECKLIST

1. The goal of peer tutoring:
❑ To complete the assignment
❑ To make sure the tutee understands the assignment and content

2. Why does the student need tutoring?
❑ Was absent
❑ Needs encouragement and motivation
❑ Does not understand the content
❑ Does not understand the directions
❑ Needs help staying on task
❑ Needs help understanding the reading

**I DO**
❑ Demonstrate how to answer the question and explain what you did.
❑ Don't simply tell the student the answer.

**WE DO**
❑ Answer the question with the student. Talk about each step together. Encourage the student to ask questions.
❑ Don't do it by yourself.

**YOU DO**
❑ Ask the student to answer the next question by him/herself and explain to you what he/she is doing at each step.
❑ Listen carefully to what the student is saying and watch what he/she is doing.
❑ Provide praise.
❑ Provide corrective feedback as needed.

*Figure 11.2* Peer Tutor Checklist.

would take to complete the tutoring session. Each session would include space for the tutor to mark that they had completed the step. The sheet would also include a list of "do's and do not's" to remind the student of what was taught during the tutoring lessons and space for the tutor to write comments. Many teachers create folders that include all of the materials that the tutor and tutee will need for the day and develop a routine for when the students should pick up the folder and what they should do with the materials.

The teacher selects the tutee based on need and selects a well-matched student who knows

Consider language and student characteristics!

Image used under license from Shutterstock. New Vectors/Shutterstock.com.

the material to teach the content. Selection of the tutee is likely to be straightforward.

The teacher selects the tutee based on need and selects a well-matched student who knows the material to teach the content. Selection of the tutee is likely to be straightforward. Students may simply work together to tutor each other (reciprocal tutoring discussed later) or the tutor could be in a lead role. For example, the teacher may select the tutee based on who was absent during an important lesson? Who is struggling with the content being taught? Who missed important instruction because they were not paying attention? Who tends to lose focus when working independently, such as Jaiden?

Selection of the tutor is not quite as simple. The teacher considers the qualities of the tutor needed to the tutor this particular student in this specific content. The first qualification for all tutors is that they understand the content being taught. This does not necessarily mean that they are high achieving students. When a low-achieving student who understands the content being taught is paired with a similarly low-achieving student who may not understand the material, then both the tutor and tutee can benefit academically. The second is that they are compassionate. In some situations, students are embarrassed to be receiving tutoring from a peer. The tutor should have the ability to understand why the student needs help, how it can be embarrassing, and how to encourage the tutee without increasing the embarrassment. It can be helpful to have online tutor training program or for school staff to have orientation and training sessions for tutors in the school in order to learn these important basics. When these do not exist, then an individual teacher may choose to work with a few students to be tutors in the teacher's classes.

Another consideration is the degree of inattention, impulsivity, and hyperactivity demonstrated by a tutee or tutor. Pairing a tutor and tutee who both demonstrate several symptoms of hyperactivity or inattention may limit their potential to accomplish much. As such, the take home message is that as a teacher, you should think carefully about the characteristics of the tutor and tutee, monitor their progress, and adjust as needed.

In addition to matching pairs of students, teachers also schedule the tutoring sessions and set some clear expectations (see Figure 11.3). As tutoring is supplemental instruction, we suggest that it take place when the tutee and the tutor will not miss additional classroom instruction. As such, it would typically not happen during Jaiden's algebra class unless there is "free" time within the class period. We have noticed that some schools have times that work best for individual peer tutoring, such as time set aside for study skills instruction, homeroom, intervention, and/or before or after school. Regardless of the time, it is important that sufficient time is set aside for the tutor to fill in learning gaps with new knowledge and practice.

*Figure 11.3* Peer Tutoring Expectations. Image used under license from Shutterstock. Gabrieuska/Shutterstock.com.

Peer tutoring expectations are similar to the teacher's classroom rules. For example, most teachers ask students to demonstrate mutual respect and trust, to remain on task, and to maintain appropriate voice levels. Although these are typical rules, it is important to have expectations specific to peer tutoring. For example, students should understand what is meant by mutual respect and trust in a peer tutoring relationship. Respect and trust are demonstrated by providing support and assistance when the tutee struggles to answer a question. Some students are tempted to laugh when a student does not know the answer to a question that they consider "simple." Tutors need to understand that laughing at the tutee's response does not help the tutee trust the tutor or lay the foundation for a respectful relationship. For example, in a tutoring relationship, if Jaiden does not pay attention and the tutor directs him back to the task several times, the tutor might find it tempting to start joking about Jaiden's struggle with attending. The tutor might say, "Squirrel" and laugh, but that would not increase trust in any way! It is likely that the joke would alienate Jaiden and lead to uncooperative behavior and disengagement. As such, it is essential that the teacher explain the expectations specific to the activity!

## Stage 2: Train the Peer Tutors

After the plan and materials are developed, the teacher trains the tutor. This step directly impacts the effectiveness of the intervention. Specifically, the teacher invites the student to be a peer tutor, explains the purpose for peer tutoring to the student and explains his role as the tutor and trains the

I will be a great tutor!

student to ask effective questions, to be a good listener, to give positive and corrective feedback, and how to respond when he does not know the answer to the tutee's questions.

Image used under license from Shutterstock. New Vectors/Shutterstock.com.

## Inviting the Tutor

The first step in training is to invite the selected student to be the tutor (in individual tutoring). The teacher presents the opportunity to the student as a privilege, explaining that she selected the tutor because she knows the content and would be an excellent tutor for the student. She tells Kenya that she is asking her to work with Jaiden, explaining that she will teach her how to tutor. She tells Kenya that tutoring should be a fun experience and that many students learn by teaching. She gives her the opportunity to accept or decline. Ms. Renette is very clear that declining the request will not hurt Kenya's grades or Ms. Renette's perception of her.

## Explain the Purpose

If the student agrees to be a tutor, then the teacher works with her individually or with a small group of students selected to be tutors for other students. Ms. Renette explains that the purpose is for someone to tutor Jaiden to help Jaiden understand the content taught and complete his classwork. She is clear that, it is not Kenya's responsibility to do the work for Jaiden, but instead to reteach content, help him understand it, and encourage him to stay on task while he is working.

## Reteach the Lesson

After explaining the purpose of the lesson, the tutor is taught to reteach the lesson taught by the teacher or a new lesson, if needed, following the fidelity checklist with the Behavioral Skills Training Model. The student is taught to explain the content, model completing the activity (algebra problems, in the case of Jaiden) and verbalizing each step, as he completes the task, asking the student to complete the task verbalizing each step, and then asking the student to work independently and providing input as needed.

## Ask Effective Questions

The tutor is taught to engage the tutee by minimizing the use of one answer questions, such as those that can be answered with a simple yes or no. The teacher trains them to ask open-ended questions as the student practices the task and ask questions while completing the task independently. For example, Ms. Renette might teach Kenya to answer questions, such as "look at this quadratic equation and tell me how you are going to answer it." Another option is to for her to ask Jaiden questions about each step of the equation, such as "what do you think should be done next?" Furthermore, tutors are trained to ask their tutees to ask questions, explain what they do not understand, and repeat back what they have learned.

## Be a Good Listener

In addition to asking effective questions, tutors are trained to be good listeners. Specifically, they are taught to listen to what their tutee asks them, reflecting to make sure they understand. For example, Kenya might say to Jaiden, "So you said that you do not understand what the three terms of the quadratic equation represent." If she does not understand exactly what Jaiden is asking, she could ask a clarifying question, such as "Tell me more about where you got confused?"

## Use Effective Prompts

In addition to asking effective questions, tutors are taught to use effective prompts. This is especially important when the tutee is an adolescent with ADHD, such as Jaiden. It is likely that Kenya will need to prompt Jaiden to continue working throughout the tutoring and session and to stay on task. Tutors are taught to provide verbal, gestural, and visual prompts to students and encouraged not to be "annoying," which can be difficult at times! Verbal prompts are simply reminders or redirections to get back on task. Tutors can simply say, "Hey Jaiden, get back on task" or ask a question, such as "What is the next step to the problem?" encouraging him to think about what he is doing. Gestural prompts are the simplest and often the most acceptable types of prompts. The tutor is taught to place her finger on the spot on the paper where the student should be working or on the materials that the student should be using. This often draws the student's attention back to task. Checklists are also a form of visual reminder. The tutor would create a checklist of the procedures for the day and the tutee would check off each step as it is completed. The checklist could be combined with a gestural prompt, with the tutor tapping the next step on the checklist with a pencil or her finger.

## Give Feedback

Teachers teach the tutors to give both positive and corrective feedback. Giving positive feedback is the act of encouraging students with genuine verbal praise when tutees are engaged and working hard, when they arrive at the correct answer, or complete their work. It is important that tutors understand that praise is motivating and not always just given for completing the assignment correctly. Another time to give positive feedback is when the tutee is struggling but continuing to work. One way to train tutors to give positive feedback is to ask them to reflect on times when they were given positive feedback. What did you do to get the feedback? Was there

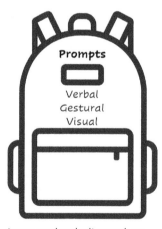

Image used under license from Shutterstock. Lidiia Koval/ Shutterstock.com.

a time when feedback was given for simply working hard? The teacher should help the tutor apply their experiences to how they work with their tutees.

Tutors are also taught to give corrective feedback. Corrective feedback is given to tutees in relation to the academic content and behavior. For example, Kenya might provide corrective feedback when Jaiden verbally describes a step in applying the quadratic formula or when he opened his phone to use his calculator and got lost in social media. The teacher could teach Kenya to explain what went wrong with the problem, reteach it, and demonstrate how to solve the problem correctly.

Tutors are encouraged to explain the problem in their own words and not try to replicate the words of the teacher. This is one of the benefits of peer tutoring, peers make things easier for tutees to understand in ways that we do not even think about as adults. Tutors are taught to think of alternative ways to explain the idea or subject and to give many examples.

Corrective feedback in relation to behavior is a bit trickier for peers to deliver. Tutors are taught to simply ask the student to change his behavior and work with them. As such, Kenya might say, "Hey Jaiden, how about you open your calculator and solve this equation." Whether positive or corrective feedback, tutors are taught not to be judgmental. Nothing about the corrective feedback reflects negative feelings on the part of the tutor. It is important that the tutor tells the student through words and her behavior that mistakes can be corrected.

**Seek Help When Needed**

Finally, tutors are taught to seek help from the teacher when they do not know the content or how to best help the tutee. Tutors must understand from the beginning that they do not have to know everything and it is okay for them to say, "I don't know" to the tutee or the teacher. At times, both the tutor and the tutee will need more explanation and/or reteaching from the teacher. In addition to explaining this to the tutor, the teacher must demonstrate that it is okay to ask for help. Teachers are busy and can get frustrated at times when asked too many questions and you think the tutor should know the answer to the questions. We encourage teachers to watch their body language and words when responding to tutor questions. We express frustration in many ways and sometimes do not realize that it is so obvious. Be careful!

## Stage 3: Implementation

Now that the preparation is done, the tutor trained and the tutee agreed to participate, implementation begins. At the designated time of the day, the tutor and tutee meet. Teachers should be discrete when talking about the tutoring pair. With individual peer tutoring, no other classmates need to know except the two peers. The tutor begins by presenting the content and or problem and following the steps outlined earlier, explain, demonstrate, have the tutee practice, and allow the tutor to complete the work alone. The tutee provides feedback while practicing the skills taught

We encourage the teacher or another trained adult to monitor early sessions until confident that both the tutor and the tutee will follow the expectation and procedures and remain on task. During these early sessions, the teacher provides feedback regarding the procedures, helps the tutor as needed, gives both positive and corrective feedback, and encourages the pair to keep working.

## Stage 4: Monitor Progress and Reward Success

During peer tutoring, teachers monitor student progress on the content being taught and the skill of the tutor and tutee. Monitoring student progress on the content could be completed through curriculum-based measures, such as teacher created tests, typically used in the class. As such, a teacher could develop a test or use a test that she typically gives to her class on the content being covered in the tutoring sessions.

The teacher monitors the skill of the tutoring pair directly through observation and indirectly via the outcomes of the tutee. Using a checklist allows the teacher to be consistent with what she is measuring. In addition to monitoring student progress, the teacher should provide reinforcers for student progress and for following the expectations and procedures. As the social interaction involved in peer tutoring is often reinforcement enough, the additional reinforcer could be something such as free time and computer time.

# Modes of Peer Tutoring

Until this point in the chapter, we primarily described individual peer tutoring with one tutee and one tutor selected to address struggles faced by the tutee. Other types of tutoring include reciprocal peer tutoring, class-wide peer tutoring, and cross-age tutoring, and these are described in the following paragraphs.

## Reciprocal Peer Tutoring

Reciprocal peer tutoring is a mode of peer tutoring in which peers alternate being the tutor. The procedures follow the same as individual peer tutoring with the exception of moving between tutor and tutee. This mode is used when students need to review information or practice skills. For example, after Jaiden has learned to solve quadratic equations, he and Kenya could study for the test together. Ms. Renette could give them a study guide to complete or instruct Kenya and Jaiden to create their own study guide. With Jaiden as the tutor, he would ask Kenya to verbally explain the procedures to solve quadratic equations. He would refer to the study guide and provide positive or corrective feedback to her response. Next, they would switch roles and Kenya would ask Jaiden to verbally describe the steps, and she would provide feedback. It is likely that the study guide would include practice problems. In this case, the pair would complete the problems on the study guide one at a time and share and discuss their calculations.

## Class-wide Peer Tutoring

Class-wide peer tutoring occurs during class time and is not a separate activity. Teachers include class-wide peer tutoring as a teaching strategy within their daily lessons. Many of the preceding procedures for individual peer tutoring apply to class-wide peer tutoring; however, additional steps are necessary. At the beginning of the class, the teacher creates two large teams of students. Each team should include students who are similar in ability, as they will be competing with one another. Within the teams, the teacher assigns tutor–tutee pairs based on her knowledge of the students. These pairs would change for each lesson in which peer tutoring is used. When the activity begins, the teacher sets a timer and at five minutes the tutor and tutee switch roles. The teacher awards points for teams when they are on-task and following the required procedures. Teams keeps score by recording points and points are documented on a class chart. The teacher can provide a reinforcer for the team(s) that met a predetermined goal or for the team with the most points. It is especially important that teachers provide verbal reinforcement to the students each time they engage in the activity.

## Cross-age Peer Tutoring

Cross-age peer tutoring is the use of older students to tutor younger students. In elementary schools, this typically looks like the students from a fifth-grade class tutoring the students from a third-grade class. As adolescents are not usually in one class all day, cross-age peer tutoring would become cross-class peer tutoring. For example, students in a geometry class, who have successfully completed algebra the prior year, could tutor students in Jaiden's algebra class. The two teachers would work together to pair students from one class with another, select the topic, schedule time for tutoring, and let the students do their work. This type of tutoring is benefi-cial for the tutor and the tutee as it involves review and practice.

# Potential Barriers and Methods of Overcoming the Barriers

## *Lack of Teacher Control*

There are barriers associated with peer tutoring. The first relates directly to teachers' sense of control over what and how they teach. As teachers do what they do because they are devoted and committed to the learning of their students, it is not surprising that many want to hold on tight to the reins. This can be a problem for several reasons. First, there is not typically enough time in the day for teachers to tutor students who are struggling, such as Jaiden. Without letting go of some control, those students may continue to fall behind. Additionally, there are times when adolescents can explain content in a way that their peers understand better than the way, we as teachers explain it. Letting go and letting tutoring happen can feel risky, but it often provides important benefits to students. If progress monitoring measures suggest that it is not helpful, then modifications can be made.

## *Hesitancy to Participate*

The second potential barrier is student willingness to participate. It is possible that adolescent tutees will be reluctant to participate in this type of tutoring. As you would expect, students are often hesitant to share their academic struggles with their peers. In fact, we frequently say that some adolescents with ADHD would rather be perceived as the student with behavior problems than the student struggling to learn. As such, it is important to clearly explain to students that everyone learns differently and some struggle to learn specific content. A classroom climate where no stigma is attached to learning struggles, disabilities, or mental health goes a long way to remove this barrier. These concepts have to become normalized within the classroom climate. The selection of the tutor can make a big difference in this area also. Tutees should be nonjudgmental and compassionate individuals helping the student learn without making them feel less than competent. Additionally, if needed, using positive reinforcement for cooperating within the tutoring session has the potential to decrease student reluctance.

## *Logistics*

Another obstacle is logistics. It can be difficult to find the time to use tutoring effectively as there can be scheduling challenges and limits on time to carefully plan. The encouraging part of this is that after the initial investment preparing materials and establishing a monitoring and training system, then some of these logistics barriers diminish and the benefits are much more efficiently achieved.

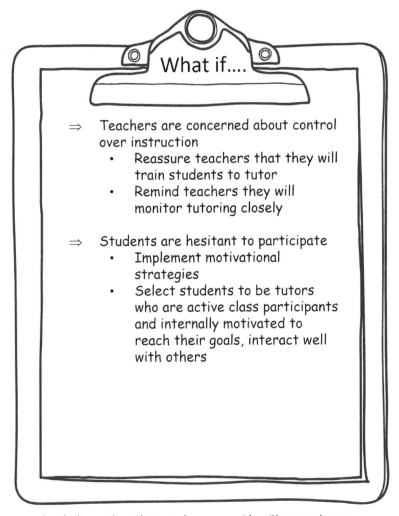

## What if....

⇒ Teachers are concerned about control over instruction
  • Reassure teachers that they will train students to tutor
  • Remind teachers they will monitor tutoring closely

⇒ Students are hesitant to participate
  • Implement motivational strategies
  • Select students to be tutors who are active class participants and internally motivated to reach their goals, interact well with others

Image used under license from Shutterstock. rangsan paidaen/Shutterstock.com.

## Considerations for Culturally Responsive Peer Tutoring

Ensuring that peer tutoring is culturally responsive can be viewed from two perspectives, the content of the lesson and the attributes of the tutoring partners. The first consideration is that the lesson be culturally relevant. Regardless of the content, according to Gloria Ladson-Billings, the teacher should ensure high expectations for all and encourage students to demonstrate cultural competence, maintaining their own culture and gaining access to others.

Furthermore, instruction should encourage students to critique the ways in which social order is maintained in society, allowing access and opportunities to some, and creating barriers for others (Ladson-Billings, 1994). All of these considerations should be made when selecting the content for the peer tutoring lesson. As such, this speaks more to the content of the lesson than the actual peer tutoring.

Additionally, teachers should carefully consider the characteristics of peers paired together. Language is an important issue when considering tutor–tutee pairs. It can be helpful if tutors for students who are English language learners know the first language of the tutee. In relation to culture, teachers should monitor how individual students respond to being in tutored by or tutoring peers from cultures other than their own. Some research indicates that students of color respond best to other students of color; however, other studies indicate that pairing students from different cultures for peer tutoring is more effective. We encourage you to monitor peer interactions for equity and to consider many student characteristics when pairing students including race, culture, gender, and social networks within your class.

## Programming

We strongly encourage teachers to advocate for the inclusion of interventions with evidence of effectiveness on any plan written for the student, such as a response to intervention plan, individualized education program (IEP), section 504 plan, and/or any other plan developed for an adolescent with ADHD. As you know, research indicates that peer tutoring can increase academic impairment and decrease disruptive behavior. Therefore, we provide examples of Jaiden's current levels, strengths and weaknesses, and

**CASEL Standards:** Social Emotional Learning Competency: Relationship skills
   Sub competency—Communication, social engagement, relationship building,
   teamwork

**Current levels, strengths, and weaknesses:** Jaiden is a ninth-grade student who
   struggles to maintain attention in algebra. During direct instruction, he will be
   on his phone rather than paying attention. When he is not on his phone, he is
   loudly shuffling his feet or fiddling with his pencil. This inattentive behavior
   has ultimately led to his failing algebra grade. After direct observation, it was
   discovered that Jaiden was off task for 37 minutes out of a 50-minute class
   period. According to Jaiden, this behavior can be attributed to his disdain for
   the subject. Currently, Jaiden and Ms. Renette are at odds over how to the
   handle the situation. This has ultimately left Jaiden resentful and unwilling to
   participate in tutoring sessions with his teacher. Considering Jaiden's popularity
   among his peers, he might benefit greatly from peer tutoring.

**Annual Smart Goal:**
- With peer tutoring, Jaiden's inattentive behavior in algebra will decrease from
  74% of time to 35% in a 50-minute period.

annual goals. In addition, we provide a description of interpersonal skills
that can be included in the accommodations/modifications section of the
plan.

#  Conclusion

Peer tutoring is a teaching strategy to help adolescents with ADHD who
are struggling with academic content or attending to task in whole group
situations. Peer tutors can reteach information, help students with ADHD
practice skills learned, and/or retain information. Through peer tutoring,
adolescents with ADHD have an opportunity to be taught by their peers and
to have additional instruction needed to assist them in mastering content
that they potentially missed when unfocused or distracted or struggled to
remember. In the current chapter, we discussed four stages of peer tutoring
and steps for implementation. We described three challenges often present when implementing peer tutoring: time for consistency, the provision
of reinforcers, and the motivating properties of the selected reinforcers and

recommendations to overcoming them. We provided strategies to increase the cultural relevance of peer tutoring, such including culturally relevant content and considering tutor and tutee characteristics. Peer tutoring is one strategy to assist students with academic impairment associated with ADHD.

# Reference List

Bowman-Perrott, L., Burke, M. D., Zhang, N., & Zaini, S. (2014). Direct and collateral effects of peer tutoring on social and behavioral outcomes: A meta-analysis of single-case research. *School Psychology Review, 43*(3), 260–285.

DuPaul, G. J., & Henningson, P. N. (1993). Peer tutoring effects on the classroom performance of children with attention deficit hyperactivity disorder. *School Psychology Review, 22*(1), 134–143.

Goodlad, S., & Hirst, B. (Eds.). (1990). *Explorations in peer tutoring.* Blackwell Education.

Ladson-Billings, G. (1994). *The dream-keepers: Successful teachers of African American children.* John Wiley & Sons.

Robinson, D. R., Schofield, J. W., & Steers-Wentzell, K. L. (2005). Peer and cross-age tutoring in math: Outcomes and their design implications. *Educational Psychology Review, 17*(4), 327–362.

# Intervention Selection

# Selecting Effective Interventions

**12**

In many of the previous chapters, we wrote about interventions for adolescents with ADHD with stages, modes, considerations for cultural responsiveness, potential barriers, and programming. In Chapter 2, we provided three guides to help you determine which intervention(s) address the academic, social/interpersonal, and behavior challenges associated with ADHD. In this chapter, we provide information to help you select interventions. Our recommendations are guided by evidence-based practices (EBP) and by the Life Course Model (Evans et al., 2014). We begin with a description and definition of both.

## What Is Evidence-Based Practice (EBP)?

EBP is a term that gets used so frequently that for many it is meaningless. It seems as if everything advertised on web pages and catalogs claims to be an EBP; however, it is likely that many of the programs advertised are not. In its purest and simplest form, EBP means that the program or practice has been studied in trials and found to be effective. When a prac-

Image used under license from Shutterstock. kozhedub_nc/Shutterstock.com.

tice is studied in a trial this means that the researchers recruit students in the age group who have the problems that the practice is designed

DOI: 10.4324/9781003109983-15

to help. They randomly divide them into at least two groups with one group receiving the intervention being tested (i.e., intervention group) and the other group(s) not receiving it. The groups not receiving the practice are considered a control condition. In school mental health research, the students in the control condition(s) may receive other services (e.g., medication, school services), but they cannot receive the service(s) being studied. The students who agree to participate in the study should be randomly assigned to one group or the other to increase the likelihood that any benefits found in the study are due to the intervention being evaluated and not due to differences in the characteristics of the students assigned to one group or the other.

Image used under license from Shutterstock. ESB Professional/Shutterstock.com.

There are many details of a study that can make the trials described here better or worse. Evidence coming from studies with a small number of students in each group (e.g., less than 20) is not considered as strong as evidence coming from studies with large numbers in each group. It is important that researchers carefully provide the intervention being tested so the intervention received by the students is consistent and adherent to the description in the manual. Another important detail that is considered when reviewing the level of evidence for an intervention is the meaningfulness of the benefits. Most researchers determine if the benefits of their study are statistically significant, and this is important to know as one can have greater confidence in benefits that are statistically significant compared to those that are not. However, there are benefits for interventions reported in some studies that are statistically significant but are not meaningful. For example, an investigator may report that the students in an intervention and control condition rated their management of emotions. Scores from those who received the intervention improved when they compared students' ratings before the intervention to their ratings after the intervention and the scores of students in the control condition did not change. This difference may be statistically significant, but if the scores only changed a small amount, the differences may not be meaningful. For example, it may be that the differences in scores between pre-test and post-test are so small that neither peers nor adults could tell a difference (even if differences are statistically significant). As a result, it is important to consider if the benefits are meaningful. Many who conduct studies of interventions skip this step and yet it is critical to consider if science is to affect practice. If research does not provide evidence of statistically significant and meaningful benefits, then the intervention should not be considered an EBP. There are many other details that determine the strength of the study (e.g., feasibility, attrition), but we will not go into them here.

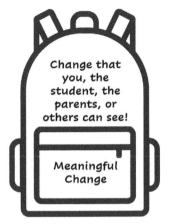

Image used under license from Shutterstock. Lidiia Koval/Shutterstock.com.

These research procedures provide the evidence necessary to make a practice an EBP. Many practices that are considered evidence-based have been evaluated in more than one trial. Interestingly though, some practices that we think about as being evidence-based have never been carefully evaluated in studies like the trials described earlier. For example, one common practice thought to be evidence-based is praise, but it has not been carefully studied for children with ADHD in a trial. A second method for calling a practice an EBP is that it is based on a scientifically sound theory. Praise is based on behavioral theory and specifically on operant conditioning (B.F. Skinner). Praise is considered a clear application of positive reinforcement, so it is often considered an EBP even though it has not been specifically evaluated. Some behavioral practices have been carefully evaluated and reported to be beneficial (e.g., daily report cards), but other EBPs are based on an evidence-based approach like operant conditioning.

Just because something is an EBP does not mean that it will work for you with a particular student. There are a variety of reasons related to the teacher or the student why an EBP may not work. Many do not work when they are not implemented consistently and according to the procedures. Others do not work for reasons associated with the student. For example, as we described earlier, praise is an EBP, but praise is unlikely to work for a student if the praise is provided by someone the student does not like or respect. Praise only works when the student cares about the opinion of the person providing the praise. It is accurate to think about EBPs as those that are more likely to work for a student than practices that are not EBPs. So EBPs are a good starting point, but like all interventions, educators should measure the student's response to the intervention and make adjustments, if after a reasonable period of time, improvements are not forthcoming.

# What Is the Life Course Model?

The Life Course Model (LCM; Evans et al., 2014) is a framework to help professionals decide what services to provide for children with emotional and behavioral problems. The authors of this model proposed that the value of an intervention is the extent to which it helps a child be able to independently meet age-appropriate expectations now and in the future. This means that the ultimate goal of an intervention is for the student to be able to perform academically, socially, and behaviorally in a manner similar to same aged peers without any interventions or supports in place. This may seem like an obvious goal, but the majority of the services that youth with emotional and behavioral problems receive are not consistent with this ideal. For example, there are medication treatments for many psychiatric disorders; however, most offer little to no benefit for youth after they discontinue taking them. Stimulants are the most common medication treatment for individuals with ADHD, yet their benefits are typically limited to the day they take the medication. Thus, even when medications allow a student to meet age-appropriate expectations, that success is partially dependent on the medication (i.e., thus not *independently* meeting age-appropriate expectations). Medications can certainly be helpful and an important part of the services a student receives; however, additional interventions are needed if independence is the goal.

Image used under license from Shutterstock. tynuk/Shutterstock.com.

The majority of services that students receive at school for help with emotional and behavioral problems are also not aligned with the ideal of the LCM. Studies revealed that the vast majority of services provided to students with emotional and behavioral problems (and students with ADHD in particular) reduce expectations. For example, providing extended time on tests and assignments reduces the expectation for timeliness. Providing students with a copy of the teacher's notes eliminates the expectation that the student learns to independently take notes.

We must maintain high expectations for all!

Image used under license from Shutterstock. New Vectors/Shutterstock.com.

When accommodations are exclusively used there is often little intention to remediate students' emotional and behavioral problems, but instead the focus is on helping them get through the demands of school without directly addressing their problems. This approach is similar to accommodations for people who have injuries that prevent them from walking. Society provides accommodations including ramps, elevators, cut-out curbs so people using wheelchairs can get to where they wish to go. The difference between this situation and the use of accommodations for children with emotional and behavioral problems is that people reliant on wheelchairs are typically unable to have their medical problem corrected so there is no available approach that would help them walk independently. There are many interventions for children and adolescents with emotional and behavioral problems that can improve their ability to independently meet age-appropriate expectations—however, they are not often used.

The guidance from the LCM is that interventions are more valuable and beneficial to students and their families than accommodations because, when effective, they help students independently meet age-appropriate expectations. However, there are limitations to interventions that diminish their value. First, interventions take more effort and time to benefit students than accommodations or some medications. For example, it can take many weeks to train a middle school student to take accurate notes; however, if an intervention team decides that the teacher will provide copies of the class notes to the student in class, then the problem is solved overnight! In the short run, giving the student copies of notes is easiest, but in the long run a student provided with copies of teacher's notes is likely to never learn to take accurate notes and therefore never independently meet age-appropriate expectations. This is similar to the proverb, "Give a man a fish and you feed him

Image used under license from Shutterstock.
Stenko Vlad/Shutterstock.com.

for a day. Teach him how to fish and you feed him for a lifetime" (this would translate to, "Give a student a copy of teacher's notes and you help him for a day. Teach him how to take notes and you help him for a lifetime").

Unfortunately, because interventions take more effort and time than accommodations it may not be possible to provide interventions for every problem identified for a student. The staff resources may not be adequate and too many interventions may be confusing to the student. Thus, the recommendation in the LCM is to choose problems that are a priority and use interventions to target those problems while accommodating the others. As the interventions effectively address the problems, then staff resources can be reallocated to interventions for other problems that were previously accommodated.

We strongly encourage you to consider the LCM and EBPs when creating IEPs, section 504 plans, or simply deciding how to help a student with emotional and behavioral problems. Federal regulations state that EBPs should be prioritized when preparing an IEP for students. Unfortunately, there are not EBPs for every possible problem students may exhibit. There is some research available to get a sense of the extent to which the LCM and EBPs are currently considered when providing services in schools.

## Do the LCM and EBPs Guide Current Selection of Services?

Examining the services that are currently provided to students with ADHD can provide clues as to the use of the LCM and EBPs when selecting services. In order to gather these data researchers obtained copies of IEPs and 504 plans for students with ADHD in multiple school districts and reported the services listed on these documents. Unfortunately, the evidence suggests that the vast majority of students do not receive services based on EBPs and are not intended to help them independently meet age-appropriate expectations.

Evidence reported in studies of types of services typically provided to adolescents with ADHD (Hustus et al., 2020; Spiel et al., 2014) indicate that the most common services provided for students with IEPs and 504 plans is extended time on tests or assignments. A frequently used rule-of-thumb related to this practice is to provide time and a half on tests and quizzes. Following this rule, when a class is given 30 minutes to complete a test, a student with this accommodation receives 45 minutes to complete it. In spite of how frequently this is used, extended time is not an accommodation and unlikely to be helpful (Harrison et al., 2022; Lewandowski et al., 2007). From our perspective, these research results are not surprising. Youth with ADHD have difficulty sustaining attention so their ability to be persistent and accurate diminishes as time advances. In addition, their frustration and boredom often increase the longer they are expected to work on something. These trends make it very unlikely that their extra time is going to be very useful and results of research on extended time with students with ADHD have reported this finding.

Our experience is that extending deadlines for submitting assignments is also counterproductive. First, our work with these students suggests that many of them have no record of the assignment and have lost any material related to an assignment on the same day that the work is assigned. In this situation, it doesn't matter if the deadline is extended a day or a year, the student has no record of the assignment so it will not be completed. For some students, the work never gets completed until either school staff or parents have sufficiently provided a "pestering intervention" that includes the adult independently obtaining the material and nature of the assignment and then standing over the student until the work is completed. This pestering intervention is often not implemented until after the assignment is late so the extended time may most practically afford adults time to learn of the assignment and force it into the student's attention. When an adult obtains the assignment and stands over the student until it is completed, then the task becomes turning it in. Some adults who specialize in working with these students simply take the assignment from the student as it is completed and give it to the teacher who assigned it. They know to not risk a repeated loss of the assignment if given back to the student to submit. Although this process may get the completed assignment submitted before

Image used under license from Shutterstock. cuttingtool/Shutterstock.com.

an extended deadline, it also leads to the second reason that this approach is a problem. This pestering intervention does nothing to help the student learn to independently meet age-appropriate expectations. In fact, the practice of this approach teaches students that they are not expected to meet age-appropriate expectations. Further, when they fail expectations, adults will rescue them. This is a terrible lesson to be teaching adolescents. Even if this approach can be sustained through high school and helps them graduate, this approach is not present in adult life and their expectations for this support could severely hurt their adult outcomes. As a result, when choosing services for a student, we encourage educators and SMHPs to consider both the short- and long-term effects of their choices.

Unfortunately, the vast majority of the services for adolescents with ADHD identified in the studies that reviewed IEPs and 504 plans are similarly problematic. Other common services that were identified in these studies included prompting, organizing materials for the student, providing students with copies of notes, reducing the length of assignments, and providing breaks. As with extended time, there is no expectation that if these services are provided for a long enough period of time, the student will better be able to independently meet age-appropriate expectations. They are intended to help the child pass the courses and they may accomplish that goal. For example, we have seen situations where secondary students with ADHD were failing a course due to consistent failure to submit homework. Justin's case is an example. He was not completing any math work outside of his math class and is failing the course. His parents were frustrated, and his teachers and parents tried intensive "pestering." The teacher offered to provide an "accommodation" to address the problem. The teacher would quit assigning homework to Justin and based his grade entirely on work completed in the classroom. This was enthusiastically embraced by Justin and his parents as it relieved a major daily frustration and stress. Overnight his grade went from failing to a C so all were quick to conclude that this worked! It did work to help Justin pass the class; however, it is full of negative long-term side-effects.

Long-term concerns for Justin included a missed opportunity to help him learn to independently manage his own assignments. There are interventions (other than the pestering intervention) that may have worked to help him achieve this goal, yet there is no urgency to provide them once the problem/ expectation is eliminated. In addition, the underlying message to Justin was that "you are broken and are not fixable." Justin could have

Handheld chalkboard. Image used under license from Shutterstock. Jack_the_sparow/ Shuterstock.com.

reasonably concluded that adults cannot help you so they will no longer try. Instead, they will give you the rewards that other students are required to earn (e.g., grades) without having to meet the same expectations. If this type of service is the primary approach taken for Justin over his years of education, he will learn to internalize these messages. He will learn that he is broke beyond repair and will never be able to be as successful as others. As you can imagine, there are numerous long-term risks associated with students believing this about themselves, including depression, delinquency, school disengagement, dropout, substance use, and suicide.

The good news is that there are alternatives that align with the LCM and EBPs. There are interventions discussed in the chapters of this book that require time and effort but can make a difference. These interventions take time and effort on the part of the classroom teacher, parents, and possibly other school support staff. These interventions are long-term investments as this is the primary focus of our education system. For example, if a child cannot read fluently by the end of first grade, educators do not quit teaching reading and just decide that this student will not be expected to read. Yet, this is essentially the approach that was taken for Justin. Developing academic competence requires a long-term invest-ment; in addition, successfully addressing the behaviors of students with emotional and behavioral problems also requires a long-term investment. Unfortunately, the current state of practice suggests that this investment is often not made for students with ADHD and other emotional and behav-ioral problems.

## So, What Can We Realistically Do to Help These Students?

Time and effort are a limited resource in schools so providing time-expensive interventions for every presenting problem of every student with problems is not possible. The goal of the teams making plans to help students is to balance available resources with the priority to make long-term investments in students. For many students with moderate to severe problems there are multiple problems that need to be addressed. There should be resources to provide interventions for some of these problems and the team should identify those that are the best candidates for intervening immediately. Typically, some of the problems are more of a priority than others based on safety, disruption to learning, and teacher frustration. These priorities could identify a starting point for interventions. Another approach is to consider which of the problems (if any) is most likely to have a fairly quick and positive response to intervention. Sometimes one of these problems are targeted first in order to establish some momentum and help with buy-in from the teaching staff, parents, and student. Once a few problems are identified (e.g., one to three problems), then the interventions are selected, and plans are made to address the other presenting problems. The approach for the other presenting problems is to provide accommodations that may lower expectations; however, this is time-limited as these problems are "in line" to be targeted with interventions. This strategy of selecting some problems to target with interventions, provide accommodations for the others, measure progress over time, and check progress and re-establish priorities and services based on data is aligned with the LCM.

Selecting interventions for the priority problems based on EBPs and the LCM can benefit students and their families in the short and the long run. According to the LCM, interventions should be selected that are likely to help the student learn to independently meet age-appropriate expectations. EBPs are those that research has identified as most likely to be able to accomplish those goals. In addition to specific EBP, some of the most effective interventions for adolescents with ADHD were based on a novel approach. For example, the organization intervention described in Chapter 7 was initially developed as part of the Challenging Horizons

Program (CHP). Following early research in the CHP, the organization intervention was studied by others (Abikoff et al., 2013) and incorporated into other programs (e.g., Homework Organization and Planning Skills—HOPS; Langberg et al., 2018). Some of our research has shown large gains in academic and social functioning for adolescents with ADHD from the organization intervention and other services in the CHP. We believe that the key to this success is the training framework that is the basis of the CHP and other currently studied interventions for adolescents with ADHD.

At the time I (SWE) began conducting treatment development work for adolescents with ADHD in the 1990s, the field started to recognize that children do not "grow out" of ADHD after puberty. As odd as this may seem now, it was the prevailing belief in the late 20th century. The challenge that accompanied this new realization was the need to develop effective treatments for adolescents with ADHD. There was some consideration of modifying the techniques used for children and evaluating their application with this older population. The most effective psychosocial treatments for children were behavioral interventions that were often provided to children as a result of parents receiving parent training and teachers receiving teacher classroom management training. Techniques such as daily report cards, time outs, effective commands, and point systems were, and still are, the tools taught to parents and teachers to help children with ADHD. There were many problems associated with attempts at upward extensions of behavioral approaches with adolescents. These include reduced adult monitoring, challenges identifying and providing salient contingencies, powerful peer influences, and increasing independence. Of course, these are all desirable and part of normal development during adolescence; however, they do make it difficult to provide behavioral interventions.

I knew that some behavioral approaches could still work, but I also knew that we needed a new approach to address the problems of adolescents with ADHD. I chose to focus intervention development on training approaches. These do not involve providing reinforcement and punishment but take an approach that is used by teachers and coaches every day. Training approaches involve four stages that are described in Figure 12.1.

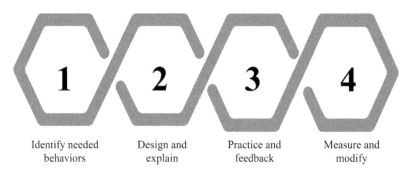

*Figure 12.1* Four Stages of Training Approach.

## Stage 1: Identify Needed Behaviors

When I developed the organization intervention and the note-taking intervention described in other chapters of this book I did it based on my observation that students with ADHD had extremely disorganized backpacks, binders, and lockers and either did not take notes in class or took notes that were so disorganized they provided no value to the student. Thus, the identified behaviors were to help students develop a system for storing and managing their materials so they would not lose things and know what was expected of them. For the organization intervention a system for tracking assigned work was incorporated into the intervention (see Chapter 7). There are other common behaviors that can be identified to address other school problems. For example, a student may disrupt the class, linger, and forget materials at the end of a class period. The behavior identified for this student could be to gather materials, put them in their proper place, and leave the class quietly and quickly. Another example involves a student whose work frequently includes careless errors. As a result, an identified behavior that could address this impairment is to carefully check work (assignments and tests) for accuracy after they are completed. The behaviors selected should be directly applicable to common school situations so the expectation to exhibit them occurs very frequently for the student.

## Stage 2: Design and Explain

Once the target behaviors are identified then it is time to design the training program. This is similar to how a coach might design training for a particular play in a sport or how instructional procedures are determined for a curriculum for a skill such as learning short and long vowel sounds. The program starts with establishing the details or steps of the new behavior (similar to the organization checklists, Figures 7.2 and 7.3). These steps should be observable so someone training the student can determine if they are being done. For the problematic behavior described earlier involving lingering in the classroom after dismissal, bothering other students,

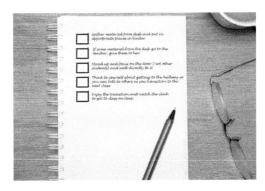

*Figure 12.2* Steps to New Behavior.
Image used under license from Shutterstock. nukeaf/Shutterstock.com.

and not gathering their materials and putting them in the correct locations in their binder, the program could include the steps in Figure 12.2.

The preceding steps are examples of steps for achieving the desired behavior. Steps 1 through 3 can be easily observed and behavior incompatible with the fourth step (e.g., talking to peers in the classroom) can also be observed. When designing the program, it is also important to consider context. The context is where and when the behavior will be expected. For the behavior in this example, the context might be in Mrs. Parker's science class when she dismisses the class. To complete the training program a person needs to be identified who will train the behavior and a decision made about when it will be done. Training a behavior like this one should take less than five minutes so an aide will take the student to Mrs. Parker's classroom at the beginning of fourth period when there are no students in the room. This is the period that the student is assigned to the resource room. The final step is to explain the program to the student. This can be a brief discussion and student input is encouraged. The student may wish to change some of the steps or the time for practice. This is also a time to discuss with the student how you will know when this training program is completed. For example, the program may be stopped when Mrs. Parker reports that the student exhibits the desired behavior consistently for two consecutive weeks.

## Stage 3: Practice and Feedback

Following the development of the training plan it is time to implement it. There are three important aspects to the training session including

1. This coach is confident that the student will succeed.
2. He relates well to the student.
3. He listens to the student.
4. He considers the students' feedback.
5. He is respected by the student.

*Figure 12.3* Characteristics of Effective Coaches.

Image used under license from Shutterstock. GaudiLab/Shutterstock.com.

relationship, repetitions, and feedback. The relationship between the coach and the student is critical to the success of the program. The coach (person doing the training) must have all of the characteristics in Figure 12.3. When these components of the relationship are present, the likelihood of the program succeeding is enhanced.

Another key is repetitions. This training should take place as many times each week as possible (daily is desirable). Although this is a relatively simple training program, its success is very dependent on repetitions. It is also important to approach this training with the expectation that it could easily take multiple weeks of training and meaningful gains could come slowly. Training interventions require frequent repetitions over an extended period of time.

The third important key of training sessions is the nature of the feedback. It should be clear from the feedback that the coach and student are on the same team. Feedback should be corrective, but also constructive and encouraging. For example, instead of the coach saying, "Wrong—go back to the desk and try again"; the coach could say, "You almost got it Justin. You left your assignment on your desk. Go ahead and give it another try. I know you can get it this time." The coach should record the student's adherence to each of the four items on a tracking sheet. Compliance with each item should only be recorded if the student does the behavior correctly on the first attempt in that repetition. For example, if the student gets up from his desk before putting the materials in his folder, but then he self-corrects and returns to his seat to get the materials, the coach should record that the first step was not done correctly. It is not helpful to "give students a break" and record a "yes" when the behavior is not done correctly the first time. The goal of repetitions is to help the behavior being trained to become automatic. In other words, the student exhibits the target behavior without thinking. In order for this to happen, practice repetitions should require perfect repetition of the target behaviors. Accepting less than perfect repetitions can actually train behaviors that are not desired. The teacher may record compliance with the departure behaviors even if it is not perfect, but within practice sessions we encourage that coaches maintain a high standard. For this sample training program, the coach may only practice three times each day and thus the entire coaching session could take less than five minutes.

## Stage 4: Measure and Modify

As with all interventions, it is important to track progress so success can be identified and celebrated. In this example training program, there will be data from the coach tracking the practice sessions and the classroom teacher can record adherence to the four stages every day at the end of math class. Mrs. Parker's data can be used to determine when the student meets the criteria established in stage one (follow the stages at the end of math class every day for two weeks). Mrs. Parker's data (Figure 12.4) along with the coach's data can be used to identify potential problems with the intervention (e.g., student misses step 3 frequently, but consistently completes the others). Identifying a problematic step could lead to increased focus on that step in training sessions and possibly adding private prompts by Mrs. Parker to remind the student of the problem step shortly before the end of class.

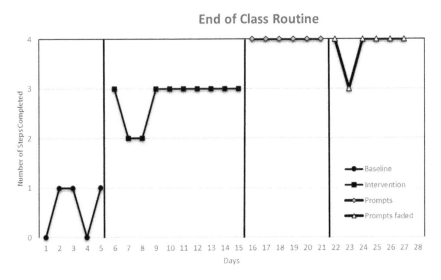

Figure 12.4 Visual Graph.

## *Notes on Training Interventions*

The example used in the description of these steps is a fairly small problem, but one that can be very frustrating for a teacher and possibly annoying to peers. A behavioral approach to this problem could include punishment for misbehavior and reinforcement for appropriate behavior. Given the nature of this behavior it is likely that verbal praise and reprimands would be the likely reinforcement and punishment used initially to address this problem. Certainly, if this is all it takes to change the problematic behavior, then the behavioral approach is the one that should be tried first. The training approach described here could be used if the praise and reprimands are inadequate. A simple problem was used here to provide an example of how the steps of a training program operate. We developed training programs for behaviors much more complex than this example. In addition to the training programs for organization and note taking described elsewhere in this book, there is also a training program for interpersonal skills to target problems getting along with peers and adults. This is the most complex training program we have seen for adolescents with ADHD.

It is important to note that there are interventions referred to as training programs that are unlikely to be effective because they do not adequately include the core requirements for an effective training intervention. For example, social skills training is an intervention frequently provided to children and adolescents with ADHD. Unfortunately, traditional social skills training programs do not appear to be effective for youth with ADHD and are not an EBP. Most social skills training programs include the identification of skills that may improve overall social functioning, but the practice and feedback is very minimal. It is common in these programs for youth to meet once a week for group sessions and a new social skill is presented at each session. The skill is explained and practiced within the group session; however, in order to be effective training programs should include numerous practice and feedback sessions over an extended period of time. Traditional social skills training is actually closer to a psychoeducation intervention than a training intervention. The primary activity in psychoeducation interventions is teaching and that is the main activity in typical social skills training. Psychoeducation interventions are an important part of many effective interventions (including training, see step 2), but teaching is unlikely to be adequate by itself to cause behavior change.

Another intervention that includes the word "training" in its name is cognitive training. These are usually presented to children as computer games and parents are told that repeated practice with these games will improve their child's problems related to ADHD. Cogmed© and EndeavorRx© are two common games that take this approach. Although neither is an EBP because of the lack of evidence of benefits, they are fairly common. These games include extensive practice and feedback; however, they appear to train a skill that is not directly transferable to daily life. They train students to improve their performance in the games; however, this improvement does not transfer to daily functioning so meaningful benefits are unlikely to appear. If you are interested in reading a detailed review of these games, then I encourage you to read this article written for practitioners (Evans et al., 2021: see Figure 12.5).

The decision of whether to use training or behavioral interventions is not an either/or choice. For example, it would have been very appropriate to add a reward to Justin's program to enhance engagement. He may have earned credit in the cafeteria or some other reward for progress with his behavior exiting the classroom or he may have been able to have a snack while practicing. In our experience rewards can be helpful for some students using a training program; however, the majority have not needed them. When they are needed it tends to be with younger students (e.g., 11- to 13-year-olds) and high school students almost never needed a reward.

It is also important to approach this with the proper mindset. Interventions take time to be effective and multiple practices each week matter. The advantage is that the practice sessions are often short. The practice sessions for Justin would have been less than five minutes and typical practice sessions with the organization training intervention can also take approximately five minutes (after the first three to six sessions). This approach of rapid-fire frequent brief sessions is unique

EVIDENCE-BASED PRACTICE IN CHILD AND ADOLESCENT MENTAL HEALTH
2021, VOL. 6, NO. 1, 116–130
https://doi.org/10.1080/23794925.2020.1859960

**R** Routledge
Taylor & Francis Group

The Efficacy of Cognitive Videogame Training for ADHD and What FDA Clearance Means for Clinicians

Steven W. Evans[a], Theodore P. Beauchaine[b], Andrea Chronis-Tuscano[c], Stephen P. Becker[d], Anil Chacko[e], Richard Gallagher[e], Cynthia M. Hartung[f], Michael J. Kofler[g], Brandon K. Schultz[h], Leanne Tamm[d], and Eric A. Youngstrom[i]

[a]Department of Psychology, Ohio University, Athens, USA; [b]Department of Psychology, The Ohio State University, Columbus, USA; [c]Department of Psychology, University of Maryland, College Park, USA; [d]Department of Psychology, University of Cincinnati College of Medicine, Ohio, USA; [e]Department of Applied Psychology, New York University, USA; [f]Department of Child and Adolescent Psychiatry, Grossman School of Medicine, New York University, USA; [g]Department of Psychology, University of Wyoming, Laramie, USA; [h]Department of Psychology, Florida State University, Tallahassee, USA; [i]Department of Psychology, East Carolina University, Greenville, North Carolina, USA; [j]Department of Psychology and Neuroscience, University of North Carolina, Chapel Hill, USA

ABSTRACT
News of a videogame that received FDA clearance to treat youth with attention-deficit hyperactivity disorder (ADHD) garnered a great deal of media attention and raised questions about the role of digital cognitive training programs for treatment. In order for clinicians and clients to understand this news for the purposes of making treatment decisions one must have an understanding of what it means for a treatment to be considered evidence-based and an understanding of what is required to obtain FDA clearance. Finally, in order to fully inform decisions about treatment, clinicians and parents must be able to consider the evidence supporting cognitive training programs in relation to other treatments available for children with ADHD. A review of these standards and the evidence supporting cognitive training in general, and the new videogame that received recent FDA clearance (EndeavorRX™) specifically, revealed an overall lack of support for this approach to treatment. There are multiple psychosocial and pharmacological treatment options with much more evidence supporting their effectiveness than any commercially available cognitive training program. The contrast between receiving FDA clearance without evidence of any observable benefits to the child is explained within a description of the FDA process for clearance and approval. Finally, these conclusions are described in the context of clinicians' decisions regarding services offered and procedures for explaining this to families who may have seen the media attention related to FDA clearance.

*Figure 12.5* Article about Cognitive Videogame Training.

Screen shot created by author.

to training interventions and this also makes it difficult to provide them in clinic settings. Those who attempt to incorporate training interventions into clinic-based treatment often try to get the parents to do the frequent practice sessions with the child between clinic sessions (e.g., Abikoff et al., 2013; Sibley et al., 2016). Given the benefits of training interventions for adolescents with ADHD, this means that educators and SMHPs have a powerful tool at their disposal that adolescents cannot get anywhere else!

## *Final Thoughts*

Letting the LCM and EBPs guide you in your selection of services for adolescents with ADHD will greatly benefit the adolescents at your school with ADHD. This will lead you to rely on training interventions like the ones described in this book or to creating your own training interventions based on the guidance provided in this chapter. No treatment works for every child, but the likelihood of adolescents becoming able to independently meet age-appropriate expectations is greatly enhanced when you use EBPs compared to reducing expectations or using services known to have little benefit for most youth with ADHD (e.g., fidget toys, cognitive training, social skills training, giving copies of notes). As described previously, using accommodations for some problems while intervening with others can be a wonderful balance of resource limitations and priority for intervening. Helping students with ADHD be successful is a long-term effort that requires consistent investment over time by staff who are invested in the success of students. The ability to effectively use training interventions puts educators and SMHPs in a powerful position to help students with ADHD learn to independently meet age-appropriate expectations.

## Reference List

Abikoff, H., Gallagher, R., Wells, K. C., Murray, D. W., Huang, L., Lu, F., & Petkova, E. (2013). Remediating organizational functioning in children with ADHD: Immediate and long-term effects from a randomized controlled trial. *Journal of Consulting and Clinical Psychology, 81*, 113–128. https://doi.org/10.1037/a0029648

Evans, S. W., Beauchaine, T. P., Chronis-Tuscano, A., Becker, S. P., Chacko, A., Gallagher, R., Hartung, C. M., Kofler, M. J., Schultz, B. K., Tamm, L., & Youngstrom, E. A. (2021). The efficacy of cognitive videogame training for ADHD and what FDA clearance means for clinicians. *Evidence-Based Practice in Child and Adolescent Mental Health*, *6*, 116–130. https://doi.org/10.1080/23794925.2020.1859960

Evans, S. W., Owens, J. S., Mautone, J. A., DuPaul, G. J., & Power, T. J. (2014). Toward a comprehensive, Life Course Model of care for youth with ADHD. In M. Weist, N. Lever, C. Bradshaw, & J. Owens (Eds.), *Handbook of school mental health* (2nd ed., pp. 413–426). Springer.

Harrison, J. R., Evans, S. W., Zatz, J., Mehta, P., Patel, A., Syed, M., Soares, D. A., Swistack, N., Griffith, M., & Custer, B. A. (2022). Comparison of four classroom-based strategies for middle school students with ADHD: A pilot randomized controlled trial. *Journal of Attention Disorders*, *26*, 1507–1519. https://doi.org/10.1177/10870547221081108

Hustus, C. L., Evans, S. W., Owens, J. S., Benson, K., Hetrick, A. A., Kipperman, K., & DuPaul, G. J. (2020). An evaluation of 504 and individualized education programs for high school students with attention deficit hyperactivity disorder. *School Psychology Review*, *49*, 333–345. https://doi.org/10.1080/2372966X.2020.1777830

Langberg, J. M., Dvorsky, M. R., Molitor, S. J., Bourchtein, E., Eddy, L. D., Smith, Z. R., Oddo, L. E., & Eadeh, H.-M. (2018). Overcoming the research-to-practice gap: A randomized trial with two brief homework and organization interventions for students with ADHD as implemented by school mental health providers. *Journal of Consulting and Clinical Psychology*, *86*, 39–55. https://doi.org/10.1037/ccp0000265

Lewandowski, L. J., Lovett, B. J., Parolin, R., Gordon, M., & Codding, R. S. (2007). Extended time accommodations and the mathematics performance of students with and without ADHD. *Journal of Psychoeducational Assessment*, *25*, 17–28. https://doi.org/10.1177/0734282906291961

Sibley, M. H., Graziano, P. A., Kuriyan, A. B., Coxe, S., Pelham, W. E., Rodriguez, L., Sanchez, F., Derefinko, K., Helseth, S., & Ward, A. (2016). Parent–teen behavior therapy + motivational interviewing for adolescents with ADHD. *Journal of Consulting and Clinical Psychology*, *84*, 699–712. https://doi.org/10.1037/ccp0000106

Spiel, C. F., Evans, S. W., & Langberg, J. M. (2014). Evaluating the content of individualized education programs and 504 plans of young adolescents with attention deficit/hyperactivity disorder. *School Psychology Quarterly*, *29*, 452–468. https://doi.org/10.1037/spq0000101

# 13 | **Final Thoughts**

This book was born from our desire to bridge the gap between research and practice. As practitioners, we have spent years in schools working with children with emotional and behavioral disorders, including those with ADHD. As such, we have contributed to the selection and implementation of strategies. We have contributed to individualized plans, informal and formal, section 504 plans and individualized education programs (IEPs) and selected strategies for our own practices. Over the years, it has become clear that strategies were often selected from a laundry list and as a "shot in the dark" with the intention of removing something in the environment that was interfering with the student's opportunity for success. We often selected strategies based on what was popular at the time without much consideration as to why the strategy was popular. For example, many times, we placed students at the front of the class with the intention of removing them from distractions. This was effective sometimes and other times students with ADHD sitting at the front of the class just served as a disruption to the students sitting behind them. Sometimes, we decided to place students with ADHD in the back of the classroom so that they would not be distracting to others and could move around at will. They were allowed to stand up, walk around, and fidget without disruption. We found that this frequently resulted in the student attending less instead of more. In sum, we found that students with ADHD could be distracted (and distracting) regardless of where they were sitting in the classroom.

We were positive that we were doing what was best for students. Our goal was to ensure that they had the same opportunities to perform as

DOI: 10.4324/9781003109983-16

those without ADHD. After all, we thought, demonstrating what they had learned in math had nothing to do with sitting still. We aimed to accommodate the student and remove all "content irrelevant variance." Unfortunately, no research evidence to date suggests that by accommodating challenges associated with ADHD, we increased student learning or performance.

Image used under license from Shutterstock. FGC/Shutterstock.com.

In fact, emerging studies indicate that some of our favorite accommodations for youth with ADHD, such as extended time and fidget items, are not helpful and might even be harmful. Regardless, accommodations were never designed or intended to teach students a skill.

Although not intentional, as we provided accommodations, we gave little consideration to the students' long-term future. How was giving them extended time preparing them for the future? I do not remember ever having that conversation. Thinking about it now, did the future employers of the students allow them to miss deadlines? It is possible. Most of us have asked for extensions on deadlines, right? Nonetheless, what are the consequences of continually making such requests in our jobs? Many times, individuals need extensions because they forgot to do something. We wonder how this forgetfulness has caused problems in relationships. Consider the adult with ADHD who forgot to pay the light bill. No doubt when the lights were turned off, his relationship with his partner was stressed. And now after the work that we have done, we wonder why we did not teach students to organize their time and materials using strategies that might have continued to benefit them throughout their lives.

As scholars and researchers, we realize we could have implemented interventions with evidence of effectiveness to teach adolescents with ADHD some of the skills they needed in hope of changing behaviors that have probably interfered with their lifelong success. It is likely that many of those students learned from negative experiences along the way that they had to find coping strategies to be successful. It seems that it would have been more productive to teach them skills for independence.

As such, we included strategies and interventions in this book with evidence of effectiveness. We began by describing symptomology and challenges associated with ADHD with the intent of framing the need for school-based intervention. In Chapter 3, we described the fundamentals of classroom organization and management that includes best practice strategies to prevent problem behaviors. Being consistent with clear expectations and routines, building positive student–teacher relationships, and providing multiple opportunities for students to respond to instruction increases the probability that students will feel comfortable and accepted in a friendly positive classroom environment. Additionally encouraging family-school partnerships, making data-based decisions, and being culturally responsive goes a long way to increasing student academic performance and achievement.

Once a healthy classroom climate is established, if students with ADHD continue to struggle, we encouraged teachers to select and implement one of the interventions in this book to teach students skills needed to overcome academic, behavioral, and social challenges. For example, many of the strategies are designed to teach students academic skills. Teaching students to write sentences, paragraphs, and essays following the procedures of SRSD helps them regulate their own writing following explicit steps. Similarly, teaching students to take notes will help them remember what was taught and teaching them to organize their materials will increase the likelihood that they will complete and submit their homework. In addition to the immediate effect of these strategies, they are likely to contribute to lifelong success. Students who know how to write, take notes, and organize their materials will have many of the tools they need to be successful in academic, vocational, and social endeavors. After all, an employer who remembers to take notes in meetings, check on employee progress, and submit payroll, along with a spouse who remembers to take the trash out and buy presents on birthdays, is likely to have a successful and happy career and relationships!

We also placed strong emphasis on adapting strategies to be culturally relevant. Our intent was to provide clear steps to adapt common interventions to increase equity and reach students from diverse cultures. We leaned heavily on the works and tenets of Gloria Ladson-Billings. Dr. Ladson-Billings described three tenets in her writing in 1995. She found that teachers who were responsive to students of color maintained high expectations for students, were culturally competent, and encouraged sociopolitical consciousness. In each intervention chapter in this book, we described adaptations that fall under one or more of these tenets. For example, when the strategy was directly related to the content being taught, such as SRSD, study skills, note taking, and peer tutoring, we encouraged teachers to demonstrate value for diverse cultures, activate cultural knowledge, and include diverse content in their lessons. One method discussed was to bring individuals from relevant cultures into the content being taught, such as professional writers and historical figures from diverse cultures. Similarly, we encouraged teachers to help students develop sociopolitical consciousness. The opportunity to critically analyze political, economic, and social forces is available when teaching content that is helped by many of the strategies in this book. We encouraged teachers to always be aware of how they are teaching content in relation to students' cultures.

When we discussed strategies designed to address behavior, we encouraged teachers to consider student behavior within the context of cultural competence. For example, we stressed that teachers should learn about cultural perspectives in terms of individualistic or collectivistic norms. For students from cultures that ascribe to collectivistic ideas, who value doing what is best for the group, we encouraged teachers to consider monitoring group behavior and developing group goals.

We strongly urged teachers to consider parental beliefs about disabilities and behavioral practices. Individuals from some cultures have misconceptions about ADHD diagnoses. It is by no means our job to convince them that their child is challenged by inattention, hyperactivity, or impulsivity. Instead, we encouraged teachers to focus on the impact of their challenges on success. Parents are more likely to collaborate with schools when we are all working toward student learning. Similarly, some parents prefer authoritarian behavioral practices, with strong values toward respect and obedience. We discussed respecting these beliefs and adapting our interventions to fit within that frame. Consequently, throughout this book we urged teachers to consider parental values in our education decisions.

Within all interventions, we emphasized that teachers must maintain high expectations for all students, including those with ADHD. Naturally, there are times, when we tend to "feel sorry" for students with ADHD and especially those from low-income environments. This is not helpful. These feelings can lead to the removal of expectations and lowering of standards. When we remove expectations, we remove the opportunity for the student to continue learning.

In addition to implementing culturally responsive strategies, we urged teachers to capitalize on recent developments in computer- and game-based implementation. Students with ADHD are more likely to be engaged with strategies that are presented in a context that they find enjoyable, such as computer programs or game-based digital applications. We encourage you to find and use technology as much as possible when is meaningfully benefits student learning and behavior.

In each intervention chapter, we described potential barriers to the intervention. Overall, time and resources are the most common barriers. Teachers are required to do a lot in a very short period of time. As we are well aware of this issue and respect teacher use of time, we encouraged teachers to implement all stages of the interventions as written, but to remember that there are others who can help. Throughout the chapters, we also reminded teachers to consider the time they will be saving in the long run by using the interventions. Although time is a commodity, the work completed upfront teaching students' skills will result in less time required throughout the academic year.

Furthermore, we provided examples of several components of programming, including statements of student current levels, strengths, and weaknesses, Common Core Standards (when applicable), CASEL standards, and annual SMART goals. We are aware that templates used by school-based teams do not always provide space to describe interventions. As such, we included the intervention in the goals as a means of ensuring that students receive the instruction they need. If the intervention is not listed on a plan, it is highly likely that it will be forgotten in the many varying and changing day to day activities.

Finally, in Chapter 12, we described the concept of evidence-based practices. For the last several decades, as educators, we heard about evidence-based practice, best practices, evidence-based interventions, all used interchangeably, rarely with much explanation. Now, we frequently read those terms in advertisements created by companies of toys or programs with very little research evidence. As such, we provided detailed information for you to be informed consumers. We strongly encourage you to select and use interventions with the framework of the Life Course Model, prioritizing training interventions to teach our student skills they will need to be successful and happy members of society. Furthermore, within this information, which at times seems quite lofty, we provided

information to help you realistic-
ally make this happen within the
context and resources in which you
live and work.

Together, the sections of this
book provided the opportunity for
you and other educators to impact
the long-term outcomes of students
with ADHD. Although challenges
will change as adolescents become
adults, the individual will likely
continue to be challenged. As
educators, if we can teach them
skills that they can generalize from
adolescence into adulthood, we
give them the tools they need to
be successful adults, which is the
ultimate goal of our professions!

Image used under license from Shutterstock.
AnnaSmirnova/Shutterstock.com.

www.ingramcontent.com/pod-product-compliance
Ingram Content Group UK Ltd.
Pitfield, Milton Keynes, MK11 3LW, UK
UKHW050346141224
452378UK00017B/59

9 780367 622404